To: Missus
From: Kit·Kat

MW00795664

THE TENNESSEE AND VIRGINIA COOKBOOK

2018 Mabry-Hazen Edition

Patrick J. Hollis, Editor

STORYHAUS MEDIA, LLC
Knoxville, Tennessee USA
2018

STORYHAUS
BUILDING YOUR STORY FROM THE GROUND UP

MABRY-HAZEN
HOUSE

2018 Mabry-Hazen Edition

Names: Hollis, Patrick J. | Hollis, Patrick J., The Tennessee and Virginia Cookbook.
Title: The Tennessee and Virginia Cookbook / Patrick J. Hollis.
Description: Limited First Edition. | Knoxville : Storyhaus Media, 2018.
Identifiers: LCCN 2018963672 | ISBN 978-0-9800553-3-7 (hardcover)
Subjects: Regional History–Nonfiction. | Appalachia–Social life and customs–19th
century–Nonfiction. | BISAC: NONFICTION / Historical. | NONFICTION / Historical /
Cuisine. GSAFD: Regional nonfiction. | Cookbooks. | Appalachia.

A WORD
FROM THE HAZEN HISTORICAL
MUSEUM FOUNDATION

On behalf of the Board of the Hazen Historical Museum Foundation, our nonprofit that runs the Mabry-Hazen House, we'd like to thank you, the reader, for your support of our important mission: to preserve the historic fabric of Mabry's Hill and Bethel Cemetery, and to educate the public about the rich history of the Mabry, Hazen, and Winstead families whose lives left lasting impressions on Knoxville, Tennessee.

This cookbook was rediscovered in our archives during conservation efforts following a fire in the Florence Meek Caretaker's Cottage on Mabry's Hill. The research efforts that followed made it possible to reinterpret this work in a modern culinary light and led to our decision to republish this book. It is our privilege to bring this glimpse of Appalachian history back into publication so that future generations can learn about the recipes and traditions of their mothers and grandmothers.

Bo Connor
President
The Hazen Historical Museum Foundation

November, 2018.

The Hazen Historical Museum Foundation

Board of Directors

Bo Connor, President
Yvette Fragile, Vice President
Karen Peterman, Secretary
Teresa Mabry, Treasurer

Ramon Halloun
Edwin Lay
Douglas McDaniel
David Nix
Terrence Schofield
Arin Streeter*
Suzy Trotta
Bob Whetsel*

*term completed in 2018

Staff

Patrick J. Hollis, Executive Director
William Oaks, intern
Emily Weddle, intern

Book Production Team

Patrick J. Hollis, Editor
Douglas McDaniel, Creative Director
William Oaks, Contributor
Christian Pennisi, Layout
Tyler Dippel, Quality Control
Stephen Zimmerman, Quality Control

FOREWORD

The women of First Presbyterian Church of Knoxville, Tennessee and Central Presbyterian Church of Bristol, Virginia did not write *The Tennessee and Virginia Cookbook* with the intention to speak to the past, present, and future of southern Appalachia. But in many respects, that is exactly what they achieved.

Published in 1911, *The Tennessee and Virginia Cookbook* is a collection of over 1,000 recipes from over 250 contributors—mostly local women from East Tennessee and southwestern Virginia, but as far away as London, England. The cookbook reflects ingredients and dishes from the region's frontier origins as well as its growing connections with a global market. It nostalgically clung to the traditional dishes and recipes of their mothers and grandmother, while simultaneously embracing new modern technologies, ingredients from around the world, the realities of changing dining styles, and the influences of science driven nutrition. For 21st century readers, *The Tennessee and Virginia Cookbook* recorded a moment in the history of Knoxville and southern Appalachian, but one it did not necessarily intend to capture. It brings to light commercial, industrial, and domestic changes and helps track them in a unique and tangible way. Beyond preserving their favorite foods and dishes, the women of First and Central Presbyterian churches preserved a way to examine region, class, economics, foodways, and womanhood in New South Knoxville.[1]

Cookbooks, in particular church community cookbooks, offer rare and often detailed glimpses into the domestic lives, tastes, and practices of the women from this era. As historian Alan Grubb notes in his study of Victorian-era cookbooks, "for historians, particularly social historians, nineteenth-century cookery and household books may actually be [the] most valuable [of period sources], for they represent a kind of 'populist' literature and enable us to observe the household from within." Using these texts, we may see many facets of late Victorian life, and the ways in which Knoxville's vibrant and dynamic post-Civil War economy, touched every part of women's lives; both in and out of the home.[2]

As Knoxville entered the second decade of the 20th century, the city seemed the "new jewel in the crown of the New South" as large retailers, merchants, bankers, factory owners, and real estate owners bandied about statistics that testified to the city's great progress and even greater potential. The city had grown exponentially in the post-Civil War era in commercial

---

1. *The Tennessee and Virginia Cookbook*, Preface.
2. Alan Grubb, "House and Home in the Victorian South: The Cookbook as Guide" in In *Joy and in Sorrow: Women, Family and Marriage in the Victorian South*, ed. Carol Bleser (New York: Oxford University Press, 1991), 159.

wealth, manufacturing activity, and population size. In 1910, Knoxville citizens organized and hosted the Appalachian Exposition; an intoxicating display of regional boosterism and "the spirit of Appalachia." During the daytime, spectators could view the strange sight of aeroplanes and dirigible balloons high above, while nighttime skies were filled with the flashes and booms of fabulous pyrotechnical displays. Former President Theodore Roosevelt even spoke and praised the "purely native American" character of East Tennessee. It was a "grand exposition" that showcased the city's progress and economic vitality and proved wildly successful. As this cookbook went to the presses, the 1911 Appalachian Exposition opened and the spirit existed to outdo the efforts of the year before.[3]

Yet even as the boosters of the New South metropolis boasted of the city's progress and potential, the phenomenal growth that they bragged about at the same time was also the source of many of Knoxville's increasing number of ills. The near universal use of coal for fuel and heat sullied the city with a grimy, sooty veneer. Street paving was still spotty at best, and cows and hogs walked the muddy city streets, bringing with them their accompanying smells. Dirt, coal dust, and unpleasant odors were common characteristics of the city at the turn of the century.

The need for labor drew a flood of Appalachian whites and blacks, and residential segregation by class and race began to divide the city. Fashionable enclaves, like West Knoxville, grew on the fringes of the city—away from the bad airs and poor streets. Finally, despite the strength of its economy, Knoxville began to experience increasing difficulty in the emerging, consolidating national economy. Once a key engine in the city's growth, the railroad brought the city, and surrounding regions, into national competition with Midwestern and Northern commodities where it was at a competitive disadvantage. East Tennessee farms and factories struggled against the huge farms and highly mechanized industries found throughout the country. Thus the impact of industrialization on Appalachia was uneven, with communities like Knoxville modernizing quickly, while others, especially in rural areas, were bypassed, and maintained traditional ways long into the 20th century.[4]

In many ways, Bristol, Virginia/Tennessee mimicked the development of Knoxville, albeit on a smaller scale. Precisely situated along the border of Tennessee and Virginia, Bristol developed into an important rail station, connecting the East Coast with southern Appalachian markets. It was a nexus for the Norfolk & Western Railway on the Virginia side and Southern Railway on the Tennessee side, an important transportation corridor. Transporting mail, freight, and people, the trains proved an engine for the hustle and bustle of Bristol and its prosperity. Between 1900 and 1910, the population grew nearly 50%. A new, uniquely styled rail station was

3. Knoxville Journal and Tribune, October 8, 1910; Richard D. Lukens, "The New South on Display: The Appalachian Expositions of 1910 and 1911." Journal of East Tennessee History Vol. 69, (1997): 1-28.
4. William Bruce Wheeler, *Knoxville, Tennessee: A Mountain City in the New South* (Knoxville: University of Tennessee Press, 2013), 28-30.

constructed in 1902 to accommodate the robust movement of persons and material along the state border. Beyond the commotion of the city center, the surrounding rural lands gained access to commodities from around the world while retaining its agricultural character. As with so many aspects of industrialization, its affect brought access to new commodities like fresh fruit to previously isolated communities, but the spread of prosperity was limited.[5]

For women of the First and Central Presbyterian churches, the progress and potential of their respective cities was on full display whenever they held services in their recently built sanctuaries. Their church buildings were less than a decade old, and yet their congregations numbered many descendants of city founders. First Presbyterian was founded in 1792 and Central Presbyterian formed in 1875—after its founders withdrew from First Presbyterian Church (Bristol) with that congregation's blessings. Their wealth had flourished alongside their cities, fostering a higher sense of social class. Many of Knoxville's first families, including Boyds, Hazens, McClungs, and Ramseys, were listed among the members of First Presbyterian. The Knoxville congregation also counted many of the city's dynamic commercial elite. Simply put, the church shepherded an influential flock.[6]

Church members emerged to work for the better of their church and community and it was often women who, as moral guides of the domestic world, strived to promote Christian values in the public realm. While church leadership remained male-dominated, membership increasingly became feminized as women began to outnumber men in overall membership, and in turn, became the face of American Protestantism. In his brief preface for the cookbook, John Park, pastor emeritus of First Presbyterian, referenced the noteworthy "benefactions of women" in the New Testament, yet reinforced their roles as stewards and followers. Christian practice and devotion, nonetheless, presented a public space outside of the home in which the women could exert their influence and voice their opinions. Women's groups were known for creating, compiling, and editing collections of recipes with a fundraising goal in mind, and with profits from sales supporting their organizations and causes. Throughout the 19th and into the early 20th century, community cookbooks provided a vehicle through which women could exert their influence, while remaining true to their domestic duties.[7]

According to *The Tennessee and Virginia Cookbook*, among the most "active and zealous in all its beneficent work," was Mrs. Isabella Reed Boyd. Born to Benjamin and Cynthia Boyd in 1831, Isabella Boyd was a member of Knoxville's pre-Civil War elite families and trained from youth to fulfill her role as a proper, southern lady. She earned a Mistress of Polite Literature

5. Allie Robinson Gibson, "We're here because of the railroads: Historians, others discuss importance of rail service to Bristol's start." Bristol Herald Courier (Bristol), April 26, 2014. https://www.heraldcourier.com/news/local/we-re-here-because-of-railroads/article_a328fa12-cdab-11e3-802e-001a4bcf6878.html

6. First Presbyterian Church, "Church History," https://www.fpcknox.org/about/history/church-history/; Central Presbyterian Church, "Central's History," http://www.cpcbristol.org/cpc/index.php/welcome/who-we-are/central-history (Accessed November, 2018).

7. Wheeler, *Knoxville, Tennessee*, 30-32. Ann Douglas, *The Feminization of American Culture*, New York: UNoonday Press, 1998).

degree at the East Tennessee Female Institute in 1847, yet higher education during the period was geared toward helping women acquire the knowledge to raise virtuous citizens while educating them how to run a household. Beyond her formal education, Isabella likely learned the craft of cookery in her family's tavern on the corner of Cumberland and Gay and during days spent walking in her grandfather John Boyd's large fruit orchards of every variety that were known for many years as "Fruit Island." In 1853, she married Samuel Beckett Boyd, and in the passing years, she bore eight children. At the age of 76, Isabella Boyd died on September 25, 1907 and was buried in Old Grey Cemetery.[8]

According to Reverend Park, Isabella Boyd "gave cheerfully and liberally of her material substance" to the church. During the 1890s, Mrs. Boyd conceived a plan to continue benefiting the church, even in death and proposed, at her own cost, to compile, edit, and publish a volume of "choice recipes from our Mothers and Grandmothers." Before her efforts could be completed, however, she "was called to rest from her labors" and two of her daughters took up the cause to complete the cookbook. Four years later, a thousand copies—with Isabella Boyd providing the funds—were published, to be equally divided between First Presbyterian and Central Presbyterian.[9]

It is unclear how many copies of *The Tennessee and Virginia Cookbook* were published beyond the initial thousand, how many actually sold, how those profits were used by the societies, or how pleasing the recipes were for reader's palates. Regardless of the cookbook's initial reception, it was designed to preserve well-tested dishes and pass along communal knowledge from a group of local practitioners to their successors. Although several contributions were supplied by professional experts or other cookbooks, the cookbook was a repository of local cuisine mixed with traditional dishes from across the country. Many of the recipes read as though they were transcribed directly from memory, with each recipe's cadence better mimicking the spoken rather than written word. In other words, *The Tennessee and Virginia Cookbook* became a memorialization of a bygone era, and an aid in bringing a new generation into a larger community of peers and history.

Isabella Boyd and her daughters compiled their cookbook with a majority of recipes contributed by local women, but in a few cases, periodicals and other cookbooks augmented the offerings. Often, the editors anonymously noted these outsider additions by stating the author as "Contributed." In other instances, however, *the Christian Observer*, *The Knoxville Cookbook*, *Pictorial Review*, or other noteworthy sources, received their due credit. Some of most prolific local authors were Mrs. Samuel B. Boyd, Mrs. Rush S. Hazen, Mrs. Joe Jourolmon, Mrs. J.H. McCue, Mrs. Hattie King Taylor, Mrs. H.H. Taylor, but countless others also imparted their culinary knowledge.

8. "Boyd Family History as related by Isabella Reed Boyd," Boyd, Samuel B., (Samuel Beckett), 1828-1890. Finding Aid for the Samuel B. Boyd Papers MS.0871. 1850 1928. [https://dlc.lib.utk.edu/spc/view?docId=ead/0012_002387_000000_0000/0012_002387_000000_0000.xml]
9. *The Tennessee and Virginia Cookbook*, Preface; Isabella Reed Boyd Diploma, 1847 July 29, MS.0096. University of Tennessee, Knoxville, Special Collections Library.

The Tennessee and Virginia Cookbook divided its content into 26 distinct chapters and was fairly typical for cookbooks of the period. In addition to the standard sections on meat, bread, and preserves, The Tennessee and Virginia Cookbook listed two less common and surprising categories—oysters and omelettes. The section on oysters was a reflection of Knoxville's food culture at the time. As early as the 1850s, fresh, live oysters were shipped to Knoxville via rail and kept cool in train cars. As a result of their prevalence, the cookbook contained 17 recipes for the popular shellfish. The inclusion of omelettes requires some unmixing. Although directly preceded by a section on eggs, separating omelettes into a distinct category likely lent the dish an air of sophistication (as did their preference for the French spelling). Additionally, the two recipes for fruit omelettes show the transformative power of rail transportation on their diets as refrigerated freight cars made it possible for fresh fruit to travel across the country.[10]

Cakes have become an icon of American culture and for good reason. No other section of The Tennessee and Virginia Cookbook boasts the number of recipes listed, and its pages accounted for nearly a sixth of the cookbook. The key cake ingredients—butter, eggs, sugar, and flour—have not changed over the course of American history, but tastes, technology, and techniques certainly have evolved and transformed.

At the start of the 20th century, Knoxvillians experienced dramatic changes to how they baked a cake; new gas cookstoves, new food products like Crisco, expanded access to exotic products like coconuts, celebrity cooking teachers, and new immigrants from around the world altered the baking formula.

Inflections of 20th century modernity resonated in the following pages with recipes like Angel Food Cake from an "Estate Gas Range" pamphlet, and Mavas, a French cake. While the new century made an impression, the techniques and technology to bake the cakes were molded by the 19th. Baked in wood- and coal-fired ovens, setting oven temperatures required a mix of experience and superstition. According to some, to properly regulate the oven required a measure of bravery—by holding your hand in oven and counting to twenty. Other cooks recommended throwing a piece of flour into the oven floor and judging the reaction. There are familiar treats like chocolate, devil's food, layer, and gingerbread, as well as more eclectic recipes like "Scripture" (ingredients could only be found by reading the Bible), "Mountain", and "Queen Vico" (a spice cake with alcohol).[11]

Despite the temperance movement triumphantly prohibiting liquor sales within Knoxville in 1907, alcoholic drinks and alcohol continued to appear as ingredients in recipes, and remained a common fixture of the food culture in Knoxville. The cookbook's section on beverages printed some non-alcoholic

10. Cynthia Moxley, "Food Writers Deliver History and Humor," May 26, 2015, at, https://blues-treak.moxleycarmichael.com/2015/05/26/food-writers-deliver-history-and-humor/; "Fruit," in The Oxford Encyclopedia of Food and Drink in America, ed. Andrew F. Smith, Vol. 1, (Oxford: Oxford University Press, 2014), 529-531.
11. The Tennessee and Virginia Cookbook, 52, 48, and 50.

options, but cordials and fruit wines made from blackberries, rhubarb, and other fruits ensured social lubricants were still available.[12]

Making tasty food was the main focus of *The Tennessee and Virginia Cookbook*, but as with nearly all of its contemporary counterparts, domestic education was a supplementary goal. For Victorian women, a well-prepared meal was an acquired skill, but a well-managed and controlled home was equally crucial. The cookbook assisted homemakers with the important role of hosting and made clear that middle and upper-class women were the intended audience. It contained full menus for banquets, large parties of up to two hundred as well as weekly menus for a healthy household. Alongside the menus, hints for home remedies, stain removal, and minimizing odors were shared to improve the health and well-being of readers. The sections on household management were natural candidates to appear alongside recipes for food as they reminded readers that achieving the lofty ideals of the middle and upper-classes began at home and within the control of women.[13]

On its own, extant copies of *The Tennessee and Virginia Cookbook* are a scarce resource with only a handful of known copies throughout the United States. But unique to the version held by Mabry-Hazen House are the handwritten recipes and notes penciled between and upon the pages. Wife to a successful wholesale grocer, Mr. Rush Strong Hazen, Mrs. Alice Evelyn Hazen likely was likely in constant contact with food and her role as a hostess of her antebellum Italianate home intimately linked her to the kitchen. On the top of the title page, Mrs. Hazen wrote her name, claiming her copy for posterity. She no doubt felt a sense pride in its publication as she contributed over a half-dozen recipes for the cookbook. Misspellings and errors were thoughtfully crossed over and corrected, and several recipes were given slight adjustments to meet the tastes of the Hazen family. The damaged binding, worn pages, and numerous stains indicate Mrs. Hazen found this book particularly useful in the kitchen. Additional recipes for "Chili Sauce" and "Caramel" were penciled-in upon the provided blank pages. Despite the wealth of material cultural artifacts preserved within the Mabry-Hazen House collection, precious few papers reveal much of the private lives of Alice and Rush Hazen. The handwritten notations from over 100 years ago give rare insight into the Hazen home and the interests of its matriarch.

Within Knoxville and the southern Appalachian region, *The Tennessee and Virginia Cookbook* was most certainly not the first community cookbook compiled and published by women. At the same time, *The Tennessee and Virginia Cookbook* was the first resource written directly for the women of First and Central Presbyterian Churches to learn the art of cookery, to form connections with the past and present, and to feel a place within their communities. It was a source of key information for preserving the traditions of their secular and religious families. The belief that these things were significant enough for publication gave voice to their collective identity, and

12. Wheeler, Knoxville, Tennessee, 33-34; *The Tennessee and Virginia Cookbook*, 7.
13. *The Tennessee and Virginia Cookbook*, 93.

each contributor helped to define and memorialize a way of life.

For modern readers and scholars, *The Tennessee and Virginia Cookbook* represents a direct line to Knoxville and southern Appalachian life in the 20th century. You are offered a glimpse into the history of women's lives and opportunities, gender roles, community building, and shared experiences. Popular cookbooks continually are revised and republished, but community cookbooks are rarely reproduced. As Knoxville undergoes a culinary renaissance in the early 21st century, remembering its food culture from a century ago may inspire new interpretations of historic recipes and give modern eaters a taste of the past.

Patrick J. Hollis
Executive Director
Mabry-Hazen House Museum
November, 2018.

ABOUT THE EDITOR

Patrick J. Hollis is the Executive Director and Curator of the Hazen Historical Museum Foundation. He is a former cook and sous chef who honed his culinary skills in Knoxville's burgeoning restaurant scene. Since childhood, he always had a taste for history and while still working in the back of house, earned his Bachelor of Arts degrees in History and Psychology from the University of Tennessee. Blending his two passions, Patrick studied public history at James Madison University where he concentrated on food, the South, and cultural conceptions of taste. He presented his research paper, "Capital Hunger: Food, Taste, and Civilization in Confederate Richmond," at the Shenandoah Valley Regional Studies Seminar in November 2015. He also designed an educational program on 18th century foodways on the Tennessee frontier for Blount Scholars initiative at the Blount Mansion in Knoxville, Tennessee.

Upon completion of his Masters of Arts in History with a concentration in Public History at JMU, he returned to Knoxville in 2016 and began volunteering at Mabry-Hazen House. A year later, he was named executive director. In his time at Mabry-Hazen House, Mr. Hollis has researched and hosted historic dinners which examined what people in Knoxville and the United States ate, who they ate with, how they ate it, why they ate it, and what it meant to them.

A self-described foodie, Mr. Hollis also possesses a deep appreciation for the history of food, and how it relates to 21st century food culture in Appalachia and beyond.

Mr. Hollis is passionate about food—from researching its history, dining out, to learning new techniques—and even more importantly, bringing friends and family around the table to share food, drink, and experiences.

PREFACE

The New Testament shows that in the primitive church the benefactions of women were noteworthy. The evangelist Luke testifies that when our Saviour went through the cities and villages, preaching and showing the glad tidings of the Kingdom of God, not only were the twelve apostles with him, but certain women, Mary Magdalene, Joanna, the wife of Herod's steward, and Susanna, and many others, who ministered unto him of their substance. The evangelist Matthew tells us that many women followed Jesus from Galilee to Jerusalem ministering unto him, and were witnesses of his crucifixion; among whom were Mary Magdalene, Mary the mother of James and Joseph, and Mary the mother of Zebedee's children. In one of his epistles the apostle Paul speaks of "women who labored with him in the gospel, whose names are in the book of life." And so it has been through every succeeding generation down to the present time wherever the church of Christ has been planted.

Among the many good women who have ministered to the cause of Christ in the First Presbyterian Church of Knoxville, was Mrs. Isabella R. Boyd, For about sixty years she was a consistent member of this church, and active and zealous in all its beneficent work. She gave cheerfully and liberally of her material substance for its maintainance and work. Having passed three score years of her life she conceived a plan to continue her benefactions after her decease, and purposed to edit and publish, at her own cost, a volume containing the choice recipes .of our Mothers and Grandmothers in housekeeping and give the copyright to the societies for Church work of the First Presbyterian Church of Knoxville, Tennessee, and the Central Presbyterian Church of Bristol, Virginia, that the proceeds from the sale of the book might be used for the cause of Christ. The work was well started in her own hands, when, in her 77th year, she was called to rest from her labors, and the completion of the book devolved upon her daughters, Mrs. James H. McCue and Mrs. John McAllen; but she had provided for the publication of 1000 copies, to be divided equally between these two societies.

It is now sent out on its mission of aiding the cause of Christ, with the prayer and hope that while doing this, it may also contribute to the comfort, health and happiness of every household into which it may win access.

James Park
April, 1911.

TABLE OF CONTENTS

KITCHEN TERMS

1 gill = ½ cup or 4 ounces or 8 tablespoons
2 gills = 1 cup or 8 ounces
1 coffee-cup = 1 cup
1 small coffee-cup = ¾ cup or 6 ounces
1 tea-cup = ¾ cup or 6 ounces
1 small tea-cup = ½ cup or 4 ounces
½ tea-cup = approx. 1/3 cup or 3 ounces
1 tumbler = 2 cups or 1 pint
1 wineglass = ¼ cup or ½ gill or 2 ounces

1 tablespoon = ½ ounce or 3 teaspoons
4 large tablespoons = ¼ cup or ½ gill or 2 ounces
1 teaspoon = 1 scant modern teaspoon
1 dessert spoon = 2 teaspoons
2 dessert spoons = 1 tablespoon
1 salt spoon = ¼ teaspoon
1 pinch = less than 1/8 teaspoon
1 dash = 1/8 teaspoon

Lump of butter = 1 tablespoon or ½ ounce
Butter or lard the size of walnut = 1 tablespoon
Butter the size of egg = 2 tablespoons or 1/8 cup
2 cups butter = 1 pound

1 egg in recipe = 1 modern medium egg
12 small eggs = 1 pound
10 medium eggs = 1 pound or 2 cups
9 large eggs = 1 pound
1 cup eggs = 4 large eggs, 5 medium eggs, 6 small eggs or 8 whites
4 cups white flour = 1 pound
2 cups sugar = 1 pound
2 ¼ cup brown sugar = 1 pound
4 cups ground suet (loose) = 1 pound
2 dry gallons = 1 peck
4 pecks = 1 bushel
1 ounce salt = 2 tablespoons
1 ounce ground allspice = 4 ½ tablespoons

1 ounce ground nutmeg = 3 ½ tablespoons
1 ounce ground cloves = 4 cloves
1 ounce ground ginger = 5 tablespoons
1 ounce ground pepper = 3 ½ tablespoons
1 ounce grated chocolate = ¼ cup
1 square of Baker's chocolate = 1 ounce

2/3 cup liquid yeast = ½ cake yeast or 1 packet yeast or scant
    tablespoon
1 Fleischmann's 0.6-ounce yeast cake = 1 packet dry yeast
1 Fleischmann's 2-ounce yeast cake = 3 packet dry yeast

A slow or slack oven = 275 - 300 degrees
A moderate oven = 325 - 375 degrees
A hot oven = 400 - 425 degrees
A quick oven = 450 degrees

RECIPE FOR
A HAPPY DAY

Take a little dash of water cold,
A little leaven of prayer,
A little bit of sunshine gold
Dissolved in morning air,
Add to your meal some merriment
And thought for kith and kin,
And then as a fine ingredient
A plenty of work there in.
Flavor it all with essence of love
And a little dash of play,
Let a good old Book and a glance above
Come the well spent day.

BEVERAGES

RECEIPT FOR ACID.

One ounce of tartaric acid to every two pounds of berries, water enough to cover the berries.

Allow this to stand forty-eight hours, Draw off the liquid very carefully. (Mash the berries as little as possible, this gives good color and fine flavor).

Sweeten to taste and allow to stand for twenty-four hours, then bottle, but do not cork.

Berries of any kind can be used-I prefer good ripe blackberries. It requires a good deal of sugar. I tie a cloth over bottle instead of corking.

MRS. C.S. NEWMAN, Knoxville, Tenn.

STRAWBERRY ACID.

Two quarts of strawberries, two quarts water, two ounces citric acid. Let this stand three hours, strain through a cloth and pour over two more quarts of berries, let stand for three hours, strain, and to every pint of juice add three-fourths of a pound of white sugar; let it come to a boil, skim, and when cool put in bottles and seal. When used as a drink add a little lemon juice and crushed ice. Also nice for making sherbet.

MRS. H.R. LENOIR, Knoxville, Tenn.

CHERRY BOUNCE.

One gallon sour cherries, two quarts of alcohol and two quarts of water, mixed. Pour alcohol and water over cherries and let them stand six weeks, then pour off the liquor; make a syrup of two pounds granulated sugar and two quarts of water, add this to liquor, mix well and strain, then bottle, (delicious).

We wash cherries and drop in a demijohn. When we make syrup, allow it to heat and boil up once or twice, till sugar is thoroughly dissolved.

MISS PASCAL HALL, Hagerstown, Md.

COLD CHOCOLATE.

Cut into small bits one ounce of unsweetened chocolate. Put this into a granite saucepan and gradually pour over it one-half pint of boiling water, stirring all the time over the fire until the chocolate is smooth. Add one pint of granulated sugar and let cool. When cold add one tablespoon of vanilla extract. Bottle and keep in a cool place.

When ready to serve it put in a tall glass one tablespoon of cracked ice, two tablespoons of the chocolate syrup, three tablespoons whipped cream, one-half cup of milk and a dash of soda water from a siphon bottle and a tablespoon of vanilla ice cream. This is a delicious drink, even if the soda water and ice cream are omitted. A plainer drink can be concocted by combining the chocolate syrup, three-fourths of a cup of milk and the cracked ice, shaking it well.

MRS. WM. J. BROWN, Bristol, Va.

PARISIAN CHOCOLATE.

Add two tablespoons of hot water, and the same of granulated sugar to one square of chocolate broken up small, stir thoroughly, let cook till smooth. Add the mixture to a quart of milk heated in a double boiler, cook from five to ten minutes. To each cup add, just before serving, a spoonful of thick whipped cream, which has been sweetened slightly and flavored with vanilla. Serve lady fingers with it or any delicate sponge cake.

CONTRIBUTED.

COCOA.

Four tablespoons cocoa, one-fourth cup sugar, few grains of salt, four cups of milk, one-half teaspoon of vanilla, three-fourths cup of boiling water.

Scald milk, mix cocoa, sugar and salt, adding enough boiling water to make a smooth paste; add remaining water and boil one minute, pour into scalded milk. Beat two minutes, using Dover egg beater, when froth will form, preventing scum, which is so unsightly. This is known as milling.

ELIZABETH O. HILLER, Chicago, Ill.

COFFEE.

The desired strength must be adjusted to individual tastes. One cup of coffee to eight or ten cups of water is about right. Pour the water fresh and boiling over the coffee in the pot; allow to stand at the boiling point (simmer) for two minutes; then move to the back of the stove for two minutes more, adding a dash of cold water to settle. A teaspoon of egg mixed with the cold water used in settling is an improvement for some people. If not to be served at once the liquid should not stand on the grounds. Serve hot. If coffee is bought parched, but not ground, it can be put in a pan, slightly warmed and a well beaten egg stirred in the coffee.

You will not need to use any egg when making. Or if no egg is on the coffee and eggs are scarce the shell of an egg may be put in with the coffee when making.

CONTRIBUTED.

COFFEE.

Two tablespoons ground coffee, teaspoon of egg, tablespoon cold water, stir well. Over this pour one pint of boiling water and let come to a good boil. Before taking off the fire put in a little cold water to settle the coffee.

CONTRIBUTED.

GRAPE FRUIT COCKTAILS.

Cut exactly into halves, six large grape fruit, carefully remove with scissors every particle of hard pithy centre and the thick, membranous skin; then with the tines of a silver fork, flake the fruit pulp into minute particles, sprinkle thickly with powdered sugar, and place directly on the ice to chill and ripen.

Half an hour before serving, pour into each portion a tablespoon of maraschino cordial, a teaspoon of bar le duc (black currant) jelly or red currant, a teaspoon of confectioner's sugar, and six small crystalized cherries; blend the fruit thoroughly in the grape fruit shell, attaching a small handle to each of twisted smilax, ornamented with a spray of holly and serve on a small dessert plate, resting on a dainty lace paper doily.

PICTORIAL REVIEW.

BLACKBERRY CORDIAL.

Two quarts blackberry juice, one pound loaf sugar, half ounce grated nutmeg, one-fourth ounce cloves, half-ounce cinnamon, half-ounce allspice. Pulverize the spices, put in muslin bag and boil all together for fifteen or twenty minutes. When cold add a pint of brandy, put in bottles and seal. This is very good for bowel trouble.

MRS. S.B. BOYD, Knoxville, Tenn.

BLACKBERRY CORDIAL.

Put two and one-half gallons of ripe berries in three quarts of water and boil till the berries are soft, strain through a bag and to one and one-half gallons of juice add five quarts of loaf sugar, cinnamon, cloves, mace, and allspice tied in a bag. Put it on the fire and boil till it thickens a little. When cool add good brandy to suit the taste. Bottle and seal and keep in a cool place.

MRS. A.P. WHITE, Knoxville, Tenn.

BLACKBERRY CORDIAL.

Two quarts of blackberry juice, one pound of loaf sugar, two grated nutmegs, one-eighth pound each of ground cloves and allspice, six sticks of cinnamon.

Simmer all together for thirty minutes in a stew pan, closely covered to prevent evaporation. Strain through a cloth. When cold add a pint of old brandy or whiskey.

MRS. JOHN BELL.

BLACKBERRY OR ELDERBERRY CORDIAL.

Set berries over a moderate fire and let simmer until they fall to pieces, strain through a jelly bag and to each pint of juice allow one pound of sugar, add cinnamon, cloves and mace to taste, boil fifteen minutes and strain a second time, set away to cool.

When cold, add to each pint of syrup one wine glass of good brandy. Bottle, cork tight and put in a cool place.

MRS. W.K. VANCE, Bristol. Tenn.

A REFRESHING DRINK.

A drink that is truly refreshing for one suffering from cold or sore throat is made by pouring a quart of boiling water over a carefully washed handful of Irish moss. First wash the moss in soda water, then through several waters. Then pour the boiling water over the moss and let it stand till the water is cool, strain through a muslin bag; add sugar and lemon juice, with a few thin slices of lemon, until it is about like a mild lemonade; a little cinnamon is considered an addition by some people.

CONTRIBUTED.

FAMILY DRINK.

Eight pounds of sugar to six gallons of water, hot, four ounces of good bruised ginger, a little spice, cloves and cinnamon boiled in a half gallon of the water; the juice of four lemons mixed in and all poured into demijohns with the water and sugar. When milkwarm, put in half a pint of good yeast and let stand two days. Then if you wish to keep it a long time, bottle and cork it. Put a raisin in each bottle and it will foam like the best of soda water.

MRS. JAMES S. BOYD, Knoxville, Tenn.

PLAIN FRUIT JUICE.

The following rule is given for preparing fruit juices for general purposes. Heat the ripe fruit slowly until you can mash and strain out the juices as for jelly. Put the juices in a preserving kettle and bring slowly to the boiling point, then skim carefully and allow to simmer for fifteen minutes. To each quart of juice add a quarter of a pint of granulated sugar. Cook slowly for ten minutes, then seal in bottles or pint glass jars.

CHRISTIAN OBSERVER.

GRAPE JUICE.

Thoroughly mash the grapes through a potato masher, put over the fire, pulp, juice and all and let it heat well, but not boil. Strain through a jelly bag, letting it drip, not squeezing. To one gallon of juice put one pound of sugar. Let this come to a good boil. Bottle and seal while hot. When ready to serve add a little lemon juice.

MRS. J.F. HICKS, Bristol, Tenn.

GRAPE JUICE.

Pick ripe grapes from the bunch, wash clean, add no water and cook on slow fire until done. Then squeeze out all the juice and set in a cool place till next day. Strain it again through a thick bag, add one cup of sugar to one gallon of juice, put on the fire, and when boiling hot, bottle, cork and seal.

ALBERTINE LUTTRELL VANCE, Knoxville, Tenn.

LEMONADE.

Put two cups sugar in saucepan, add one-half cup of water, place on range and bring to boiling point, boil three minutes: Pour hot syrup over the thin rind of lemon from which all the white, bitter portion has been removed, let stand till cold. Add the juice of six lemons to two quarts of water and combine with cold syrup; let stand in a covered vessel two hours to ripen before serving. All fruit juice except currant, grape, raspberry and pineapple are more palatable uncooked.

ELIZABETH O. HILLER, Chicago, Ill.

ALWAYS READY LEMONADE.

Extract the juice from six large lemons, grate the rind of three of them, add to the juice, let the mixture stand over night, closely covered. In the morning make a syrup of three pounds of granulated sugar and as little water as possible; when it has cooled stir in the lemon juice and put up in bottles and jars, making it air tight. In making lemonade with the syrup put in a little crushed ice, add a couple of teaspoons of the syrup and fill with water.

MRS. CHARLES LEONHARDT, Knoxville, Tenn.

APOLLINARIS PUNCH.

Two cups sugar, one cup water, one cup cold tea, five lemons, five oranges, one pint strawberry syrup, one can grated pineapple, one quart bottle Apollinaris water, iced water to make a gallon of liquid. Boil the sugar and one cup of water ten minutes slowly. When it is cold add the tea and the juice of the fruit. Let this stand awhile to extract the flavors; then when it is time to serve add the Apollinaris and enough water to fill a gallon measure. This makes eighteen glasses full. As Apollinaris is expensive, cheaper waters may be used.

MRS. J.H. McCUE.

FRUIT PUNCH.

Two and one-half dozen oranges, two and one-half dozen lemons, two cans grated pineapple, one dollar bottle Maraschino cherries, four pounds granulated sugar, twelve bottles seltzer water.

Sufficient for one hundred and seventy-five people.

KNOXVILLE COOKBOOK.

FRUIT PUNCH.

Pour one cup of strong tea over one cup of sugar, add three-fourths cup of orange juice, one-third cup lemon juice, one pint ginger ale, one pint Apollinaris water (or you can use White Rock), strain into a punch bowl over a large piece of ice and decorate with slices of orange.

DR. VOORHEES, Ft. Myers, Fla.

FRUIT PUNCH.

Five dozen lemons, three large oranges, four small cans pineapple, grated, eight scant pints granulated sugar, one jar of Maraschino cherries (one-half gallon). Boil sugar in four pints water, cool, then add six quarts of water to the lemon juice and add the other ingredients. When ready to serve add four quarts of White Rock or Apollinaris water and pour over a block of ice. This is sufficient for one hundred persons.

KNOXVILLE COOKBOOK.

FRUIT PUNCH.

One-half dozen lemons, four large oranges, a small bottle of Maraschino cherries, a small can of grated pineapple, one quart bottle of seltzer water, sugar to taste. This is sufficient for twenty people.

MRS. T.J. CAMPBELL, Bristol, Va.

GREATER KNOXVILLE PUNCH.

Four cups of cold water, one cup of sugar, one-half cup Canton ginger; three-quarters of a cup of orange juice, one quarter of a cup of lemon juice, three tablespoons ginger syrup, one quart Apollinaris water.

ELIZABETH O. HILLER, Chicago, Ill.

SALPICON OF FRUIT.

A delicious salpicon is made by cutting all kinds of fresh fruits in small pieces, sprinkling with lemon juice and sugar, then heaping into glasses and placing a spoonful of frozen water, ice or cream on top.

CONTRIBUTED.

ENGLISH TEA.

About five minutes before you wish to use the tea, have freshly boiling water. Use English Breakfast black tea, pour a little boiling water in the teapot, throw it out and put a small teaspoon of tea to two persons, pour over a pint of water, let it stand for a few minutes, not boil, then serve.

MRS. H.N. SAXTON, Knoxville, Tenn

ICE TEA.

The best way is to pour freshly brewed tea over a large lump of ice, then pour into glasses half-filled with shaved ice. A more economical way is to make a small quantity of rather strong tea several hours before using, cool and place in the refrigerator and weaken to the desired strength with iced water just before serving. Serve the tea in glasses half-filled with cracked or shaved ice, and if lemon is used it is best to adopt the Russian plan of grating the rind of a lemon and pouring hot tea over it. If you pass the lemon when tea is served, rut it in lengthwise sections. Mint leaves or lemon verbena added to iced tea, besides the lemon give a delicious flavor, and it is also good with a little ginger syrup. The thinner and more slender the glass, the more refreshing the tea tastes.

CONTRIBUTED.

RUSSIAN TEA.

Three teaspoons tea, two cups boiling water, candied cherries, slices of lemon.

ELIZABETH O. HILLER, Chicago, Ill.

STRAWBERRY VINEGAR.

Put four pounds of very ripe berries into one quart of best cider vinegar, let stand closely covered three days. Drain through a jelly bag and pour on the same quantity of fresh berries. Ditto after three days the third time. To each pound of liquor thus obtained, put a pound of loaf sugar. Bottle and let stand for a week, then cork tightly and put in a dry place.

MRS. JAMES S. BOYD, Knoxville, Tenn.

BLACKBERRY WINE.

Take ripe blackberries and mash them, and to every two quarts berries, add one quart of tepid water. Let them stand twenty-four hours, stirring two or three times, then strain and to every gallon of juice allow three pounds of sugar. Fill jars or bottles to the top, skim twice a day and keep filled with juice till fermentation ceases-it will be some weeks. Strain off into a clean vessel, add a lump of sugar and in one week strain into bottles and seal.

MRS. S.B. BOYD, Knoxville, Tenn.

BLACKBERRY WINE.

Take ripe blackberries, or dewberries, and press them, let stand for thirty-six hours to ferment, and to every gallon of the juice add a quart of water and three pounds of sugar. Let this stand in a vessel with a cloth over top for twenty-four hours. Skim and strain; put in jugs till March, when it should be carefully drawn off and bottled. Keep in a cool place.

MRS. H.R. LENOIR. Knoxville, Tenn.

CATAWBA WINE.

Mash the grapes with a small mallet, let stand all night and press the juice in open vessels, let it stand until the scum rises, breaking in cracks, showing a little white foam. Skim it off, pour out the wine, adding two pounds of sugar to one gallon of juice. Put the bung in loosely and let stand three weeks, then tighten and let remain till February. Bottle and keep in a cool place.

MRS. E.A.R. BRECK, Knoxville, Tenn.

GRAPE WINE.

Take ripe grapes and mash them, and to every gallon of grapes add one-half gallon of warm water. Let them stand twenty-four hours, stirring two or three times, then strain, and to every gallon of juice allow three pounds of sugar.

Place in jars or bottles, skim twice a day and fill to the top with the juice, till fermentation ceases.

Stop tightly for three months, then pour off into a clean vessel, add a lump of sugar, in one week strain off into bottles and it is ready for use.

MRS. S.B. BOYD, Knoxville, Tenn.

RHUBARB WINE.

One gallon of water to one gallon of rhubarb, cut in small pieces, remove strings, cover it and let stand three or four days. Pour off the water, (do not use the rhubarb), add three and one-half pounds granulated sugar, and one-half of five cents isinglass, put in demijohn that will hold it all and cork tight. Let stand six weeks or longer, then drain off clear and bottle, corking tight does not ferment, so need not tie corks.

MRS. M.V. DOUGLAS, Washington, D.C.

BREAD, BISCUIT, CAKE, ETC

SUGGESTIONS IN MAKING BREAD.

Before mixing bread it is better to warm the flour slightly.

Use any kind of good yeast; a good compressed yeast should be free from strong odor, clear, and of uniform color and consistency. The pleasant yeasty odor of a fresh cake cannot be confounded with strong, stale yeast.

The first step in preparing bread is to measure butter, lard, sugar and salt in the mixing bowl. Then add the scalded milk, if used, and water. Let it cool until lukewarm. This is very important, for a higher temperature will surely kill the tiny yeast plants. If bread be started at night, one-fourth of a cake will be sufficient, while a whole cake will be required for the quick process five-hour bread.

When water alone is used in making bread, add one tablespoon of sugar to every two cups of water. This provides food for the yeast plant at once, otherwise the yeast is forced to change some of the starch in the flour to sugar and thus it takes longer for the plant to grow.

In kneading, flour the board well and toss the dough on this.

Knead with the palm of the hand, pushing the dough from you. Do not bear down on the dough too hard, as it tends to make the loaf coarse and tough. The longer the bread is kneaded, the more thoroughly the yeast plant is distributed throughout the dough and the finer grained the bread will be.

The blisters which come during kneading are caused by the air that is inclosed each time the dough is folded over. Knead as lightly as possible. Wash the mixing bowl and oil it slightly before returning the bread to be raised. When the bread has doubled its bulk, it is cut down and kneaded to stop further generation of gas; if too much of this gas is made it allows the acetic acid bacteria to grow and they cause sour bread. But bread need never sour, if kept cut down, as the acetic fermentation cannot start without an excess of alcohol.

In baking bread a very hot oven is needed. The bread should not begin to brown for fifteen or twenty minutes. Remove bread from pans as soon as baked. and cool on cake racks is possible. A very little butter may be rubbed on the crust if it is desired tender. Do not fold bread in cloths, but keep in an air-tight, well-sunned bread box.

GOOD HOUSEKEEPING.

BAKING POWDER BISCUIT.

Three pints of flour, one and one-half tablespoonsful of lard, one teaspoon of salt, three teaspoons of baking powder, raise them high, a pint and one-half of sweet milk. Mix flour, salt and baking powder, then lard, mix the milk in with a fork and as soft as you can. Work very little, roll out about three-quarters of an inch thick, cut out (do not stick), let rise ten or fifteen minutes, then bake in a very hot oven.

ELIZABETH WILKERSON.

BEATEN BISCUIT.

One quart of flour, two ounces of lard, a little salt. Mix with cold water into a stiff dough, leaving out a little flour to beat in, to make the biscuit light and flaky.

MRS. B.J. STEPHENSON, Knoxville, Tenn.

BEATEN BISCUIT.

To one pound of flour put two and one-half ounces of lard, make a stiff dough with cold water and beat well.

MRS. A.P. WHITE, Knoxville, Tenn.

BEATEN BISCUIT.

One quart of flour, one-half cup of lard, one cup of sweet milk, or milk and water, one teaspoon salt. Mix well and work till the dough blisters, then bake in a hot oven.

MRS. W.K. VANCE, Bristol, Tenn.

BEATEN BISCUIT.

One pound flour, two and one-half ounces of lard, one level teaspoon salt, cold water to make a stiff dough. Mix flour, lard and salt thoroughly, then add water to make a stiff dough. Add water carefully; if you get your dough too slack, you cannot make good biscuit; if you have to add more flour it destroys proportion.

Beat your dough until it is perfectly smooth and pops as you roll it out; it should blister, if good. Cut biscuit one-third of an inch thick and bake in a moderate oven about twenty minutes. Much depends upon the baking.

MRS. E.S. McCLUNG, Knoxville, Tenn.

CRACKER BISCUIT.

One quart of flour, one tablespoon of lard, one teaspoon of salt, water enough to make a stiff dough, work well and bake in a quick oven.

MRS. ANN BELL, Knoxville, Tenn.

DIXIE BISCUIT.

One pint sweet milk, one teaspoon lard, two teaspoons butter, two teaspoons sugar, one teaspoon salt, one cake yeast, one egg, six cups flour. Put milk in double boiler with butter, lard, sugar and egg, scald, then add salt. Set aside to cool, dissolve yeast in a little cold milk or water and stir in warm milk. Take two and one-half cups of flour and stir in warm milk to stiff batter. Let rise, then work in the rest of the flour for sponge, then let rise, when you work down, roll out and cut out for the biscuit. Grease the tops well with butter, let rise again and bake.

MRS. ALLEN S. MEBANE, Knoxville, Tenn.

DROP BISCUIT.

Three cups flour, two teaspoons baking powder, two tablespoons of lard, rubbed well with the flour, salt to taste, Make into a soft dough with one and one-half cups of milk. Bake in muffin rings or drop in small heaps on a flat tin. Ten minutes in a quick oven will bake them.

MRS. WILL HALLER, Portsmouth, Va.

FRENCH BISCUIT.

Four pints flour, four eggs, leaving out yellows of two, four teaspoons of white sugar, one tablespoon butter, or sweet lard, a little salt, one pint of sweet milk, one teacup of good yeast, make into a dough and work well. Let it rise, work again and then roll out thin and cut into biscuit, lard on one side and lay another on that already greased with lard, let them rise again and bake in a rather quick oven.

CONTRIBUTED.

LIGHT BISCUIT.

Four pints flour, one egg, four tablespoons sugar, one tablespoon butter, a little salt, one pint new milk, make into dough and work well. Let it rise, work again and then roll out thin and cut into biscuit, lard on one side and lay another on that already greased with lard, let them rise again, bake in a quick oven.

MRS. H.H. TAYLOR, Knoxville, Tenn.

LIGHT BISCUIT.

One heaping pint sifted flour, one heaping teaspoon Royal baking powder, one scant teaspoon salt. Sift all together in a bowl. Then mix thoroughly with these ingredients, a heaping tablespoon of lard, until the materials are like crumbs, moisten with enough sweet milk to make a soft dough.

Work lightly and roll and cut into biscuits. Bake in a moderately quick oven for about ten minutes.

MRS. A.S. BIRDSONG, Knoxville, Tenn.

TO MAKE LIGHT BISCUIT.

Three teacups flour, add half teaspoon soda, small quantity of salt, pure leaf lard, size of an egg, knead it thoroughly, then stir in sour milk with a spoon until it is dough. Roll out, cut and bake in a hot oven until a light brown.

MISS MATTIE CAMDEN, Knoxville, Tenn.

POTATO BISCUIT.

One-half cake Fleishman's yeast, one egg, one-half cup each of butter, sugar, sweet milk and hot mashed Irish potato and flour for a nice batter. Make up about two o'clock in the afternoon.

Melt the butter in the milk, and when cool mix all together. After tea, beat in as much flour as you can with a spoon. Set it to rise, in the morning beat down, adding no more flour. Two hours before dinner roll out on a floured biscuit board, cut with a biscuit cutter and place two together, greasing between in a greased pan, let rise about one and one-half hours and bake in a quick oven.

MRS. SPAULDING, California.

SODA BISCUIT.

One quart flour, one-half pint thick buttermilk, one tablespoon of lard, one-half teaspoon soda, one-half teaspoon salt.

AUNT HENRY.

SODA BISCUIT.

Rub one tablespoonful of shortening into one quart of flour, add half a teaspoonful of salt, dissolve half a teaspoonful of soda in two tablespoonsful of warm water and stir into half a pint of sour milk, stir this into the flour. You may have to add a little more milk, but do not add any more soda, knead quickly, roll out, cut into biscuits and bake in a quick oven twenty minutes.

MRS. J.H. McCUE

WAFER BISCUIT.

To one pint of flour, put one-fourth pound of lard and one egg, mix with water or milk and beat well. When the dough is smooth, roll thin and cut out size of a biscuit, then roll again very thin, stick well with a fork and bake in a quick oven.

CONTRIBUTED.

BREAD MADE WITH A STARTER.

First make a starter by soaking one yeast calm (Magic) in about three-fourths cup of lukewarm water, one cup mashed Irish potatoes, one tablespoon sugar, one teaspoon salt.

For Bread—One cup mashed Irish potatoes, four tablespoons sugar, one level tablespoon salt, one quart boiling water. When lukewarm, add the starter and set in a warm place over night. Next morning take out one-half pint of starter for next baking, then thicken the remainder to a batter, when foamy add lard, size of a small egg, add flour and knead till smooth, let raise; then make into loaves, raise and bake.

MRS. S.H. KEENER, Knoxville, Tenn.

BATTER BREAD.

One quart buttermilk, one egg, one teacup waterground meal, one tablespoon sugar, one teaspoon salt, one-half teaspoon soda, one tablespoon butter, melted.

Beat well together, turn into a baking dish and bake until solid.

MRS. DAVID DUNN, Bristol, Tenn.

BATTER BREAD.

Three-fourths of a pint of meal, scalded, one and one-half pints buttermilk, two eggs, one large dessert spoon lard, one-half teaspoon soda, salt to taste.

Make the meal, buttermilk, eggs, into batter, then pour the lard melted into it. Bake quickly, first on the rack, then in the bottom of the oven. Use shallow pans.

MRS. EDWIN H. FAY, Knoxville, Tenn.

BROWN BREAD.

Three cups corn meal, one cup flour, two cups sweet milk, one cup buttermilk, one egg, one and one-half cups sorghum molasses, one and one-half teaspoons soda, one teaspoon salt.

Beat all together, pour in a mould and steam four hours. Just fine.

MRS. ELLA P. ANDERSON, Knoxville, Tenn.

BROWN BREAD.

One and one-half cups corn meal, one and one-half cups graham flour, three-fourths cup molasses, one pint buttermilk, one level teaspoon soda dissolved in buttermilk, one teaspoon salt. Steam three hours.

MRS. RICHARD P. JOHNSON, Knoxville, Tenn.

BROWN BREAD

Three cups meal, one cup flour, two cups sweet milk, one cup sour milk, one teaspoon each of salt and soda, one egg, one-half cup molasses. Steam three hours in closely covered bucket.

MRS. W.O. GREEN, Knoxville, Tenn.

BROWN BREAD.

Two cups graham flour, one cup white flour, one teaspoon soda in buttermilk, one-half cup brown sugar, one teaspoon salt, one pint buttermilk, steam three hours.

MISS MARY FRANCISCO, Knoxville, Tenn.

BROWN BREAD.

One egg, one cup molasses, one teaspoon of salt, one-half teaspoon of soda, one cup of buttermilk, two cups of sweetmilk, three tablespoons of flour, three cups of meal, steam four hours.

JULIA HARRISON BOYD, Knoxville, Tenn.

BROWN BREAD.

Two cups of sour milk, one-half cup of molasses, one pint of meal, four tablespoons of flour, one teaspoon of soda, piece of butter size of an egg, one cup of graham flour, one egg, steam three hours.

MOSELLE PORTER.

BROWN BREAD.

Two cups sweet milk, one cup buttermilk, three cups corn meal, one cup flour, one egg, one teaspoon salt, one teaspoon soda, one-half cup molasses, steam three hours, then turn out and dry in the oven.

MRS. J.W. OWEN, Bristol, Tenn.

BROWN BREAD.

Three cups meal, one cup white or graham flour, two cups sweet milk, one cup sour milk, one-half cup molasses, two eggs, one tablespoon lard, one teaspoon soda, dissolved in the sour milk. Steam three hours in well greased bucket, set in vessel of water.

MRS. WILL HAZEN, Knoxville, Tenn.

BROWN BREAD.

Two quarts of graham flour (unsifted), one quart of sour milk, three-fourths quart of molasses, one teaspoon of salt, one teaspoon of soda dissolved in milk. Bake one and one-half hours in moderate oven. Currants or raisins can be added.

MRS. GEORGE McCULLEY, Knoxville, Tenn.

BROWN BREAD.

Three cups meal, one cup flour, one cup buttermilk, two cups sweet milk, one egg, one-half cup brown sugar or molasses, a little salt and soda. Steam three hours in a tightly covered, greased bucket. To be eaten while hot. Cut at table with a white silk thread.

MRS. R.A.J. ARMSTRONG, Caswell, Tenn.

BROWN BREAD.

Two cups sweet milk, one cup butter, two cups corn meal, one cup flour, one cup molasses, one teaspoon soda, two teaspoons salt, two tablespoons melted butter, steam three hours.

MRS. RUSSELL, Knoxville, Tenn.

BOSTON BROWN BREAD.

Two cups flour, two cups meal, one cup molasses, cane preferred, three and one-half cups sweet milk, one teaspoon of soda and baking powder together, two eggs, a pinch of salt. Steam five hours.

MRS. FLOYD H. ROBERTS, Bristol, Va.-Tenn.

BOSTON BROWN BREAD.

Two cups Indian meal, one cup graham flour, one cup wheat flour, one quart sweet milk, one teaspoon salt, one and one-half cups New Orleans molasses, two teaspoons cream of tartar and one teaspoon of soda or two heaping teaspoons of baking powder.

Steam in covered baking powder cans for four hours. Water must be kept boiling all the time.

MRS. JOHN PEYTON MOFFETT, Knoxville. Tenn.

MRS. LINCOLN'S BROWN BREAD.

Two cups corn meal, one cup rye flour, one cup wheat flour, two teaspoons salt, two tablespoons soda, one pint sour milk, one cup molasses and add a little water, two tablespoons melted butter.

Mix dry ingredients and add to milk and molasses. When thoroughly mixed, put in baking powder cans. Fill half full ,and surround with hot water and steam three or four hours. Take out, remove lid and dry in oven for a few minutes.

CONTRIBUTED.

PREMIUM BROWN BREAD.

Two cups of meal, two cups of graham flour, three cups of sour milk, one cup of Porto Rico molasses, one cup of raisins, one teaspoon of salt, three even teaspoons of soda.

Pour liquids on solids, sprinkle raisins in after you begin pouring in greased mould or bucket. Steam four or five hours.

MRS. J.J. HAGER, Bristol, Tenn.

RAISIN BROWN BREAD.

Two cups buttermilk, one cup corn meal, two cups graham flour, one and one-half cups seeded raisins, one rounding teaspoon of soda dissolved in one cup of molasses, one teaspoon salt.

Put in baking powder cans, steam three hours and brown in oven five minutes.

MRS. H.P. WYMAN, Bristol, Tenn.

RAISIN BROWN BREAD.

Sift together two cups of graham flour, after removing bran, a teaspoon each of salt and soda and baking powder, mix into this two-thirds cup of raisins, half cup molasses and one and one-fourth cup of sour milk. Beat one egg well and add to the mixture and pour into a greased mold, after pressing raisins about the surface, steam for two hours. If a dark colored bread be preferred a little kitchen bouquet may be added.

MRS. MATTIE CAMDEN, Knoxvlle, Tenn.

CORN BREAD.

Two quarts of meal, three pints warm water, one tablespoon of sugar, a large tablespoon of yeast. Let rise five hours or until it is well-risen, then add about three-fourths pint of wheat flour and one-half pint warm water. Let rise one and one-half hours. Pour into a well-greased pan, let raise a few minutes and bake one and one-half hours in a moderate oven.

MRS. HUGH W. TAYLOR, Bristol, Tenn.

EGG BREAD.

One pint corn meal, one and one-half pints buttermilk, two eggs, one tablespoon melted lard or butter, a little soda and salt. Baked in moulds makes nice muffins.

MRS. E.J. BROWN, Bristol, Va.

EGG CORN BREAD.

One quart sifted meal, one quart of buttermilk, two eggs, one tablespoonful of lard, one teaspoonful of soda, light, if milk is not very sour, one teaspoon salt, one teaspoon of sugar, one-half cup of water. Put the water and lard in a pan on the stove, let come to a boil, stir a few spoonsful of the meal into the water and lard and then remove from the fire, pour on half the buttermilk, then meal, into which the soda has been sifted, the salt, the sugar and the half of the buttermilk, and lastly, the eggs, which have been beaten very light. Beat all well together and pour into a well-greased pan and bake in a very hot oven.

MRS. S.B. BOYD, Knoxville, Tenn.

GOOD CORN BREAD.

One pint meal, one egg, salt, flat teaspoon of soda, one-half table spoon of lard, not quite a pint of buttermilk.

MRS. PETWAY, Knoxville, Tenn.

HUCKLEBERRY BREAD.

One-half cup of butter, one cup of sugar, one quart of flour, one pint of huckleberries, salt to taste, and milk enough to make a stiff batter, (using either soda or baking powder, according to the kind of milk), two eggs.

Rub the sugar and butter together, adding the eggs which are not beaten, stir together, then the milk and flour, reserving enough flour to rub through the berries, which you add last. Bake in cake or biscuit pans and eat hot, just as you would rolls. If you use it as a pudding, take one and one-half cups of sugar and serve with hard sauce.

MRS. HENRY A. CHAMBERS, Chattanooga, Tenn.

LIGHT CORN BREAD.

Two quarts of corn meal, one quart graham flour, one pint sugar or molasses, one cup yeast, salt. Pour boiling water upon corn meal until thoroughly scalded, then cool, add graham flour, molasses, yeast, salt and water sufficient to make batter like muffin batter. Place in a well greased bucket or mould and let rise two hours or more, then steam three hours.

MRS. MARY HAZEN, Knoxville, Tenn.

NUT BREAD.

Scald one cup rolled oats with two cups boiling water and one tablespoon lard. When cool add one-half cup sugar, one quart of flour, one teaspoon salt, one-half cake yeast, dissolved in one-half cup warm water. Let rise over night. In the morning add one cup flour, one cup chopped English walnuts. Let rise again. Bake forty-five minutes in two loaves.

MRS. G.S. RINGLAND, Fort Dodge, Iowa.

AN OLD BACHELOR'S LIGHT BREAD.

Put in a gallon stone jar, one quart boiling water and one pint of fresh milk, two tablespoons sugar and one teaspoon of salt, stir in enough flour to make a stiff batter, then set in a warm place to rise. When it foams on top, knead in it flour enough to make a stiff dough, adding one even teaspoon of soda and one tablespoon of sugar. Set to rise in a warm place, and bake in a moderate oven.

MRS. GEORGE NETHERLAND, Grand Island, Fla.

OLD MAID'S BREAD.

Two and one-half tablespoons yeast, three eggs, one cup sweet milk, one tablespoon each of lard and butter, work in flour to make a soft dough and let it rise, then make it out in rolls, let rise and bake.

MRS. J.W.S. FRIERSON, Knoxville, Tenn.

POCKET BOOKS.

Take the usual quantity of yeast for three pints of flour, add three-fourths of a pound of butter, three eggs, and milk sufficient to make a dough. When well-risen roll out the dough one-half inch thick and cut into strips four inches wide, then divide these into pieces six or eight inches long, butter each piece, fold into the shape of a pocket book, let them rise the second time and bake quickly.

MISS MARY PLEAS McCLUNG, Knoxville, Tenn.

BREAD OR ROLLS.
Three medium sized Irish potatoes boiled soft, butter size of an egg, one egg, one teaspoon sugar, yeast as ordinarily used for one quart of flour.

Beat the egg separately, mash the potatoes while warm with the butter, sugar and yelk, then add the yeast, and last, the white beaten stiff. Let stand to rise about fifteen minutes, then pour into the flour and work well. After it is risen, make into lapovers or single rolls.

MRS. E.J. BROWN, Bristol, Va.

BREAD PANCAKES.
Two cups of broken bread, soaked over night in a cup of hot milk. The next morning put through a sieve, add one heaping teaspoon of sugar, one teaspoon of salt, two tablespoons melted butter, and two well-beaten eggs. Beat thoroughly, then sift in one cup of flour sifted with one teaspoon of soda. Lastly add one cup of sour milk and bake.

CONTRIBUTED.

SALT RISEN BREAD.
In the afternoon, or evening, according to the time of year, take a level teaspoon of sugar, two good teaspoons of flour and four teaspoons of meal and put in a glass. Put on the fire, a gill of fresh sweet milk and let it come to a boil, then pour over the mixture in the glass and beat well, tie a paper over the glass and put in the outside part of a double boiler, dry, and put on the lid. Put in a warm place and the next morning you will see through the glass that it is well-risen. Then put on a pint of sweet milk and let it come to a boil, set aside till blood-warm, then stir it in about a quart of flour, one-half teaspoon of salt and add the yeast in the glass. Set in warm water and in a warm place to rise, which it will do in a short time.

Take four quarts of flour, a teaspoon of salt, and a big tablespoon of lard, work the lard in the flour, then push aside a part of the flour and wet the rest in the pan with boiling water, working it up and putting it out on the board, making about a pint, the rest must have the yeast poured into it with a pinch of soda and be worked up into bread, then mix with the other and put on the board and work for fifteen minutes, or till it blisters.

Make into loaves, grease the tops and put in well-greased pans and set to rise in a warm place, when the loaf has little seams over the top it is ready to bake. Have the oven tolerably hot at first and add more heat. Turn out of the pan and set on end at open window to cool.

MARGARET WISDOM.

SALT RISEN BREAD.
Put half a pint of new milk on the fire and let it come to a boil. Thicken with meal and set in a warm place to rise. Do this about supper time. The next morning when the yeast is light, take half a pint of boiling water and dissolve in it a level teaspoon of sugar and one of soda, then fill up with a half pint of cold water. Make a tolerably thick batter with flour, let it be thick enough to drop from a spoon, then add the yeast and set in a warm place to rise. When risen make a sponge using half tepid water and half tepid milk, adding butter, or lard and salt, about a tablespoon of lard and a teaspoon of salt to three quarts of flour. Let this sponge rise, keeping it in a warm place, then work it down, working it a good deal. Put in pans, greasing the tops of the loaves with softened lard and set in a warm place to rise. When ready to bake it will be very light and have little seams over the top. Bake in a hot oven and stand in the air to cool. When cold put in bread box to keep moist, but do not wrap a cloth around it.

MISS GREEVER, Burk's Garden, Va.

SALT RISEN BREAD.
Two pints of sifted flour, one and one-half pints fresh sweet milk, three tablespoons scalded meal. Enough salt to taste in the batter. Boil milk and set aside to cool, while you scald your meal, stir in your meal first, then the flour, beat all to a smooth batter and put to rise in a moderately warm place. When this yeast has risen make up your bread, using flour according to the number of loaves you wish. It takes about one quart of flour to make one loaf.

MISS ANN BELL, Knoxville, Tenn.

SALT RISING BREAD.

One teacup of meal, one teaspoon each of salt and sugar, one tablespoon of flour, stir up with a pint of boiling water, leaving out about an inch of boiling water and filling up with cold water. Put in a double boiler and set in a warm place to rise. In winter make up about two o'clock, in warm weather make up in the evening.

In the morning, stir in a pinch of soda (when the yeast is light) and make a pretty thick batter with flour, beat well and put in a warm place to rise. Then take four quarts of flour, a teaspoon of salt and a tablespoon of lard, rubbed well in the flour, add the yeast and whatever milkwarm water the flour requires, work for fifteen minutes and make into loaves. Put in greased pans and grease well the tops of the loaves and put in a warm place; when it rises and cracks open in little seams it is ready to bake. Do not have too hot an oven. With this quantity of yeast you can make more bread, but will have to add more salt and lard, or if you wish only a little bread, make up half the quantity of yeast.

MRS. HUGH W. TAYLOR, Bristol, Tenn.

SALT RISING BREAD.

Take a teacup of new milk at night; let it come to a boil and stir in two or three tablespoons of corn meal to make a batter. Set in a warm place, next morning thin with warm water and add two or three tablespoons of flour, a pinch of salt and same of sugar. Put in a warm place; it will rise in two hours. Take two quarts of flour, one tablespoon of lard, one teaspoon of salt, make up with the yeast and if necessary use tepid water, knead well, set in a warm place to rise, and bake in a moderately hot oven.

MRS. T.S. WEBB, Knoxville, Tenn.

SOFT BATTER BREAD.

One quart sweet milk, one pint corn meal, one pint thick, sour cream, one teaspoon soda, one dessertspoon of salt, six eggs, lump of butter size of an egg.

Heat the milk to near boiling, then add the meal gradually, put on stove and stir till like smooth thin mush, do not let it boil. Add the salt and butter and let the mixture cool. When cool enough, add the sour cream, in which you have dissolved the soda, then the eggs, well beaten. Bake in a moderate oven, cover until it has risen and is nearly done, then uncover and brown. Half this quantity is enough for a small family.

MRS. MARY A. BYARS, Bristol, Va.-Tenn.

SPOON CORN BREAD.

One quart fresh buttermilk, into which beat one teaspoon of soda. Beat two eggs very light and stir into the buttermilk and soda; have ready one scant pint of sifted meal, into which put a teaspoon of salt and stir the meal slowly into the milk. Add one teaspoon of lard or butter and bake in an earthen dish in hot oven one hour.

MRS. LENA LAYMAN, Daleville, Va.

SPOON CORN BREAD.

One pint of corn meal, scalded with boiling water, two eggs, beaten till very light, three tablespoons melted butter, a pinch of salt; enough sweet milk to make a thin batter.

Bake in earthen dish nearly one hour. Serve while hot from baking dish with a spoon.

MRS. G.M. BURNS, Knoxville, Tenn.

STEAMED CORN BREAD.

One cup buttermilk, two cups, sweet milk, or water, one-half teaspoon each of salt and soda, three cups corn meal, one cup flour, one-half cup molasses, one egg, steam three hours.

MRS. ELLEN WRIGHTT, Damascus, Va.

STEAMED CORN BREAD.

One cup flour, three cups meal, one teaspoon salt, two cups sweetmilk, one cup sour milk, one teaspoon soda, one cup molasses.

Dissolve the soda in one tablespoon water, mix and steam three hours in a steamer.

MRS. JOHN W. CATES, Maryville, Tenn.

STEAMED CORN BREAD.

Two cups sweet milk, one cup sour milk, three cups corn meal, one cup flour, one-half cup dark sugar or molasses, one egg, one teaspoon soda, one of salt. Steam in double boiler three hours.

MRS. J.N. MOORE, Knoxville, Tenn.

STEAMED CORN BREAD.

Two eggs, beaten separately, three cups meal, two cups sweet milk, one cup flour, one-half or three-fourths cup New Orleans molasses, one-half cup lard, two teaspoons soda.

Put in a bucket with a tight lid and boil in a kettle of water for three hours.

MRS. MORRIS, Chattanooga, Tenn.

STEAMED CORN BREAD.

Two cups of sweet milk, one cup of sour milk, three cups of corn meal, one cup of flour, one-half cup of molasses; one egg, one teaspoon of soda, one teaspoon of salt; steam four hours.

MRS. KATE WALKER, Ebeneezer, Tenn.

STEAMED PONE.

Three cups meal, one cup flour, one cup sour milk, two cups sweet milk, two-thirds cup of molasses, one teaspoonful of soda, dissolved in one tablespoon of water, salt to taste. Steam three hours.

MRS. CATES, Maryville, Tenn.

BREAD STICKS.

Add one-fourth of a cup of butter, one and one-half tablespoons of sugar, and one-half teaspoon of salt to one cup of scalded milk; when lukewarm add one yeast cake dissolved in one-fourth of a cup of lukewarm water, the white of one egg, well-beaten, and three and three-fourths cups of flour.

Knead, let rise, shape, let rise again, and start baking in a hot oven, reducing the heat that the sticks may be crisp and dry. To shape the sticks first shape as small biscuits, roll on the board (where there is no flour) with the hands from five to eight inches in length, as desired, keeping of uniform size and rounded ends, which may be accomplished by bringing fingers close to, but not over the ends of the sticks. Pile the sticks when baked, log-cabin fashion on a plate covered with a doily.

FANNIE MERRITT FARMER, *Woman's Home Companion.*

UNLEAVENED BREAD.

Two cups flour, one teaspoon salt, one teaspoon sugar, one tablespoon butter, sweet milk for a stiff dough. Roll one-fourth of an inch thick and mark off into squares.

MRS. HATTIE KING TAYLOR, Bristol, Tenn.

FRENCH BUNS.

One quart flour, two tablespoons of good yeast, two eggs, one teaspoon of salt, one tablespoon of sugar, a lump of lard, or butter, the size of a hen's egg.

Sift the flour, rub in the lard and salt, beat the eggs very light and add to the flour with the yeast, and add enough sweet milk to make a stiff batter. Let it rise eight or nine hours and work over two hours before baking in a quick oven. The buns should not touch each other in the pan. One quart of flour will make one dozen buns.

MRS. EDWIN H. FAY, Knoxville, Tenn.

BUCKWHEAT CAKES.

Sift together one quart of buckwheat flour and a teacup of corn meal. In cool weather make up a moderately thin batter with lukewarm sweet milk, salt to taste, add half a tumbler of good yeast. Make in a jar, covering closely, at nine o'clock at night. The next morning, beat in three eggs. Let it stand fifteen or twenty minutes. Just before frying, stir in a small teaspoon of soda, just sprinkling it over the batter. Bake any size you like. Serve with melted butter and nice syrup. Reserve half a cup of this batter for the cakes next morning.

MRS. A.P. WHITE, Knoxville, Tenn.

BUCKWHEAT CAKES.

One pint meal, two pints buckwheat, one pint milkwarm water, one teaspoon salt, one teacup yeast, mix all together. It will make a very stiff batter.

In the morning, stir one teaspoon of soda into one pint of milk warm water and stir in the buckwheat batter, beat thoroughly until the batter is smooth. Put soda in fifteen minutes before frying the cakes. Half this quantity is sufficient for a small family.

MRS. S.B. BOYD, Knoxville, Tenn.

CREAM CAKES.

Beat three eggs very light, stir them into a quart of cream, alternately with a quart of sifted flour, and add one wine glass of yeast and a salt spoon of salt.

Cover the batter and set it near the fire to rise, when it is light, stir in a large tablespoon of butter that has been warmed. Bake the cakes in muffin rings and serve hot. Split with your fingers and butter.

MRS. R.S. HAZEN, Knoxville, Tenn.

BATTER CAKES.

One egg, one dessert spoon of butter one pint flour, three-fourths of a pint of sweet milk, a teaspoon of soda dissolved in a little warm water added just before cooking.

MRS. H.H. TAYLOR, Knoxville, Tenn.

MUSH CAKES.

Beat three eggs well, separately, of course. Take one pint of flour and one pint of cold mush, one quart of milk, one spoonful of butter or lard, beat all well together and bake in a griddle. Make the mush the night previous. Rice batter cakes are made the same way, using cold boiled rice instead of the mush.

MRS. GEN'L A. ANDERSON, Knoxville, Tenn.

CONES.

Four eggs, one quart sugar, four heaping cups flour, water enough to make thin like molasses, one spoonful of vanilla.

C.H. JENKINS, Ocean Grove. N. J.

CORN DODGERS.

One quart of meal, level teaspoon of soda, teaspoon of salt, level tablespoon of lard, one pint of sour milk. Mix well and make out into pones and put in pan, pressing down with the hand.

SADIE COPELAND, Knoxville, Tenn.

OLD FASHIONED CORN DODGERS.

To a light quart of meal, with a teaspoon of soda, and one-half teaspoon salt sifted in it, add one pint fresh buttermilk. Make in dodgers and bake in a moderate oven.

CONTRIBUTED.

BACHELOR'S LOAF.

Pour on three-fourths of a pound of sifted corn meal, one pint of boiling hot new milk, stirring well together. Beat the whites and yellows of three eggs separately, reserving the whites for the last. Add a little salt and a spoonful of lard. Pour into greased pans and bake over an hour.

ANNIE HARDIMAN.

SWISS LIPS.

One-half cake Fleishman's yeast, beaten with an egg and one-half cup sugar, half cup butter, one cup mashed Irish potatoes, one of scalded and chilled sweet milk, flour for a stiff batter. Set at two o'clock in the afternoon, after tea, beat in all the flour you can, next morning after breakfast beat down with spoon. It is not necessary to add more flour or touch it with the hand.

One and one-half hours before dinner, put on a slightly floured board, work half a minute, roll half an inch thick, cut with a biscuit cutter, lay in buttered pan, place on top each biscuit another turned-over in softened butter, let rise an hour in moderate heat and bake in quick oven twenty minutes.

In the winter, this dough will keep three days in a cool place. In summer time begin in the morning for tea in the evening.

MRS. HATTIE KING TAYLOR, Bristol, Tenn.

SALLY LUNN.

One pint of sweet milk, three eggs, one teaspoon of sugar, one and one-half pints sifted flour, one teaspoon salt, one ounce butter, one gill of good yeast, or one-fourth of a compressed cake.

Scald the milk, add to it the butter and stand on one side until lukewarm, then add the yeast, salt, sugar and flour, beat continuously for five minutes, cover and stand in a warm place for two hours, or until very light; then beat the eggs separately until very light, add first the yelks and then the whites; stir them in carefully; stand again in a warm place for fifteen minutes; then turn into a greased Turk's head and bake in a moderately quick oven forty minutes.

MRS. RORER.

SALLY LUNN.

One pint new milk, four eggs, large spoon butter, or butter and lard mixed, flour to make a good batter, pinch of salt, tablespoon sugar, teacup good yeast.

Put shortening into milk and warm, stir eggs, flour, yeast, etc., into this beat well, and put in a warm place to rise. Beat a second time and put into a pan or mould for second rising. Bake in moderate oven. It will take from forty-five minutes to an hour to bake thoroughly. The first rising should take about six or eight hours, the second about one and one-half hours.

MISS MARGARET PRESTON, Seven Mile Ford, Va.

SALLY LUNN.

One pint sifted flour, one cup white sugar, one small cup butter, one cup milk, three eggs, two teaspoons cream of tartar, one teaspoon soda, a little salt, stir all together, bake twenty minutes.

MRS. R.S. HAZEN, Knoxville, Tenn.

SALLY LUNN.

One pint flour, three eggs; small lump of butter, one tablespoon of sugar, make the dough a little softer than light biscuit.

MRS. T.W. FLEMING, Knoxville, Tenn.

SALLY LUNN.

At nine o'clock in the morning make a batter of one small yeast cake, dissolved in a teacup of tepid water with flour enough to make a tolerably stiff batter, set in a warm place to rise. By noon it will be perfectly light, then make a batter of four eggs, well beaten, ten ounces of butter, light weight, four ounces of sugar, one good tumbler of yeast, and one of sweet milk, with flour enough to make a stiff batter and let stand in a warm place till it rises. Then beat down and pour into the pan it is to be baked in. When it rises again, bake in a moderate oven. Excellent.

MRS. A.P. WHITE, Knoxville, Tenn.

SALLY LUNN.

Beat two eggs, add one-half cup each of cold water, yeast and sugar melted and cooled, butter size of an egg, two and one-half cups of unsifted flour. Set at twelve. Two or three hours before supper pour into a cake pan, raise outside the stove one or more hours, bake an hour.

MRS. GREENWAY, Abingdon, Va.

SALLY LUNN.

Sponge, two eggs, four tablespoon sugar, two tablespoons butter, three teaspoons salt, one and one-half to two cups flour. To the risen sponge add the beaten eggs, the salt and the sugar. Pour in the melted butter and add enough flour to make a stiff batter. Beat well and pour into buttered tins to rise.

CONTRIBUTED.

SALLY LUNN.

Two eggs, one-half cup each of sugar and sweet milk, tablespoon of butter, one ounce lard, two cups very light yeast, batter and flour to make a very stiff batter.

Beat sugar and eggs very light before adding other ingredients, then beat all well together and set to rise. When light beat down and let rise again, after which pour into well buttered pans or baking dishes, let rise an hour, or till light and bake in a moderate oven. This is not so rich, but very light and nice.

MRS. JOHN M. BROOKS, Knoxville, Tenn.

SALLY LUNN.

One quart flour, one teaspoon salt, one tablespoon white sugar, rub in a heaping tablespoon of butter and lard in equal parts, then rub in one Irish potato, mashed fine, half a teacup yeast, three eggs well-beaten.

Make up the dough to the consistency of light bread dough, with warm water in winter, and cold in summer. Knead half an hour. When it has risen light, handle lightly, put into a cake mould and bake without a second kneading.

MRS. R.G. HANSON, Bristol, Va.-Tenn.

SALLY LUNN.

Two eggs, beaten separately, one-half pint sweet milk, one tablespoon butter or lard, two tablespoons sugar, flour to make a stiff batter, then add a tablespoon of good yeast, let rise several hours, make into rolls, let rise again and bake.

MRS. LIZZIE BECK, Knoxville, Tenn.

SALLY LUNN.

Two and one-fourth cups flour, one cup butter, five eggs, one cup new milk, one tablespoon sugar, one and one-half cups potato yeast. Stir well until the sponge will leave the spoon, let rise the second time before baking.

Bake one hour in moderate oven. This makes a large cake.

MRS. R.V. DAVIS, Abingdon, Va.

SALLY LUNN BISCUIT.

Three pints of flour, two eggs, two large tablespoons of shortening, one-half teacup of white sugar, one teacup liquid yeast. Mix well, set to rise, work down, let rise again and roll out and cut in biscuit, let rise and bake.

MRS. J.A. RAYL, Knoxville, Tenn.

ROCKBRIDGE SALLY LUNN.

Four eggs, four ounces sugar, ten ounces butter, light weight, a tumbler of sweet milk and one of very light yeast batter, with enough flour to make a very stiff batter.

Cream the butter, beat the eggs well, before adding sugar, then pour them on the butter and beat well together, after which add the yeast, milk and flour and beat well until smooth. Set to rise, when light, beat down and let it rise again, then pour into well buttered pans or baking dishes, let this rise an hour and bake in a moderate oven. This is very rich.

MRS. JOHN M. BROOKS, Knoxville, Tenn.

MUFFINS.

Three eggs, beaten separately, one pint sweet milk, one pint flour, lard size of a walnut, salt, add whites of eggs last thing. Bake quickly.

MRS. E.S. McCLUNG, Knoxville, Tenn.

MUFFINS.

Beat four eggs well together, then stir in a pint sweet milk, and beat in two and one-half pints flour, one tablespoon lard, melted, a little salt and again one and one-half pints milk, one tablespoon lard, melted, a little salt and again and one-half pints milk.

Bake in moderately hot oven.

MISS SUE DEADERICK, Knoxville, Tenn.

MUFFINS.

Sift together one cup of flour, slightly rounded, a good half pint, and one generously heaped teaspoon baking powder and a salt spoon of salt, add one-half cup of sweet milk and one well-beaten egg, and bake immediately in a very hot oven.

If the white and yelk of the egg are beaten separately, the muffins will be lighter. This quantity is sufficient for half a dozen muffins.

MRS. J.S. McDONOUGH, Knoxville, Tenn.

MUFFINS.

Two eggs well beaten, one cup of sweet milk, one tablespoon of lard, one tablespoon of butter, two teaspoons of baking powder, one tablespoon of sugar and a good pinch of salt.

First beat eggs, then put in milk, then sugar and salt and then melted butter and lard, lastly put in the flour. The baking powder must be put in the flour and then sifted twice, beat batter well and bake in a hot oven.

MISS CONWAY, Niagara Falls, N. Y.

MUFFINS.

Warm one pint of sweet milk with one-half cup of butter, add three eggs, a little salt, one teaspoon of sugar, one-half cup of yeast, or one-half yeast cake, flour to make a very stiff batter, let rise ten or twelve hours, add one-half teaspoon of soda, pour into rings or a pan and let rise about an hour and bake.

MRS. BRIGHT, Canada.

BREAD MUFFINS.

Cover one pint stale bread crumbs with one pint sweet milk a half an hour before using, then add yelks of two eggs well-beaten, one tablespoon melted butter, one teaspoon salt and about one cup of flour with two teaspoons baking powder, lastly the well-beaten whites. Bake in gem pans in a moderate oven, thinned a little can be made into cakes.

CONTRIBUTED.

BROWNED CRUMB MUFFINS. (ORIGINAL)

Brown bread slowly, so as to dry out. Then grind in Enterprise meat grinder, keeping light bread and biscuit separate.

Take one quart buttermilk, one teaspoon soda, one egg, one pint of flour, adding enough of the browned crumbs to make a stiff batter, heaping tablespoon lard or butter, salt to taste.

Bake in iron gem. If using biscuit crumbs it takes less shortening. These crumbs make fine batter cakes, using some flour with crumbs. I prefer them to cracker crumbs for minced oysters.

MRS. J.P. McMULLEN, Knoxville, Tenn.

CORN MUFFINS.

One pint buttermilk, one egg, heaping half pint meal, salt, one tablespoon of melted lard, one level teaspoon soda, bake in quick oven.

MRS. JAMES PARK, Knoxville, Tenn.

CORN MUFFINS.

Two eggs, one quart buttermilk, one quart meal, three spoons of lard poured in while hot, a level teaspoon soda.

MRS. B.J. STEPHENSON, Knoxville, Tenn.

CORN MEAL MUFFINS.

One egg, one pint buttermilk, scant teaspoon soda, saltspoon salt, one pint meal.

Beat the egg, add milk, salt and soda, beat, then lastly the meal and pour into muffin rings piping hot and bake in a quick oven, always use water-ground meal, if possible.

MRS. JOHN RICHARDS, Knoxville, Tenn.

GRAHAM MUFFINS.

One pint of graham flour, not sifted, two eggs, one-half cup of brown sugar, a little salt, two teaspoons baking powder, a piece of lard, size of an egg, or a heaping tablespoonful. Beat the eggs well, add a little sweet milk and all the graham flour, then the sugar and salt and lard, melted, beat thoroughly, then add enough more milk to make batter as stiff as ordinary corn muffins, lastly put in the baking powder, mixed in an equal quantity of graham flour. Bake in a quick oven.

MRS. HENRY A. CHAMBERS, Chattanooga, Tenn.

PHOEBE'S MUFFINS.

One pint meal, one big spoon flour, one teaspoon sugar, one and one-half teaspoons baking powder, one-half teaspoon soda, one or two eggs, one-half tablespoon lard, pint buttermilk, add more milk if you wish to make cakes, one-half teaspoon salt.

PHOEBE JINES, Knoxville, Tenn.

WHEAT MUFFINS.

Three cups sweet milk, three eggs, beaten separately, three cups flour and a lump of butter or lard size of a walnut, rubbed into it, salt to taste. The whites of the eggs must be put in last. Bake in a hot oven.

MRS. HENRY A. CHAMBERS, Chattanooga, Tenn.

WHOLE WHEAT MUFFINS.

Two cups whole wheat flour, two tablespoons olive oil or butter, one tablespoon molasses, three teaspoons baking powder, one level teaspoon salt. Add warm water or milk to make thick batter, and bake quickly. An egg may be used. Oven hot, pans warmed.

MRS. RICHARD P. JOHNSON, Knoxville, Tenn.

WHITE FLOUR MUFFINS.

Two tablespoons butter, two tablespoons sugar, two cups flour, two teaspoons baking powder, two eggs, one-half teaspoon salt, one cup milk.

Cream the butter and sugar in warm mixing bowl; in a sieve place two cups sifted flour and on top of this the baking powder; beat the eggs and salt to a thick cream; over the creamed butter and sugar sift the flour; over the flour pour the beaten eggs, then the milk. After creaming the butter and sugar do not stir a stroke until you arrive at this point, but now blend the ingredients barely enough to moisten the flour, but not enough to make a smooth batter, the lumps will take care of themselves. The object is to get the batter into the oven as quickly as possible after the liquids are added.

E.B.

BAKING POWDER.

One pound cream of tartar, one-half pound soda, one-fourth pound flour, mix and sift six times. I put alternate spoons of each in the sifter the first time. Seal the cans not in use with a strip of cloth wet with white of egg.

MRS. JOS. T. McTEER, Knoxville, Tenn.

THE VERY BEST BAKING POWDER.

Get one-half pound of bicarbonate of soda, one pound of pure cream of tartar and one ounce of corn starch. Sift two or three times. Use about one tablespoonful for each pound flour.

MR. HOLMDEN, London, England.

ROGERSVILLE PUFFS.

One quart of sweet milk and four eggs, one quart of flour and a piece of butter as large as an egg. Rub the butter in the flour, have the milk a little warmer than new milk, but not hot, beat the eggs thoroughly and separately, add half the milk and all the flour and beat well, then add the remainder of the milk. Have your moulds hot before pouring in the batter and bake in a quick oven. Half this quantity is enough for a small family.

MRS. HENRY A. CHAMBERS, Chattanooga, Tenn.

ROLLS.

One quart flour, one tablespoon lard, one level teaspoon each of salt and sugar, one cup of "Mothers Yeast" or any good yeast.

Mix all together to rather soft dough. If the yeast does not make it soft enough, use tepid water. Make up at eleven o'clock for six o'clock tea, at four o'clock make into rolls, brush with softened lard, put in pans for baking let rise and bake.

MRS. E.S. McCLUNG, Knoxville, Tenn.

ROLLS.

Two cups bread sponge, one-half cup sugar, one-half cup lard, one-half cup warm water. Mix together, add sufficient flour to work well, then let rise and make into rolls. Let rise again and bake. This makes about twelve large rolls.

MRS. S.H. KEENER, Knoxville, Tenn.

ROLLS.

One quart milk, one-half cup butter, two tablespoons white sugar, one cake yeast (Fleishmann's), one teaspoon salt, two quarts or more of flour.

Scald the milk and butter together; when partly cool make a thin sponge with part of the flour and other ingredients, set to rise. When ready, in about an hour or so, mix in the rest of the flour, knead and let it rise again. Roll, cut out, put in pan and let rise the third time. Bake in a hot oven. If wanted at six P.M., can start about 11 A.M.

MRS. JON. PEYTON MOFFETT, Knoxville, Tenn.

ROLLS OR BREAD.

One-half cup scalded milk, one-half cup boiling water, one-half tablespoon lard, one-half tablespoon butter, three-fourths teaspoon salt, one teaspoon sugar, one cake Fleishmann's yeast dissolved in one-eighth cup lukewarm water, three cups flour.

To hot milk add sugar, salt, butter and lard. Let cool, add yeast, dissolved in water. then flour. Keep dough soft. Put in pan for one loaf bread. or make into rolls. While rising keep at about seventy degrees.

If more than one loaf is wanted, increase all ingredients proportionately except the yeast.

MRS. RICHARD P. JOHNSON.

BAKING POWDER ROLLS.

These rolls are dainty and inviting for tea if made of the usual baking powder dough, cut into round biscuit, brushed with melted butter and folded over into "pocket book" rolls. Bake in a brisk oven and serve at once.

MRS. DANIEL BRISCOE, SR., Knoxville, Tenn.

FRENCH ROLLS.

Two pints of flour, one teaspoon of sugar, a little salt, one-half pint of water, milkwarm in winter, one-half tablespoon of butter or cottolene, one-half teacup of yeast. If you wish it a little richer, you may add one egg, white and yelk beaten separately. To prepare the yeast: take one-third of a cake of any good yeast, dissolve in half a cup of lukewarm water, when soft stir in flour to make a pretty thick batter, make the yeast in the. evening, next day it will be ready to use.

For supper make up about ten o'clock. Two pints will give you rolls and a small loaf of bread.

MRS. S.B. BOYD, Knoxville, Tenn.

GRAHAM FINGER ROLLS.

Into four cupsful of graham flour, stir one level teaspoon of salt, and one and three-quarters of a cup of sweet cream. Sift graham flour on the kneading board; roll a tablespoon of the dough under your palms to the desired thickness and length, bake in a moderate oven.

CONTRIBUTED.

LIGHT ROLLS.

Three medium Irish potatoes, peel and boil in one quart of water. When done mash and pour the potato water over them, let them stand till lukewarm. Dissolve one-fourth of a cake of any good dry yeast with a little of the potato water, then mix it with the potatoes and let stand in a warm place till light, and before setting it to lighten add one teaspoon of salt and one tablespoon of sugar.

For the Rolls— Take one quart of flour, lard size of a hen's egg, one level teaspoon of salt and a half teaspoon of sugar. Mix with one-fourth of the yeast, well stirred and add water if necessary. Work till smooth and set to rise. After it has risen make into rolls; and after these have risen, bake in a moderate oven.

MRS. C. W. McCUE, Huntington, W. Va.

LIGHT ROLLS.

Peel, slice and boil four medium sized Irish potatoes in one quart of water, when soft mash to a cream. Take three teacups of sifted flour and scald with the potato water, add potatoes and more boiling water, if necessary, to make a batter a little thinner than mush. When milkwarm, add one cake of Magic yeast that has been dissolved in a small amount of lukewarm water. This is the yeast.

For the Bread— Take one quart of flour, add to the flour one rounded tablespoon each of lard and sugar and one teaspoon of salt, one tablespoon of yeast, and tepid water to make a stiff dough, so no other flour will be required. Work and put to rise. Next morning roll on the board, not too thin and cut with a baking powder can. Rub tops and pans with softened lard not melted and raise slowly. Bake in a moderate oven.

MRS. MARY CARTER, Knoxville, Tenn.

LIGHT ROLLS.

Two quarts flour, one tablespoon lard, two teaspoons sugar, two eggs, one teacup yeast, or half cake of Fleischmann's yeast, one good sized Irish potato rubbed into the flour, knead well. Set to rise in the morning or over night. When risen, make into rolls, handling lightly, grease tops and set to rise again, and when risen bake.

MRS. R.G. HANSON, Bristol, Va.-Tenn.

WINTER ROLLS.

Scald one quart of buttermilk, one cup of lard, pour over three quarts of flour, beat well. Add one quart cold water, one cup potato yeast; now set to rise; add salt and flour to make a dough, when risen set to rise again, covering tightly in a cool place. When needed roll out thickness of soda biscuit, put in iron oven to bake.

MRS. J.G. CHAFFIN, Knoxville, Tenn.

RUSK.

One cup of yeast, three eggs, one-half pound brown .sugar, one pint milk, lump butter, size of a hen egg.

Let the milk, butter and sugar come to a boil, then let them boil, add the eggs whites and yelks beaten separately and enough flour to make a sponge, set to rise. Next morning, when light, add more flour and let rise again, then make into rolls and let rise, and when light bake.

MRS. J.A. RAYL, Knoxville, Tenn.

RUSK.

To three well-beaten eggs add one and one-half cups sugar, one of butter, three of light yeast batter and flour enough to make a stiff batter. When this is risen very light, (it is best when set to rise over night), add flour to make a soft dough, knead well and set to rise again. When light make into rolls. Let rise and bake. Beat a little sugar into some cream and put this smoothly over the top of the rolls just before taking them from the oven.

MRS. JOHN M. BROOKS, Knoxville, Tenn.

RUSK.

One pint new milk, three-fourths pound sugar, butter size of a large egg, three eggs, one cake yeast, teaspoon salt, flour enough to make a pretty stiff batter.

Put milk, sugar and butter on the stove and let come to a boil, when nearly cool add the eggs, beaten separately, and the yeast dissolved in a little warm water, then the salt and flour. Put in a warm place and when light make into rolls and let rise again. Before baking break an egg into a cup and with soft rag put on tops of rolls.

MRS. ALICE DEADERICK McCLUNG, Knoxville, Tenn.

RUSK.

Seven eggs, one and one-half pounds sugar, one quart sweet milk, one-fourth pound butter, put in and warmed, two tablespoons yeast and flour sufficient to make a stiff batter. Make this up at night and let it rise until morning, then make it into a stiff dough and let it stand for several hours until light, when it must be made into rolls, let rise again and bake.

For Doughnuts—Take part of the dough, cut in any shape or form you may fancy and fry in an oven with sufficient lard to let them swim. In this way you can have rusks and doughnuts at the same time, though in summer when the lard becomes a little strong the doughnuts should be omitted.

MISS SUE DEADERICK, Knoxville, Tenn.

RUSK.

In the evening take one pint sweet milk, three-fourths pint sugar, butter size of an egg, put them in a saucepan and let come to a boil, then take off till milkwarm. Beat the whites and yelks of three eggs till light, stir one quart of flour into the milk and add the beaten eggs, which are beaten separately, add five spoonsful of yeast and set to rise.

In the morning when light, stir in flour till it becomes thick batter, then set to rise again, when risen make out into rolls, using as little flour as possible, for if stiff they are not so nice, put to rise and when light bake in a quick oven.

MRS. J.G.M. RAMSEY, Knoxville, Tenn.

CREAM SCONES.

Mix and sift two cups flour, four teaspoons baking powder, two teaspoons sugar, one-half teaspoon salt, rub into dry ingredients with tips of fingers four tablespoons of butter; add three eggs beaten thick and lemon colored; add one-third cup rich cream; toss on floured board, pat and roll to three-fourths inch in thickness; cut in squares then crease diagonally and brush over with white of egg, sprinkle with sugar and bake in hot oven twenty minutes.

ELIZABETH O. HILLER, Chicago, Ill.

SCOTCH POTATO SCONES.

One and one-half cups of flour, one-third cup butter, one cup mashed potatoes, two teaspoons baking powder, one-half teaspoon salt, one egg.

Sift the flour, salt and baking powder together, and after adding the mashed potatoes rub in the butter lightly. Make a soft dough by adding the egg well beaten, and, if necessary, a little milk. Make the dough of the right consistency to roll out. If the potato happens to be moist, no milk will be required. Divide the dough into three parts and roll into rounds about half an inch thick. Cut these across twice, so as to make four parts, but do not cut it quite through. Bake in a quick oven, or on a griddle, and when they are done, split and butter and serve hot.

WOMEN'S HOME COMPANION.

CREAM EGG TOAST.

Toast and butter three slices of bread. Put in a saucepan one teacup of rich milk, one tablespoon of butter, white pepper and salt to taste. Beat well two eggs, when the milk boils, pour over the eggs, set in a pan of hot water and stir constantly for a few minutes, when thick, pour over the eggs and serve at once.

MRS. BARNETT, Atlanta, Ga.

DATE WAFERS.
Roll some of the dough made as directed in the "Graham Finger Rolls" as thin as possible and spread with a layer of washed and seeded dates. Cover these with a stratum of dough of the same thickness as the lower. Cut into squares and bake. These are fine and better for children than cookies or cakes.

CONTRIBUTED.

WAFFLES.
Place three heaping pints sifted flour in mixing bowl, one-half teaspoon salt, two eggs, three if eggs are small, stir gently until well mixed, add three kitchen spoons melted lard, and lastly, one-half teaspoon soda dissolved in a little hot water. Stir gently until well mixed, as beating makes batter tough. Fry in well greased waffle irons. Serve hot.

MISS IDA HOOD, Knoxville, Tenn.

WAFFLES.
One level pint of flour and one tablespoon corn meal, one level teaspoon soda and half teaspoon salt, one heaping teaspoon baking powder, one-half pint fresh buttermilk, one egg.

Sift the soda, flour and meal together, taking out a little of the flour to be mixed with the baking powder and added at the last, mix with the buttermilk, then add the well beaten egg and melted butter. Stir in lightly the remainder of the flour into. which the baking powder had been sifted and begin baking the waffles at once.

MRS. J.S. McDONOUGH, Knoxville, Tenn.

WAFFLES.
Two cups flour, one teaspoon baking powder, one-half teaspoon salt, three eggs, pint milk, half cup cream. Sift flour, baking powder and salt together, beat yelks of eggs well, add cream and milk; lastly stir in carefully the well-beaten whites of three eggs, bake in well greased waffle irons a nice brown. Excellent.

MRS. CHARLES LEONHARDT, Knoxville, Tenn.

WAFFLES.
Two eggs, beat separately, two and one-half cups buttermilk, not very sour, one tablespoon melted lard. Mix the yellows and milk with one teaspoon, a light one, of soda and a teaspoon of salt.

Put in a quart of flour, stir gently, then put in lard, lastly add the whites, which have been beaten to a stiff froth, stir just enough to get together, don't beat. This batter can be baked as muffins if desired.

CORDIE CARMICHAEL, Rogersville, Tenn.

WAFFLES.
One quart flour, level teaspoon baking powder, level teaspoon soda, one tablespoon melted butter, level teaspoon salt, one egg, well beaten, one pint buttermilk. Have irons hot enough to brown nicely.

SADIE COPELAND, Bristol, Tenn.

WAFFLES.
One quart of flour in a bowl, put salt in yellows of two eggs, tablespoon melted butter, milk enough to beat it with, beat very hard, just before baking, put in a half teacup of buttermilk with a light teaspoon of soda dissolved in the milk, and lastly, the whites of two eggs beaten very light, bake quickly.

MRS. H.H. TAYLOR, Knoxville, Tenn.

QUICK WAFFLES.
Four tablespoons of mush, one egg, tablespoon of lard, one one pint of sweet milk, flour enough to make the consistency of cake batter, one teaspoon of baking powder, last thing, sifted in with the flour, salt to taste.

MRS. BEARDEN.

SPECIAL CAR WAFFLES.
Two eggs, one pint sweet milk, five tablespoons flour, well-beaten together, one tablespoon butter. Just before pouring into irons, stir in quickly one teaspoon Royal baking powder, dissolved in a little sweet milk.

MRS. WM. J. BROWN, Bristol, Va.

WINNIE'S WAFFLES.

Four teacups flour, measured after sifting, three cups buttermilk, one-half pint melted grease, lard and butter mixed, the butter being about the size of a small egg, one level teaspoon of soda, unless the milk is very sour, then use a little more, one egg, and salt to taste.

Break egg in the milk, then stir in flour and beat well. Then add melted lard and butter, and stir well. Add soda and salt. Cook on a greased hot waffle iron.

CONTRIBUTED.

YEAST.

Take three Irish potatoes, wash, but do not peel, put them in half-gallon of water along with a handful of hops, boil till the potatoes are done. Put one pint of flour in a pitcher or crock, and strain the hop and potato water on it. Let stand till milkwarm, then add a teacup of yeast, do this at night, in the morning when risen, stir in enough corn meal until thick enough to roll out into cakes. Place cakes on dishes or a large waiter, over which a thick cloth has been laid and dry in the shade, turning the cakes twice a day. When dry, put in a bag.

MRS. S.B. BOYD, Knoxville, Tenn.

YEAST.

One tablespoon yeast in a large teacup of lukewarm water. When dissolved, add flour to make a stiff batter. After it has risen enough, add corn meal to make a crumbly mass and dry in the shade.

MRS. O.H.P. ROGAN, Knoxville, Tenn.

YEAST.

One dozen Irish potatoes, one teacup each of sugar and salt, two tablespoons hops. Pare the potatoes and boil, put the hops in a muslin bag and boil with potatoes in water sufficient to make a gallon when done. Mash the potatoes well, add sugar and salt and mix well, put the water in which the potatoes were boiled over and let it stand until milkwarm, then mix-in a cup of good yeast.

MRS. McCRUMB, Virginia.

YEAST

One dozen potatoes, peeled, and two tablespoons hops boiled in sufficient water to make one gallon when done. Mash the potatoes when done and add one teacup sugar, one teacup salt and pour over them the gallon boiling water, when cool add a cup of good yeast, bottle and keep in a cool place.

MRS. SOPHIE K. HUNTER, Knoxville, Tenn.

YEAST.

Take two cakes of good yeast, pour on them one pint warm water, when soft enough to mash, add one-fourth teaspoon salt and flour enough to make stiff batter. Set in warm place, it will rise in a few hours, then stir in corn meal until it can be rolled out, cut into cakes. Spread on dishes to dry in the shade, turn over every morning until thoroughly dry. This will be good for two or three months, it can be continued for years without the addition of hops. Tie up in a bag.

To make light biscuit with this yeast—Sift three pints flour in a bowl, put into this, salt, one egg, beaten, tablespoon white sugar, small tablespoon lard. Have one cake yeast dissolved in pint tepid water, mix bread with this, adding more water if necessary; make into a soft dough, set in warm place. When risen, add half table.spoon lard, more flour, work well, roll out, cut into biscuit, when risen, bake quickly.

MRS. E.S. McCLUNG, Knoxville, Tenn.

HOP YEAST.

Boil four medium-sized Irish potatoes in one-half gallon of water, with one-half cup of hops tied in a bag. When the potatoes are done take them from the water and mash in a dish. Remove the hops and put potatoes back in the water, adding one cup white sugar and one-half cup of salt. When lukewarm add one cup of made yeast. Set in a warm place to rise for twelve hours. Keep in a cool place. One cup of this yeast makes two quarts of bread.

MRS. MARY LEE WINSTON, Bristol, Va.-Tenn.

LIQUID YEAST.

Grate two large Irish potatoes, pour on them three pints of boiling water, stirring all the time, add one tablespoon of salt and half a cup of sugar. When cold, add one-half teacup of old yeast and set in warm place to rise, then keep in the refrigerator. When going to use, shake well, and use one-half cup to a quart of flour.

MOSELLE PORTER, Marietta, Ga.

LIQUID YEAST.

One pint boiling water, one cup hops, one cup mashed potatoes, three-fourths cup of sugar, one-half cup salt, two tablespoons flour, one yeast cake, one-half gallon boiling water. Pour the pint of water over the hops and steep ten minutes, add to the liquid, the potato, sugar, salt and flour. Beat and add the half gallon of boiling water; and when cool, put in the yeast cake. Let rise twenty-four hours, removing the skim several times. Bottle and keep in a cool place. Use this liquid with an equal quantity of water in making bread.

CONTRIBUTED.

MOTHER'S YEAST.

Wash thoroughly and boil four large Irish potatoes with the peelings on; mash them smooth with four tablespoons of flour, then add enough of the water they were boiled in to make a batter; add to that two pints of cold water; lastly one cake of any good dry yeast, dissolved in a little milkwarm water. Make this yeast about eight o'clock, stir it well at eleven and it should be well risen at four o'clock. The peelings will all rise to the top and it will be well fermented. Then strain through a sieve, pressing everything through, except the peelings. Put this in a jar with a top and place in the refrigerator. This will keep for a week and is splendid yeast.

MRS. E.S. McCLUNG, Knoxville, Tenn.

POTATO YEAST.

Wash and peel six Irish potatoes, have half a gallon of boiling water on the stove with a large kitchen spoon of salt in it; grate the potatoes and put them in the wafer, let them boil until well done; have a cake of National yeast well dissolved in warm water; take the potatoes from the stove and before they are altogether cool, stir this yeast in them. Set it away in a cool place, and it will soon be ready for use.

MRS. J.T. McTEER, Knoxville, Tenn.

YEAST AND ROLLS.

Three tablespoons of any yeast, three teacups of lukewarm water, four or five Irish potatoes, peeled and mashed, three tablespoons sugar. Put all in a tight glass jar and set in a warm place to rise. It does not seem to rise, but will bubble. It is then ready for use. Let it stand twenty-four hours to rise.

Three pints flour, sifted, one or two eggs, well beaten, two tablespoons granulated sugar, butter or lard the size of an egg, salt and enough of the liquid yeast out of the glass jar well stirred up, to wet it well. Work it well. Roll out, cut with biscuit cutter, grease pans, put the rolls in, cover with cloth and set in a warm place to rise, which they will do in four or five hours. Make them up, roll and cut them' out and set to rise all night for breakfast, and bake as you do biscuit. Omit sugar, lard and eggs and it makes an excellent loaf of bread.

MRS. O.H.P. ROGAN, Knoxville, Tenn.

CAKES

ANGEL FOOD CAKE.

Three tumblers sugar, two tumblers flour, two teaspoons of cream of tartar, whites of twenty-two eggs. Sift the flour four times, then measure, add cream of tartar and sift again, sift sugar four times, then measure. Beat eggs very light, then add sugar, a little at a time, then flour, a little at a time, lastly two teaspoons of, vanilla. Bake in a tolerably hot oven, leave in pan three days and not to be eaten for four days. Do not grease the pan, bake forty-five minutes, when cool loosen it around the pan.

MRS. H.H. TAYLOR, Knoxville, Tenn.

ANGEL FOOD CAKE.

One cup flour, sift three times, one and one-fourth cups granulated sugar, roll and sift once, one and one-fourth cup of white of egg, one level teaspoon cream of tartar, pure, one-third teaspoon salt. The salt will freshen the eggs and assist in the beating; should be put in the egg before beating.

When eggs are about half beaten add the cream of tartar and extract, your choice, but vanilla preferred. When eggs are fully beaten, but not too stiff, then sift in sugar. Up to this point beat with a strong
continuous stroke. Add flour last, simply folding it in with a few strokes, just enough to mix well.

Put into pan at once and then into Gas Range oven. Place the pan on rack about three inches above the bottom of the stove. The oven should be lighted (both burners) about two minutes, no longer, before placing cake in oven.

Immediately on placing cake in oven turn out the front burner and turn down the back burner to one-half its capacity. The cake should be kept in the oven one hour. Pure cream of tartar must be used and be careful not to use too much gas and thus spoil the cake.

"ESTATE GAS RANGE."

ANGEL FOOD CAKE.

One glass of whites of eggs, one and one-half glasses of sugar, one glass of flour, level teaspoon of cream of tartar, one teaspoon of vanilla flavoring.

Beat white of eggs to a stiff froth, sift flour and sugar separately, add sugar first, then fold in flour gently, add flavoring and cream of tartar. Line a biscuit pan with paper, pour in your batter, bake forty-five minutes in slow oven. When cold cut in diamond shapes. and ice.

MRS. WALTER McCOY, Knoxville, Tenn.

APPLE SAUCE CAKE.

Cream together one cup of sugar, one-half cup of shortening, add one salt spoon of salt, one-half teaspoon cloves, one teaspoon cinnamon, a little nutmeg and one cup raisins, seeded and chopped.

Dissolve one teaspoon soda in, a tablespoon of warm water, stir it into a cup of sour apple sauce, letting it foam over the ingredients in the bowl. Beat all thoroughly and add two cups of sifted flour. Bake in a loaf tin forty-five minutes. If the apple sauce is not very sour add a little vinegar or cream of tartar.

EDNA L. BROWN, Knoxville, Tenn.

CINCINNATI BALTIMORE CAKE.

One cup butter, two cups sugar, three and one-half cups flour, one cup sweet milk, whites six eggs, two teaspoons baking powder, one teaspoon rose water.

Cream butter and sugar, then add the milk and flavoring, beating all the while, then add flour into which the baking powder has been sifted and lastly the stiffly-beaten whites, which should be folded lightly into the batter. Bake in three layer cake pans in an oven that is hotter than it would be for loaf cake.

Filling—Dissolve three cups of granulated sugar in one cup of boiling water, cook till it threads, then pour over the stiffly-beaten whites, stirring constantly, add one cup chopped raisins and one cup pecans and five chopped figs. Ice top and sides.

CONTRIBUTED.

BLACK CAKE.

One pound each of flour, sugar and butter, twelve eggs, two pounds each of raisins and currants, one pound citron cut up, two tablespoons of mixed mace and cinnamon, two grated nutmegs, a large glass of wine, a glass of brandy, half a glass of rose water.

Stir sugar and butter to a cream, add beaten yelks and then stiffly beaten whites and flour alternately, flour, fruit and add in the spices before putting in fruit. It requires four hours to bake.

MRS. R.B. McMULLEN.

BLACK CAKE.

One pound flour, one pound sugar, one pound of butter, twelve eggs, two pounds of raisins, two pounds of currants or two pounds of seedless raisins, one pound of citron, one-half tablespoon of cinnamon, two teaspoons of mace, two nutmegs, grated, one-half teaspoon of cloves, one gill of brandy, one gill of wine, one gill of rose water, two heaping teaspoons of baking powder.

Cream butter and sugar, add beaten yelks, sift flour, baking powder and spices together and mix with chopped fruit, add to butter, sugar and yelks, beat well, add brandy, wine and rose water, and lastly the well-beaten whites. Bake carefully.

MRS. S.B. BOYD, Knoxville, Tenn.

BLACK FRUIT CAKE.

Twelve eggs, one pound butter, one pound sugar, one pound flour, one tablespoon ginger, one tablespoon cinnamon, one teaspoon cloves, one teaspoon allspice, one nutmeg, grated, one saucer black molasses, into which mix one level teaspoon soda, one tablespoon whiskey, one wine glass black wine, two pounds raisins, two pounds currants, one pound citron, flour the fruit and add last to the batter. Bake six hours.

MISS NELLA C. MOSS, Knoxville. Tenn.

PLAIN BLACK CAKE.

Four cups sugar, eight and one-half cups flour, two cups milk, seven eggs, three teaspoons baking powder, or soda when sour milk is used, one teaspoon salt, one pound each raisins and currants, half pound citron, one-half pound candied peel, two cups butter, spices to taste. This makes two cakes in pound pans.

MRS. O.H.P. ROGAN, Knoxville, Tenn.

BRIDE'S CAKE.

Four cups flour, three cups sugar, one and one-half cups butter, whites of sixteen eggs, two teaspoons Royal Baking Powder. Gold cake the same with the addition of one cup of sweet milk. Flavor.

MRS. RUSSELL, Knoxville, Tenn.

BUCKEYE CAKE.

One cup butter, two cups sugar, four cups flour, five eggs, beaten separately, one cup sour milk, one teaspoon soda, one pound seeded raisins, chopped. Beat the butter and sugar to a cream, add the beaten yelks and milk, then stir in the flour with the soda, well mixed in it, then the whites, beaten stiff, lastly the raisins, floured. Bake an hour and a half.

MRS. MARY CARTER, Knoxville, Tenn.

CARAMEL CAKE.

Four eggs, three and one-half cups flour, one cup sweet milk, two cups sugar, one and one-half teaspoons baking powder, flavor with vanilla. Bake in two or three layers, put together when cold with this filling.

Two cups brown sugar, one cup white sugar, one cup new milk. Stir until the sugar is well dissolved in the milk before putting on the fire. Cook until it drops well from spoon, add one and one-half tablespoons butter just before removing from stove and one teaspoon vanilla, stir and beat until thick enough to spread on cake. This makes a large cake. Add one-fourth pound of English walnuts if you wish a nice finish.

MRS. SAM CAMPBELL, Bristol, Va.-Tenn.

CHEAP CAKE.

One cup sugar, half cup butter, one cup milk, one pint flour, one egg, one teaspoon soda, two of cream of tartar.

MRS. WILL INGLES, Knoxville, Tenn.

CHOCOLATE CAKE.

Two cups of sugar, one and one-half cups of butter, one and one-half cups of sweet milk, five and one-half cups of flour, four eggs, beaten together, four and one-half teaspoons of baking powder. Stir chocolate mixture in and bake as a loaf or in jelly pans.

Chocolate Mixture—One cake of chocolate, grated, one cup of sugar, one cup of milk, boil until thick and let cool.

MRS. JAMES CARTER, Knoxville, Tenn.

CHOCOLATE CAKE.

One-half cup butter, three eggs, one cup sugar, two and three-fourths cup of flour, three-fourths cup sweet milk, two and one-fourth teaspoons baking powder.

Chocolate Mixture—One-fourth cake Baker's chocolate, grated, one cup sugar, one-half cup sweet milk, yelk of one egg, mix and boil until thick, when cold pour in cake batter. Mix well and bake in layers.

Filling—Two pounds light brown sugar, one cup butter, one cup sweet milk, one-fourth cake Baker's chocolate, one teaspoon vanilla, boil until like caramel, stir constantly until cold.

MRS. S.B. BOYD, Knoxville, Tenn.

CHOCOLATE CAKE.

One cup butter, not quite full, two cups sugar, three cups flour, one-half cup sweet milk, one teaspoon soda, two teaspoons cream of tartar, whites of eight eggs.

Take one-third of this batter and spice it, using two tablespoon of cinnamon, one teaspoon of spice and one teaspoon of cloves. Use this for the middle layer.

Filling—One section of chocolate, two cups sugar, one-half cup butter, one-half cup of sweet milk. Put the sugar, milk and butter together and when dissolved and near boiling, put in the grated chocolate, let boil until nearly candy and flavor with vanilla.

MRS. EMMA EVANS, Knoxville, Tenn.

CHOCOLATE CAKE.

Whites of eight eggs, four cups flour after sifted, two cups sugar, three-fourth cup butter, cup of sour cream, two heaping teaspoons baking powder sifted in flour, vanilla to taste.

Cream butter and sugar, add cream, whip whites of eggs stiff and add flour and eggs alternately, flavor and beat till it bubbles. Bake in pan or jelly tins.

Filling—One-half cake Baker's chocolate, one cup cream, one and one-half pints of brown sugar, butter size of a hen's egg, Cook till it forms a soft ball in cold water, take off and beat till creamy, and then spread on cake.

CONTRIBUTED.

CHOCOLATE CAKE.

I use the Silver Cake batter and put into it as much of the Baker's chocolate, as you like, sweetened and grated. I usually make what I call a cake and a half, which is twenty-one eggs and to that amount I use nearly the whole cake, which costs twenty cents, and half a pound of sugar to sweeten it, or about that. I use my own judgment somewhat, as I have no regular recipe. I bake it some longer than the silver cake.

MRS. O.P. TEMPLE, Knoxville, Tenn.

CHOCOLATE CAKE.

One scant cup butter, two cups sugar, three cups flour, one cup milk, whites of six eggs, one-fourth pound of Baker's chocolate, melted, teaspoon baking powder, flavor.

Cream butter and sugar, melt chocolate in pan placed over hot water, let cool, then add flour, milk, eggs and chocolate alternately, baking powder and flavoring last. Bake rather slow.

Filling—Three cups brown sugar, one cup milk, butter size of egg, one-fourth pound chocolate, cook until it drops from spoon, then beat until it begins to cream.

MRS. WALTER McCOY, Knoxville, Tenn.

CHOCOLATE CINNAMON CAKE.

One-half cup butter, two-thirds cup sugar, two eggs, one and one-half cups flour, two level teaspoons baking powder, three level teaspoons cinnamon, one-half cup sweet milk, pinch of salt, bake in layers.

Filling—Beat together thoroughly whites of two eggs and enough powdered sugar to make a rather soft frosting, about one and one-half cups, stir in one square of chocolate previously melted, beat all well together before using.

MRS. H.P. WYMAN, Bristol, Tenn.

COCOANUT CAKE.

One pound sugar, three-fourths of a pound flour, one teaspoon baking powder in the flour, one-fourth pound butter, six eggs, one teacup milk or cream, two small or one large cocoanuts grated and mixed into the batter.

MRS. HENRY A. CHAMBERS, Chattanooga, Tenn.

COCOANUT DROPS.

One pound grated cocoanut, one pound sifted white sugar, the whites of six eggs beaten to a stiff froth. You must have enough whites to wet the whole stiffly. Drop on buttered plates, making them about the size of a cent and bake immediately.

CONTRIBUTED.

COCOANUT MACAROONS.

Two cups prepared cocoanut, one cup powdered sugar, one tablespoon of flour, one well beaten white of egg. Mix dry ingredients and stir into the well-beaten white. Drop on buttered paper and bake fifteen minutes in a slow oven.

MISS LUCY HALL, Knoxville, Tenn.

COFFEE CAKE.

One quart flour, one egg, one-half teacup melted butter and lard, three-fourths of a cup of sugar, one cup sponge or yeast, one-half teaspoon salt, enough warm sweet milk to make a stiff batter.

Make a hole in flour and put all ingredients in and beat well, put in pan, grease top, let rise and bake.

MRS. DAVID DUNN, Bristol, Tenn.

GERMAN COFFEE CAKE.

Two cups sponge, two cups sugar, two eggs, one cup milk, four tablespoons butter or lard, one tablespoon salt, flavor with nutmeg or lemon.

Cream the butter and sugar, add salt, eggs, milk, sponge and flavoring. Mix thoroughly with enough flour to make a stiff dough. May add currants or raisins to the dough. Spread with the spoon in greased tins, about three-fourth of an inch thick. Brush with melted butter and sprinkle with sugar and cinnamon. Let rise and bake.

This may be made into apple or peach cake by omitting the raisins and currants and placing sliced fruit in rows on top. When it is risen sprinkle with sugar and cinnamon.

Another good covering is made by chopping apples with currants. When risen, sprinkle with sugar and cinnamon and bake.

CLARA W. HASSLOCK, Nashville, Tenn.

CORN STARCH CAKE.

Six eggs, one pound sugar, one-half pound butter, ten ounces of corn starch, six ounces of flour, one-half teacup of sweet milk. one teaspoon baking powder, flavor with lemon or bitter almond.

Beat yelks and half the sugar, butter and other half, then mix these, add whites and sift flour, corn starch and baking powder together, add these, lastly the milk and flavoring and bake.

MRS. E.S. McCLUNG, Knoxville, Tenn.

CORN STARCH CAKE.

Eight eggs, five ounces of corn starch, three ounces of flour, one-fourth of a pound of butter, one-half pound of sugar, teaspoon of yeast, powdered, sifted through the flour, small teacup of sweet milk stirred in last.

MISS MARY PLEAS McCLUNG, Knoxville, Tenn.

COOKIES.

One cup sugar, two-thirds cups of butter, two teaspoons baking powder, two tablespoons sweet milk, one tablespoon vanilla, two cups flour for mixing and rolling out, two eggs.

CONTRIBUTED.

COOKIES OR TEA CAKES

Nine cups sifted flour, four cups sugar, two cups butter or lard, five or six eggs, one teaspoon of soda in half a cup of sour milk, cinnamon or nutmeg to taste.

MRS. HENRY A. CHAMBERS, Chattanooga, Tenn.

FRUIT COOKIES.

Three eggs, one and one-half cups sugar, one cup butter, one cup of raisins chopped not very fine, two teaspoons of cinnamon, two teaspoons of spice, one teaspoon of cloves, one large teaspoon soda, flour enough to roll, which will be about three pints.

MRS. J.H. JOUROLMON, Knoxville, Tenn.

FRUIT COOKIES.

One cup butter, one and one-half cups sugar, one cup chopped raisins, one teaspoon each of cinnamon, cloves, spice, soda, three beaten eggs. Flour.

MRS. J. WRIGHT CULTON, Knoxville, Tenn.

GINGER COOKIES.

Two cups molasses, one cup lard, two eggs, one cup sugar, three-fourths cup sour milk, one tablespoon ginger, three teaspoons soda stirred in flour and one teaspoon soda in milk, flour to roll nicely.

MRS. RICHARD P. JOHNSON, Knoxville, Tenn.

GINGER COOKIES.

One cup molasses, one cup brown sugar, one cup butter or part lard, one cup cold water, three teaspoons soda, one teaspoon ginger, one teaspoon cinnamon, salt to taste, five and one-half cups flour. Bake in thin layer and cut in squares.

MRS. J. WRIGHT CULTON, Knoxville, Tenn.

NUTMEG COOKIES.

Three-fourths cup butter, two cups sugar, two-thirds cup sour milk, one-half teaspoon soda, two eggs, nutmeg for flavor, flour for soft dough. Bake in quick oven.

MRS. RICHARD P. JOHNSON, Knoxville, Tenn.

OATMEAL COOKIES.

Two cups sugar, one cup butter, one cup lard, three eggs, four cups rolled oats, four and one-half cups flour, one teaspoon baking powder, one-half teaspoon soda, one-half cup milk, sweet or sour, one pound raisins seeded, cut fine, one tablespoon cinnamon.

Mix thoroughly, drop tablespoonful of this mixture into a slightly greased pan three inches apart and bake in a moderately quick oven.

MISS MARGARET McDANNEL, Knoxville, Tenn.

OATMEAL COOKIES.

One cup buttermilk, one cup shortening, one cup sugar, two eggs, one teaspoon soda, two cups flour, two cups raw oatmeal, one cup seeded raisins or currants, spice to taste, a pinch of salt.

Stir well together and drop on pans to bake.

MISS BERTHA PIERCE, Detroit, Mich.

SUGAR COOKIES.

One cup butter, two cups sugar, one cup milk, two eggs, three teaspoons baking powder, one-half teaspoon vanilla, flour for thin dough.

MRS. RICHARD P. JOHNSON, Knoxville, Tenn.

CREAM CAKE.

Four eggs, two cups sugar, two heaping cups flour, one cup rich sweet cream, one teaspoon soda, two of cream of tartar.

For white cake use the whites of eight eggs and the same proportion for sponge cake the yelks, using sweet milk instead of cream. This makes a good big cake. Bake quickly.

MRS. JAMES S. BOYD, Knoxville, Tenn.

FRENCH CREAM CAKE.

Boil nearly a pint of sweet milk, take two tablespoonsful of corn starch, dissolved in a little milk, to this add the whites of two and the yelk of one egg with an even teacup of sugar. When the milk boils pour all in slowly, stirring all the while till very thick, and just before taking off the fire add one-half teacup butter.

Cake for the above filling—Six eggs, two cups sugar, three cups flour, two teaspoons baking powder, four tablespoons of cold water. Bake in layers and spread with the above filling, flavoring to suit the taste.

MRS. HUGH W. TAYLOR, Bristol, Tenn.

CREAM PUFFS.

Put four ounces of butter in a kettle with one-half pint water, bring to a boil, then stir in six ounces of sifted flour, and set one side to cool. Add six eggs, two at a time. Do not beat very much. With a spoon drop on a tin, about three inches apart, the size of a large walnut, and bake in a medium hot oven about twenty minutes. This makes about two dozen puffs. When cold cut open a little on the side with a sharp knife and till with cream made as follows:

Cream for Puffs—Put into a pail ten ounces of sugar, three large teaspoons of cornstarch and four eggs. Beat well and add one quart of milk, stir well, then set the pail into a kettle of boiling water and stir till thick, when cold, add extract of vanilla to taste.

MRS. HOLMDEN, London, England.

CRULLERS.

One-half pound butter, one pound sugar, six eggs, two pounds flour, a grated nutmeg, teaspoon cinnamon, tablespoon rose-water. Beat butter and sugar well, then the yelks, which add, then the well beaten whites, add the spices and mix well together.

MRS. S.M. PARK, Knoxville, Tenn.

CRULLERS.

One-half pint sour milk, two teacups sugar, one cup butter, three eggs, teaspoon of soda, one-half nutmeg, grated, flour to make a smooth dough. Roll thin, cut in shapes and fry in boiling lard.

MRS. T.W. FLEMING, Knoxville, Tenn.

CRULLERS.

One-half pint sour milk, one cup butter, two cups sugar, three well beaten eggs, one teaspoon soda, dissolved in a little hot water, work in as much flour as will make a smooth dough, work well together, cut in shapes and fry in hot lard.

MRS. J.A. RAYL, Knoxville, Tenn.

CRULLERS.

Three eggs, one cup sugar, one-half cup butter and flour enough to make a soft dough. Fry in lard and roll in powdered sugar.

MRS. HENRY A. CHAMBERS, Chattanooga, Tenn.

CRY BABIES.

One cup hot water, one cup brown sugar, one cup molasses, one cup melted lard, one egg, one teaspoon soda, salt, five cups flour, extract of lemon. Drop with teaspoon on a buttered tin, leaving room to rise.

MRS. ARCHER A. PHLEGAR, Bristol, Va.

CREOLE KISSES.

Whites six eggs, one pound pulverized sugar, beat together one minute, add teaspoon cream of tartar, beat ten minutes, or till it is stiff, add a cupful of chopped nuts and one teaspoon of vanilla. To bake, line the pan with brown paper, but do not grease.

CONTRIBUTED.

CUP CAKE.

Four eggs, two cups sugar, one of butter, one-half of milk, three of flour, one teaspoon cream of tartar, one-half teaspoon of soda.

MRS. WILL INGLES, Knoxville, Tenn.

CUP CAKE.

One cup sugar, one-half cup each of butter and sweet milk, one and one-half cups of flour, two eggs, one-half teaspoon of soda, one teaspoon of cream of tartar, a little nutmeg or lemon.

MRS. E. BOLLI, Knoxville, Tenn.

CUP CAKE.

Two cups sugar, one cup butter, yelks of five eggs and whites of two, one cup sweet milk or water, three and one-half cups flour, two teaspoons baking powder.

FILLING FOR THIS—Whites of the three eggs saved out of the five eggs, one and one-half cups sugar, three tablespoons chocolate, one teaspoon vanilla, or plain, flavored with lemon.

MRS. WILL HAZEN, Knoxville, Tenn.

CUP CAKE.

Three eggs, two cups sugar, three-fourths of a cup butter, three cups flour, one heaping teaspoon of baking powder, three-fourths cup sweet milk.

MRS. RACHEL ROGERS, Knoxville, Tenn.

CUP CAKE.

One cup butter, two cups sugar, three cups flour, one cup sour milk, one teaspoon soda and four eggs. This recipe makes a very nice spice cake by adding spices to suit your taste.

MRS. J.T. McTEER, Knoxville, Tenn.

CURRANT SLICES.

Three-fourths of a pound of butter, ten eggs, one pound sugar, one pound flour, one pound currants, one teaspoon each of allspice and cinnamon, one-half nutmeg, grated, two teaspoons baking powder.

Beat sugar and butter together, add yelks of eggs, then the flour and whites of eggs beaten stiff. Afterwards put in the spices and the currants well floured.

MRS. EDWIN H. FAY, Knoxville, Tenn.

DELICATE CAKE.

Whites of seven eggs, one pound each of flour and sugar, one half pound butter, teacup buttermilk, one teaspoon of cream of tartar and one-half teaspoon of soda, flavor to taste.

MRS. WILL INGLES, Knoxville, Tenn.

DELICATE CAKE.

One-half cup of butter, two cups of sugar, three cups of flour, three-fourths cup of sweet milk, whites of six eggs, one and one-half teaspoons of baking powder or one level teaspoon of cream of tartar and one-half teaspoon of soda.

MRS. HATTIE KING TAYLOR, Bristol, Tenn.

DELICIOUS CAKE.

Two cups sugar, one cup butter, three and one-half cups flour; one cup sweet milk. one teaspoon baking powder, three eggs. Bake in patty pans.

MRS. ARCHER A. PHLEGAR, Bristol, Va.-Tenn.

DELICIOUS CAKE.

One cup butter, two cups pulverized sugar, or one and one-half cups of granulated sugar, three cups flour, whites of eight eggs, or four whole eggs, one cup of sweet milk or cream. three teaspoons baking powder.

Filling—One pint sweet milk, one cup of butter, two cups of very dark brown sugar, half dipper cold water; boil about twenty minutes, stirring occasionally to keep from sticking. Flavor when done with two tablespoons of vanilla. Cool and put on cake before entirely cold. Stir or beat until nearly cold.

MRS. IRWIN.

DEVIL'S FOOD CAKE.

One egg, one cup sugar, two-thirds cake chocolate, two-thirds cup sweet milk, cook until it thickens, then set aside to cool. When cold take two eggs, one-half cup butter, one cup sugar, two cups flour, one-fourth of a pound of English walnuts, one-half teaspoon soda, dissolved in one-third cup milk. After mixing this add the first part and bake.

MRS. D.F. McCARTY. Bristol, Va.-Tenn.

DEVIL'S FOOD CAKE.

Three squares of one-half pound package of chocolate, melt over the teakettle, pour over it one-half cup boiling water and let cool.

Cake—Two cups sugar, one-half cup butter, one-half cup sour cream or sour milk, one-half teaspoon soda, three eggs, two and one-half cups flour, add melted chocolate and flavor with vanilla. Put together with boiled icing or lemon filling.

MRS. JOS. S. DONNELLY, Shoun's, Tenn.

DOLLY VARDEN CAKE.

Fruit or dark stripe; yelks of five eggs, one cup sugar, two cups flour, one and one-half cups butter, one-half cup water, one pound citron, one-half pound raisins, one-half cup whiskey, spices to taste, two teaspoons baking powder.

White Part—White of five eggs, three-fourths cup of butter, three-fourths cup water, two cups sugar, three cups flour, one teaspoon baking powder. Bake in jelly tins and spread with lemon cream, made of the juice and rind of two lemons, two cups sugar, two eggs, beaten separately, mix together and cook till thick, being careful not to scorch. Spread between the layers first white and then dark and bake a meringue over it.

MRS. JAMES KENNEDY, Knoxville, Tenn.

DOLLY VARDEN CAKE.

White Layer—Five whites of egg, three-fourths cup of water, three-fourths cup of butter, three cups of flour, sifted, two cups sugar, two teaspoons of cream of tartar, one teaspoon of soda.

Dark Layer—Four yelks of egg, one-half cup of water, one-half cup of butter, one cup of sugar, two cups of flour, one-half pound each of raisins and citron, spices, one teaspoon of cream of tartar, one teaspoon of soda.

MRS. HATTIE KING TAYLOR, Bristol, Tenn.

DOLLY VARDEN CAKE.

White Stripe—Five eggs, three-fourths cup butter, two cups sugar, three cups flour, one teaspoon cream of tartar, one-half teaspoon soda, three-fourths cup water.

Fruit or Dark Stripe—Four eggs (yelks), one cup sugar, two cups flour, one-half cup butter, one-half cup water, one pound raisins or currants, one-half cup brandy, spices to taste, one teaspoon cream of tartar, one-half teaspoon soda.

MISS BRANCH KEEBLER, Bristol, Va.-Tenn.

DOUGHNUTS.

One cup each of sugar and sweet milk, two eggs, one-half nutmeg, grated, one-third cup shortening, one-half teaspoon soda, one teaspoon cream of tartar, flour enough to make a soft dough. Roll out half an inch thick and cut with a doughnut cutter, fry in deep fat.

MRS. J.A. RAYL, Knoxville, Tenn.

DOUGHNUTS.

Five eggs, three cups sugar, one cup sour cream, two cups butter, milk, flour enough to make a stiff dough, flavor to taste.

MRS. ROBERT VESTAL, Knoxville, Tenn.

DOUGHNUTS OR' "FORSNORS".

Put one pint of sweet milk, one teacup of butter and one teacup of sugar on the fire and let stay till the butter melts, then set off to cool. Beat seven eggs till light, whites and yellows separately and add to the mixture of milk, butter and sugar, after it has cooled, also half a teacup of yeast, and flour enough to make a soft dough. Let stand over night and in the morning, when light, roll out thin, cut in strips, diamonds or squares and fry in deep lard.

MRS. S.B. BOYD, Knoxville, Tenn.

FEATHER CAKE.

One cup sugar, one-half cup water or milk, one and three-fourths cup of flour, one egg, butter the size of an egg, two teaspoons of baking powder.

CONTRIBUTED.

KATIE'S FEATHER CAKE.

One egg, one cup sugar, two cups flour, one-half cup sweet milk, two tablespoons butter, one and one-half teaspoon baking powder, flavor with lemon.

MRS. A.P. WHITE, Knoxville, Tenn.

FIG CAKE.

White Part—Two cups sugar, two-thirds cup butter, three-eighths cup sweet milk, whites of eight eggs, one teaspoon baking powder, three cups flour. Beat sugar and butter to a cream, add the milk and flour, lastly the eggs, bake in two pans.

Gold Part—One cup sugar, three-fourths cup butter, one-half cup sweet milk, two teaspoons baking powder, two cups flour, yelks of eight eggs, two teaspoons cinnamon, one of allspice. Put half the batter in the pan, take half a pound of figs, sliced and lightly floured, spread over the top, then spread over that the rest of the batter and bake.

Put the layers together with icing, with the fig cake between the white layers. The pans must be one inch deep.

MISS ADDIE CARTER. Knoxville, Tenn.

FOUR EGG CAKE.

Yelks of four eggs, whites of two eggs, two cups sugar, half cup butter, one cup milk, three cups flour, heaping teaspoon baking powder, flavor to taste.

Filling—Whites of two eggs, one and one-half cups sugar, cook sugar until it hairs from spoon, pour over beaten whites, beat until perfectly cold, stir in cup of chopped raisins or pecans.

MRS. McCOY, Knoxville, Tenn.

FOURTH OF JULY CAKE.

Two whole. eggs, one cup sugar, one-fourth cup butter, two-thirds cup sweet milk, two cups sifted flour, two teaspoons baking powder, flavor to taste, add a few raisins and nut meats, beat eggs separately. Bake in loaf, or layer, or little patty pans.

MRS. H.P. WYMAN, Bristol, Tenn.

FRUIT CAKE.

One pound each of sugar, butter and flour, three pounds of raisins, one pound currants, one pound figs, one pound dates, one and one-half pounds citron, one pint of New Orleans molasses, four tablespoons cinnamon, one tablespoon cloves, two tablespoons allspice, three small nutmegs, rind of one lemon, chopped fine, two tablespoons baking powder, one wine glass brandy, ten eggs. Put flour in last and do not stir much after it is in.

MRS. J.A. McKELDIN, Knoxville, Tenn.

FRUIT CAKE.

Two eggs, one-half cup butter, one cup each of sour milk, sugar and molasses, four cups flour, one-half teaspoon soda, as much fruit as one likes.

MISS BRANCH KEEBLER, Bristol, Va.

FRUIT CAKE.

One and one-fourth pounds each of butter, sugar and flour, sixteen eggs, one teaspoon of baking powder, one-half teaspoon each of mace, cinnamon and cloves, four pounds of raisins, two pounds of currants, one pound of blanched almonds, one and one-fourth pounds of citron, one slice of preserved pineapple, one-half cup of brandy, one-half cup of molasses, one tumbler of ripe grape jelly, one-third of a pound of conserved cherries.

Put spices and powder with the flour and sift over the fruit.

MRS. HATTIE KING TAYLOR, Bristol, Tenn.

CHRISTMAS FRUIT CAKE.

Five pounds good seeded raisins, two pounds washed currants, one pound sliced citron, seven large or eight small eggs, one pound of best butter, one pound of brown sugar, one pound of flour, one cup of molasses, one wine glass of wine, one wine glass of brandy, two grated nutmegs, one tablespoon of cinnamon, half teaspoon of cloves. Mix well, bake in a large shallow pan three or four hours in a very slow oven.

Fruit cake must not be baked hard, but just let dry out. I use only for the purpose a granite roasting pan, as I prefer to cut fruit cake in thin squares, rather than from a large cake pan.

MRS. GEORGE WILLIAMSON, Brooklyn, N. Y.

FRUIT AND FEATHER CAKE.

Six eggs, two small cups sugar, butter twice the size of an egg, two cups flour, two teaspoons cream of tartar and one of soda, mix as usual. Take out a little less than half, into this stir half pound each of raisins and currants, two tablespoons sliced citron, and the same quantity of candied lemon or orange peel, one teaspoon grated nutmeg, one teaspoon cinnamon, one-half glass brandy, teacup molasses, two cups flour. Bake in jelly pans, first the plain, then the fruit, cover each with jelly, pile one on the other and ice the top. Fruit should always be mixed with the flour.

MRS. BARTON KELLER, Knoxville, Tenn.

LAYER FRUIT CAKE.

One cup of citron, two cups of raisins, one cup of jam, two cups of sugar, one cup of butter, one cup of strong coffee, three teaspoons of baking powder, six eggs, two and one-half cups of flour, spices of all kinds. Put together with boiled icing.

CONTRIBUTED.

WASHINGTON FRUIT CAKE.

Mix with one pound each of flour, sugar, raisins, currants, twelve ounces of butter or half pound butter and half a cup of sweet milk, eight eggs and spices to suit your taste.

MRS. J.T. McTEER, Knoxville, Tenn.

WHITE FRUIT CAKE.

One pound flour, fifteen eggs, whites only, three-fourths pound butter, one pound sugar, one cocoanut, three-fourths pounds citron, three-fourths pound blanched almonds, one teaspoon Royal Baking Powder, flavor with bitter almond, or any extract you may prefer. Cream butter, then add sugar, then eggs, then flour, last add baking powder to flour which you have mixed well with the chopped fruit. Bake in a loaf.

MRS. CARRICK PARK, Knoxville, Tenn.

WHITE FRUIT CAKE.

One pound each of flour and sugar, one pound raisins after they are seeded, one-half pound butter, three-fourths pound citron, whites fifteen eggs. Two teaspoons of baking powder put in the flour before it is sifted.

Cream the sugar and butter together very light, beat the whites to a stiff froth, stir in some of the flour and the whites alternately, stir the fruit in the rest of the flour and stir it in, beating very hard, flavor with a teaspoon vanilla, cut the citron in long thin slices.

MRS. J.W. FRIERSON, Knoxville, Tenn.

WHITE FRUIT CAKE.

Whites of twelve eggs, one pound each of butter and sugar, one pound flour, two pounds citron, some sliced and some chopped fine, one pound blanched almonds, two grated cocoanuts, one wine glass of wine, one tablespoon of mace, one tablespoon cinnamon, two teaspoons of baking powder. Do not bake as long as black cake.

MRS. JAMES KENNEDY, Knoxville, Tenn.

GINGER CAKES.

Yelks of four eggs, one pint of honey or molasses, three tablespoons brown sugar, one heaping tablespoon of ginger, one level tablespoon of cinnamon, one teaspoon of soda, dissolved in a little warm water, one teacup butter and enough flour to make a very soft dough. Work very little and bake in a quick oven.

GINGER CAKES.

Yelks of six eggs, one and one-half pints of syrup, one teacup of brown sugar, one-fourth cup melted butter, one heaping tablespoon ground ginger, one teaspoon of ground cinnamon, one teaspoon of soda dissolved in four spoonsful of water, flour to make soft to roll. Bake quick. To glaze them, brush the tops with a beaten egg before putting in oven.

GINGER CAKES.

To four cups flour add four eggs, two cups molasses, one cup sugar, one cup butter or lard, one cup sweet milk, two teaspoons baking powder, ginger and nutmeg to taste.

MRS. J.T. McTEER, Knoxville, Tenn.

GINGER CAKES.

One quart molasses, four pints flour, one cup butter, one tablespoon of ginger, one of cinnamon, one of spice, one teaspoon of soda in a teacup of buttermilk, six eggs, beaten separately. Mix the molasses with the yelks and spices, then the cup of butter, flour and whites of eggs, lastly the soda and milk. Can be eaten with sauce.

MRS. S.B. BOYD, Knoxville, Tenn.

GINGER CAKES.

Four yelks, one pint of New Orlean molasses, or honey, two tablespoons of brown sugar, one teacup of lard or butter, rubbed well into enough flour to make a soft dough, one and one-half tablespoons of ginger, one leaping teaspoon of soda, dissolved in a little warm water.

MRS. JAMES G. MITCHELL, Knoxville, Tenn.

HONEY GINGER CAKES.

Yelks of four eggs two-thirds of teacup brown sugar, one pint of honey, one-half teacup melted butter, tablespoon of ginger, two-thirds teaspoon cinnamon, one-half of a small nutmeg, teaspoon of soda dissolved in one-fourth teacup of cold water and put in the last thing before the flour, add flour enough to this mixture to make a smooth dough and glaze over the top with the yelk of an egg. Work in just enough flour to make it leave the hands.

MRS. H.H. TAYLOR, Knoxville, Tenn.

LIGHT GINGER CAKES.

Nine eggs, one pint molasses, one cup sugar, one-half pound butter, two tablespoons ginger, one dessert spoon of soda, dissolved in a little warm water. Mix all the ingredients well together and add sufficient flour to make a batter a little thicker than pound cake.

MRS. H.A. CHAMBERS, Chattanooga, Tenn.

QUICK GINGER CAKE.

One cup each of molasses, brown sugar, and butter, four eggs, three cups flour, one teaspoon soda stirred in molasses, two teaspoons of ginger.

MRS. BARNETT, Atlanta, Ga.

GINGER NUTS.

One pint molasses, one teaspoon soda, one tablespoon butter, one egg, ginger to taste, mix with flour, roll thin and bake quick.

MRS. T.W. FLEMING, Knoxville, Tenn.

GINGER NUTS.

Dissolve six ounces of butter and four ounces of sugar in a pint of molasses, when cold, add two tablespoons of ginger and one of mixed cloves and mace, one teaspoon of salt, add flour enough to make a soft dough. Mix well, roll thin and cut into small cakes. This quantity does not make many cakes.

MRS. HENRY A. CHAMBERS, Chattanooga, Tenn.

GINGER SNAPS.

Put a kettle on the stove and pour into it a pint of molasses, sift into it one tablespoon of soda, stirring a few minutes until it lightens. Have ready some flour, say one quart, with a tablespoon of lard and a tablespoon of ginger, pour the molasses while rising into the flour. Use flour enough to roll out and cut into cakes.

MRS. JOE JOUROLMON, Knoxville, Tenn.

GINGER SNAPS.

One pound sugar, one-half pound each of lard and butter, one-fourth pound powdered ginger, teaspoon cloves, teaspoon of salaratus, one quart of molasses. Mix these together, then add flour until the dough is stiff enough to roll out and cut into shapes and bake with quick oven.

MRS. McTEER, Knoxville, Tenn.

GINGERBREAD.

To two quarts flour, add lard the size of an egg, pour in one pint molasses, New Orleans preferred, one heaping tablespoon of soda dissolved in one-half pint of water, add one tablespoon of ginger.

Mix and pour into a baking pan and bake in a slow oven.

MRS. C.E. WINSTON, Bristol, Va.

BALTIMORE GINGERBREAD.

Seven pounds of flour, one quart of molasses, one and one-third pounds of sugar, one pound of lard, two heaping tablespoons of soda, dissolved in half a pint of sour milk, ginger and spices to your taste. Roll very thin and cut out and bake in a quick oven.

MRS. IDA McDANIEL, Knoxville, Tenn.

EGGLESS GINGERBREAD.

Five cups flour, one heaping tablespoon butter, one cup each of molasses and sugar, sour milk, two teaspoons soda dissolved in hot water, one tablespoon ginger, one tablespoon cinnamon.

Mix molasses, spice, butter and sugar together and beat until light, add the milk, then the soda, mix thoroughly and put in the flour. Bake in a biscuit pan. To be eaten with hot sauce.

MRS. WILL HAZEN, Knoxville, Tenn.

EXCELLENT GINGERBREAD.

One cupful each of butter, sugar, molasses, sour cream, three eggs, one-half tablespoon of soda, two tablespoons ginger, cloves and cinnamon to taste, flour until the spoon will almost stand alone.

MRS. H.H. TAYLOR, Knoxville, Tenn.

EXCELLENT SOFT GINGERBREAD.

One cup nearly full of butter, creamed with two cups of molasses, then add one egg beaten well and a very scant cup of boiling water, in which a tablespoon of soda has been dissolved, stir an even tablespoon of ginger into this mixture, add enough flour to make a good soft dough. Butter a baking pan and bake in a hot oven.

MRS. M.M. SPURGEON, Bristol, Va.

GINGERBREAD (HALLOWE'EN).

One cup New Orleans molasses, one-half cup creamed butter, one-half cup brown sugar, two eggs well beaten, one cup sour cream or buttermilk, one teaspoon ground cinnamon, one-half teaspoon ground cloves, one-half teaspoon ground nutmeg, two tablespoons grated chocolate, one and one-half tablespoons ground ginger, one and one-half teaspoons soda sifted in three cups flour. Beat well, and just before putting in to bake add one and one-half cups seeded raisins, dredged with pulverized sugar. Many prefer this cake with the chocolate and raisins left out.

MRS. A.P. WHITE, Knoxville, Tenn.

LIGHT GINGERBREAD.

Four eggs, two cups each of butter, sugar and molasses, one of sour cream, six of flour, one teaspoon of soda, three tablespoons ginger, and two each of allspice and cinnamon.

MRS. JOHN M. BROOKS, Knoxville, Tenn.

OLD-FASHIONED GINGERBREAD.

Put into mixing bowl one cup molasses, two large spoons softened butter, one teaspoon soda, dissolved in three tablespoons boiling water, one teaspoon ginger, add flour for kneading well, not too stiff a dough.

Roll into sheets and bake in quick oven. While still hot brush over top with a teaspoon sweet milk mixed with a teaspoon molasses, this glazes it.

MRS. RICHARD P. JOHNSON, Knoxville, Tenn.

SOFT GINGERBREAD.

Five cups flour, one and one-half cups butter, two cups molasses and one cup sugar, one cup milk, five eggs, one and one-half teaspoons of soda, two tablespoons ginger.

MRS. JENNIE HOUSE, Knoxville, Tenn.

SOFT GINGERBREAD.
One cup butter, one cup white sugar, one cup syrup, three eggs, one tablespoon each of cinnamon, allspice and ginger, three cups sifted flour, one cup sour milk, one teaspoon soda.

Beat butter and sugar to a cream, add syrup, beat eggs well and add, then spices and flour, lastly, the soda dissolved in the milk.
MRS. G.M. BURNS, Knoxville, Tenn.

SOFT GINGERBREAD.
Two cups sugar, two cups butter, one cup sour cream, four eggs, five cups flour, one teaspoon soda, two tablespoons each of ginger and allspice, one tablespoon cinnamon. Bake in a pan and eat with sauce or use as cake.
MRS. JOE JOUROLMON. Knoxville, Tenn.

SOFT GINGERBREAD.
One cup New Orleans molasses, one egg, one teaspoon soda, beaten five minutes, add six tablespoons sour milk, two cups flour, sifted, four tablespoons melted butter, a pinch of salt, cinnamon and ginger to taste. Bake in pan.
MRS. H.P. WYMAN, Bristol, Tenn.

SOFT GINGERBREAD.
One cup butter, one cup sugar, one cup molasses, three eggs, three cups flour, one tablespoon ginger, one tablespoon cinnamon, one teaspoon spice, one teaspoon soda dissolved in one cup sweet milk last thing. Bake slowly.
MRS. RICHARD P. JOHNSON, Knoxville, Tenn.

GOLD CAKE.
Beat yellows of five eggs twenty minutes, add one-half cup of butter, creamed with one cup of sugar, add one-half cup of sweet milk, two cups flour, sifted first, and a small teaspoon of baking powder.

Filling—Four heaping tablespoons of grated chocolate, butter size of an egg, three cups of sugar, one cup of sweet milk, boil till it "soft balls" in water, then take off, beat till thick and flavor.
MRS. HATTIE KING TAYLOR, Bristol, Tenn.

GOLD CAKE.
Yelks of sixteen eggs, one cup butter, two cups sugar, one cup sweet milk, two and one-half cups flour or more, if necessary, four heaping teaspoons baking powder, sifted in the flour, one teaspoon, extract of lemon.
MRS. HENRY A. CHAMBERS, Chattanooga, Tenn.

GOLDEN CAKE.
One pound of flour, one pound of sugar, ten ounces of butter, yelks of fifteen eggs, one cup of sweet milk, one teaspoon of cream of tartar, one-half teaspoon of soda, flavor with lemon.

SILVER CAKE.
Three-fourths of a pound of flour, one pound of sugar, one-half pound of butter, whites of fifteen eggs, flavor with vanilla or bitter almond.
MRS. S.B. BOYD, Knoxville, Tenn.

GOLDEN CAKE.
One pound sugar, one pound flour, ten ounces butter, yelks of fourteen eggs, large coffee cup of sweet milk, two teaspoons baking powder, flavor with lemon.
CONTRIBUTED.

GOOD CAKE.
Four eggs, two cups sugar, one cup sweet milk, one-half cup butter, three cups flour, two teaspoons baking powder, one teaspoon vanilla. Beat eggs and sugar together until very light, cream butter, put it into eggs and sugar, add milk and vanilla and then flour and baking powder.

Filling—One whole egg, beaten, butter size of an egg, one pound, pulverized sugar, juice and grated rind of one lemon. (Delicious.)
MISS PASCAL HALL, Hagerstown, Md.

HERMITS.

One cup sugar, one-half cup butter, cup seeded raisins, chopped or ground, two eggs, a teaspoon of cloves, one teaspoon nutmeg, one-half teaspoon soda, two tablespoons wine or water, flour to make a soft dough, just so you can roll it out. Bake in a quick oven.

MRS. H.P. WYMAN, Bristol, Tenn.

ICE CREAM CAKE.

Use Washington cake batter which is six eggs, one pound each of sugar and flour, one-half pound butter, one teaspoon baking powder, sifted in the flour, one small teacup of sweet milk, flavor with lemon, bake in jelly cake pans.

Filling for Ice Cream Cake—One pound and five ounces of sugar, put in a pan with teacup of water, set on the stove, boil until it ropes well, have beaten the whites of three eggs, pour the boiling syrup slowly over these eggs, flavor with vanilla, add one-third teaspoon of citric acid, beat until thick and spread between cakes.

MRS. E.S. McCLUNG, Knoxville, Tenn.

ICE CREAM CAKE.

Make a white cake. Whip one quart of cream sweetened and flavored with vanilla, put into this one pound of sliced or pounded almonds.

Slice the cake in layers and spread the mixture between, cover the top and sides with the cream, stick over at regular intervals one-fourth of a pound of whole blanched almonds.

MRS. WILL HAZEN, Knoxville, Tenn.

JAM CAKE.

One cup butter, one and one-half cups sugar, two cups flour, seven eggs, one teaspoon soda in two tablespoons of thick sour cream, one teaspoon cinnamon, one teaspoon cloves, one-half nutmeg grated, one cup jam, two tablespoons molasses.

Put together with icing, makes a large cake.

MRS. JOS. S. DONNELLY, Shoun's, Tenn.

JAM CAKE.

One cup butter, two cups sugar, three cups flour, one cup jam, one-half cup buttermilk, three eggs, one teaspoon mixed spices, one teaspoon soda, one cup pecans and as much citron (if you like it). Bake in layers and put together with icing, chocolate or caramel, any of these are good.

MRS. R.A.J. ARMSTRONG, Caswell, Tenn.

JAM CAKE.

Three eggs, one cup sugar, three-fourths cup butter, two cups flour, one cup jam, three tablespoons sour cream or milk, one teaspoon soda, spices. Put together with chocolate frosting.

MRS. H.P. WYMAN, Bristol, Tenn.

JAM CAKE.

Four eggs, save whites of two for icing, one-half cup butter, one cup sugar, nine tablespoons buttermilk, one heaping teaspoon soda, one-half teaspoon baking powder, one cup jam, one teaspoon each cloves, spice, cinnamon, two cups flour, put the whites in last, add the jam just before. Will make three layers. The icing is just plain boiled icing, one cup sugar to each white.

MRS. JOHN H. CALDWELL, Bristol, Tenn.

BLACKBERRY JAM CAKE.

Three eggs, one cup sugar, three-fourths cup butter, one and one-half cups flour, one cup jam, three tablespoons sour milk, one teaspoon soda, one teaspoon spice, one teaspoon cinnamon, one-half nutmeg.

MRS. ELLA. P. ANDERSON, Knoxville, Tenn.

"JUDY CAKE."

One-half cup butter, four eggs, one and three-fourths cup sugar, two and one-half cups flour, two and one-half teaspoons baking powder, three-fourths of a cup of sweet milk.

MISS JULIA WAGNER, Mountain City, Tenn.

JUMBLES.

One-half pound of butter, three eggs, three-fourths pound of sugar, and flour added to make it stiff enough to squeeze through the moulds. Flavor.

JUMBLES.

One pound white sugar, two pounds flour, three-fourths pound butter, creamed, four eggs, beaten separately, a teaspoon of soda, flavor to your taste.

MISS SUE DEADERICK, Knoxville, Tenn.

JUMBLES.

Two pounds of flour, one pound sugar, brown, half pound of lard and butter, mixed, good weight, five eggs, half cup buttermilk, one teaspoon soda in the milk, do not have the dough either too soft or too stiff, squeeze through a mould and bake in a quick oven.

MRS. GEORGE M. WHITE, Knoxville, Tenn.

LOAF CAKE.

Three pounds flour, set aside one-half pound for the last mixing, two pounds butter, or one each of butter and lard, two pounds sugar, two pounds raisins, seven eggs, one pint fresh milk, nearly a pint of the best yeast, one-half glass each of wine and brandy, two nutmegs, grated, one-half ounce cinnamon. Warm the milk and mix with the flour, yeast and half of the butter and sugar, rub well together, put in a tin bucket well-covered and set it in a warm place to rise. When risen work in the remaining half of butter and sugar, then the flour and raisins, then the wine, brandy and eggs, and when well mixed add a teaspoon of soda. Butter the pans; put in the batter and let it stand to rise the second time, then bake.

MRS. JAMES KENNEDY, Knoxville, Tenn.

WHITE LOAF CAKE.

Two cups sugar, one cup butter, three cups flour, one cup milk, two teaspoons baking powder, whites of eight eggs, beaten stiff, one-half teaspoon each of lemon and vanilla flavoring.

Frosting for Same—Two-thirds cup sugar, one-half cup water, cook until it threads, pour over whites of two beaten eggs.

MRS. J. WRIGHT CULTON, Knoxville, Tenn.

LADIES CAKE.

The whites of sixteen eggs, three pounds sifted flour, three-fourths (nearly) of butter, one pound white sugar, three ounces bitter almonds or peach kernels, two wine glasses rose water.

Blanch the almonds in scalding water, then pound them in a mortar, pouring in the rose water as you pound, a few drops at a time, make them light to keep them from sinking to the bottom of the cake. When they are all pounded to a paste, cover them and set them in a cool place. It is best to do this the day before they are wanted. Cream the butter and sugar together, then gradually stir in the almonds, then the whites of the sixteen eggs, beaten to a stiff froth are stirred in with the sugar and butter alternately with the sifted flour, a little at a time. Stir the whole very hard; put into a buttered pan, set immediately into an oven of moderate heat and bake. It requires more than two hours to bake, cool it gradually.

MRS. MOODY CHURCHWELL, Knoxville, Tenn.

LADY CAKE.

Whites of ten eggs, four heaped cups of sifted flour, three even cups sifted white sugar, one cup butter, lacking half inch of being full, little more than half cup of buttermilk or sour cream, one and one-half teaspoons cream of tartar, sifted through the flour. Cream, sugar and butter together, add eggs and flour alternately, pour in milk. Before putting in all the flour dissolve half teaspoon of soda in a little warm water and pour in the batter just before baking, flavor with bitter almond.

MRS. CARRICK PARK, Knoxville, Tenn.

LADY CAKE.

Whites of twelve eggs, four cups sifted flour, two light cups granulated sugar, one light cup butter, one and one-half teaspoons cream of tartar, sifted through the flour.

Cream the butter and sugar together, stir the flour and eggs in alternately, dissolve one-half teaspoon of soda in cold water, add flavor with lemon.

MRS. JOE JOUROLMON, Knoxville, Tenn.

LADY BALTIMORE CAKE.

Eight eggs, four teaspoons baking powder, half pint sweet milk, one-half pound butter, one pound sugar, one pound flour, almond flavor. Cream butter and sugar, add milk slowly, beat eggs separately, add yelks to butter and sugar and then whites of flour alternately, mix thoroughly and add extract.

Filling—Three cups sugar, whites of four eggs, one-half gill of boiling water, lemon juice to taste. Pour the water over the sugar and lemon juice and boil ten minutes, or till it threads, then pour hot syrup over beaten eggs, beat till cool and flavor with one cup English walnuts and two cups of seeded raisins.

CONTRIBUTED.

LAYER CAKE.

Four eggs, one cup butter, one cup milk, two cups sugar, three cups flour, flavor to taste. Beat well.

Filling—Two cups brown sugar, one cup sweet milk. one large lump of butter, let it cook until it makes a soft ball in water, then take off and beat till creamy and spread over the layers of cake.

MRS. TOM McMILLIAN, Beverly, Tenn.

LEMON SNOW CAKE.

Three cups each of sugar and sweet milk, one cup butter, three eggs, three pints flour, three teaspoons soda, six teaspoons cream of tartar, flavor with the juice and grated rind of one lemon.

Rub butter and sugar to a cream, add the well beaten eggs, then the milk with the soda dissolved in it, then the flour with the cream of tartar sifted through it, lastly the lemon, and bake.

MRS. J.A. RAYL, Knoxville, Tenn.

LOIS CAKE.

One-half cup of butter, one and one-fourth cups of brown sugar, yelks of two eggs, two-thirds of a cup of sweet milk, two and one-fourth cups of flour, three and one-half teaspoons of baking powder, one teaspoon of orange extract and one teaspoon of vanilla, two tablespoon of sherry wine, one-half cup of raisins, seeded and cut in pieces, one-half cup of walnut meats, one-half cup of currants, two tablespoons of candied orange peel, finely cut, whites of two eggs, mix in the order given and bake one and one-quarter hours in a slow oven.

MRS. CRAMER, Orange River, Fla.

MARBLE CAKE.

White Batter—One cup white sugar, one-half cup butter, one-half cup sweet cream, two teaspoons baking powder, whites of four eggs, two and one-half cups sifted flour.

Dark Batter—Same as white part, using the yellows, raisins, spices, cloves, allspice, cinnamon, nutmeg.

Bake in a loaf, putting first a spoonful of white and then one of dark batter in the pan.

MRS. JOS. S. DONNELLY, Shoun's, Tenn.

MARGUERITES.

Select fresh long, unsalted wafers, make an icing with whites of two eggs and one cup of powdered sugar, spread over the crackers and dust with cocoanut, grated, slip in the oven and brown. You can use chopped nuts if you prefer instead of cocoanut.

MRS. CRUTCHER, Kentucky.

MAVAS OR WONDERS.

Two eggs, two tablespoons of melted butter, or lard, pinch of salt, two tablespoons sweet milk. Mix very hard with sifted flour, roll very thin. cut with large cake cutter, then cut several slits lengthwise, fry in deep hot lard. The lard should not smoke, but be hot enough for cake to float on top when put in. When frying do not let them touch, sift powdered sugar on while hot. Serve with chocolate.

This is a French cake and is delicious. I always cut them all out before I begin to fry, then there is no danger of the lard burning.

MRS. HOWARD ANDERSON, Beverly, Tenn.

METHODIST CAKE.

Two eggs, one cup of sugar, one cup of sweet milk, one-half cup of butter, two teaspoons of cream of tartar, one teaspoon of soda, two cups of flour. Bake in three layers; put raisins, currants and spices in the middle layer, put frosting between one layer and jelly between the other and frosting on top.

CONTRIBUTED.

MINUTE CAKE.

One cup sugar, four tablespoons melted butter, two tablespoons of laundry starch dissolved in a good half cup of milk, whites of two eggs, one full cup of flour, one teaspoon of baking powder.

Put all in the bowl together and give a good stir, bake in a slow oven.

MRS. McELROY.

MOLASSES CAKE.

One cup each of molasses and sour milk or cream, one-half cup butter, three eggs, a large teaspoon soda and one of ginger, flour to make as thick as pound cake batter, add nutmeg, cinnamon and spice, eat hot with sauce.

MRS. JENNIE S. HOUSE, Knoxville, Tenn.

MOLASSES BARS.

Sift lightly three cups flour, one-half tablespoon ginger, one-third teaspoon nutmeg, one-eighth teaspoon cloves, one teaspoon salt;

Mix one-half cup sugar, one-fourth cup lard, one-fourth cup butter, one-half cup molasses, one-fourth cup of boiling water, one teaspoon soda, unite and chill over night. The next morning roll out one-fourth inch thick and sprinkle with walnut meats (English), one cup. Cut with a knife. Use Porto Rican molasses.

ANNA PAULINE DOUGHTY

MOUNTAIN CAKE.

Stir to a cream one cup of butter, two cups of sugar, the whites of six eggs, beaten to a stiff froth, one and one-third cups of sweet milk, three and one-third cups of sifted flour, one-half teaspoon of soda, one teaspoon of of tartar, flavor with lemon and bake in a moderate oven.

MRS. RUSH S. HAZEN, Knoxville, Tenn.

SPICED MOUNTAIN CAKE.

To the yelks of five eggs well beaten, add one cup of sugar, one-half cup each of butter and sweet milk, one teaspoon ground cinnamon, one teaspoon grated nutmeg, the whites of two eggs well beaten, one and one-half cups flour, one teaspoon baking powder, bake in jelly cake pans. When cold, spread each layer with an icing made with the whites of three eggs, beaten stiff, and one and one-half cups sugar.

MRS. LUCY J. BROWNLEE, Knoxville, Tenn.

WHITE MOUNTAIN CAKE.

Whites of eight eggs, three cups of sugar, six cups flour, one cup each of butter and sweet milk, two teaspoons cream of tartar, one-half teaspoon of soda, flavor with lemon, bake in jelly cake pan.

For the Icing—One pound sugar, whites of four eggs, half a cup of cold water, boil until it drops from the spoon fine as hair, then pour, beating hard, over the whites, which have been slightly beaten. Beat until cold and flavor with either lemon or vanilla. Spread the icing between the layers of cake, ice outside of the whole.

MRS. B.J. STEPHENSON, Knoxville, Tenn.

MUFFIN CAKES.

One cup butter, two cups sugar, three and one-half cups flour, four eggs, one cup milk, two teaspoons baking powder. Bake in pans.

MRS. RICHARD P. JOHNSON, Knoxville, Tenn.

NOUGAT.

Melt, but do not boil, one cup of grated chocolate, one cup brown sugar, one-half cup sweet milk, stir all the time. Make a batter of one-half cup butter, one scant cup brown sugar, yelks of three eggs, one teaspoon soda, one-half cup sweet milk, two cups flour and lastly put in the chocolate mixture. When cool, use the whites for the icing, flavor with vanilla.

MRS. JOSEPH OWEN, Bristol, Tenn.

NOUGAT.

Three eggs, one and one-half cups sugar, one-half cup butter, one-half cup milk, two cups flour, one teaspoon vanilla and one teaspoon baking powder, one-half cup English walnuts.

Filling—Two cups brown sugar, three-fourths cup milk, butter, size of a walnut, boil till it makes a soft ball in water, pour off and beat till thick, then spread between the layers of a cake.

MRS. JETT, Bristol, Va.

CHOCOLATE NOUGAT.

Two squares of sweet chocolate, two tablespoons of sugar, one-fourth cup of cold water, one-third cup of sweet milk. Grate chocolate, add sugar and water, stir over fire till thick and creamy, add one-third cup of milk and put away to cool.

Two tablespoons of butter, one cup of sugar, two eggs, two cups of flour, two teaspoons of baking powder, one-fourth teaspoon of vanilla, two-thirds cup of milk, add yelks, beaten till thick, the flour and baking powder sifted together, the remainder of two-thirds cup of milk, add cooked chocolate and beaten whites of eggs.

MRS. HERBERT CONOVER, Knoxville, Tenn.

NUT CAKE.

Two cups sugar, one cup butter, four cups flour, four eggs, two cups chopped raisins, two cups chopped walnuts, one cup milk, three teaspoons baking powder.

Beat butter to a cream, add sugar gradually, when light add eggs well beaten, then milk, then flour in which baking powder has been mixed. Mix quickly and add nuts and raisins. Bake in a large shallow pan.

MRS. H.M. SIMMONDS, Knoxville, Tenn.

NUT LOAF.

One egg, a big spoon of butter, one-half cup sugar, four cups flour, one cup chopped mixed nuts, one and one-half cups milk, four level teaspoons baking powder, set in a warm place to rise twenty minutes, bake in a slow oven fifty minutes. Have pan well greased.

MRS. RACH DAVIS, Knoxville, Tenn.

ONE EGG CAKE.

One cup sugar, piece of butter size of an egg, pint of flour, cup sweet milk, teaspoon soda, two teaspoons cream of tartar. Cream the butter with half the sugar, beat one egg, adding the other half of sugar, mix the two, pouring in half the milk, put the soda in the remainder of the milk, pouring in last before baking. Sift the cream of tartar through the flour. Double this quantity makes a pudding for dinner and some for supper. Eat with a liquid sauce.

MRS. A.M. FRENCH, Knoxville, Tenn.

ORANGE CAKE.

One-half cup butter creamed, one cup sugar, one-half cup milk, one and two-thirds cup flour, two and one-half teaspoons baking powder, two eggs, beaten separately.

Every measure is level, measure a spoon and take off half lengthwise, three teaspoons make a tablespoon, cream butter, add sugar, then part of milk with butter and sugar, then milk and flour, whites last. Always sift dry ingredients, mix wet ingredient and unite the two, fold the whites in so as not to lose any of the air beaten in. If the cake is thin anywhere, let it be toward the centre, as the edges bake faster.

Filling—One-half cup sugar, two and one-half tablespoons flour, stir in the sugar, one-half tablespoon of lemon juice, grated rind of half an orange, one egg, beaten slightly, cook about ten minutes in a double boiler.

Frosting—Rest of the grated rind of the orange, one teaspoon of brandy, one-half teaspoon of lemon juice, one tablespoon of orange juice, stir in enough confectioner's sugar to spread, about one-half pound. If you get it too stiff, thin with a little orange juice, when ready to spread.

ANNA PAULINE DOUGHTY.

PERFECTION CAKE.

Three cups sugar, one cup of butter and one cup sweet milk, three of flour, one of corn starch, whites of twelve eggs, beaten to a stiff froth, three teaspoons baking powder.

Dissolve the corn starch in the milk and add it to the sugar and butter well beaten together, then the flour and baking powder and whites of eggs.

MRS. LUCY J. BROWNLEE, Knoxville, Tenn.

WHITE PERFECTION CAKE.

Three cups sugar, one of butter, and one of sweet milk, one of corn starch, whites of twelve eggs, beaten well, two teaspoons of cream of tartar, mixed in the flour, one teaspoon of soda, dissolved in half the milk, dissolve the corn starch in the rest of the milk, add it to the sugar and butter, well beaten together, then the eggs and flour, a little of each at a time, then the milk and soda.

MISS ADDIE CARTER.

PHILADELPHIA CAKE.

White Batter—Three-fourths of a cup of butter, two cups of sugar, one cup of sweet milk, one cup of corn starch, two cups of flour, whites of eight eggs, two teaspoons of baking powder, flavor, almond or vanilla. Makes three layers.

Dark Batter—Yelks of eight eggs, one cup of butter, two cups of brown sugar, three cups of flour, one-third cup of brandy, one cup of milk, sweet, two teaspoons of baking powder, one pound of raisins, chopped, all kinds of spices, makes three layers.

Cream for Filling—Two cups of sour cream, two cups of sugar, six eggs, two heaping teaspoons of corn starch in six tablespoons of sweet milk, cook in double boiler till thick, take from fire and add one-quarter pound blanched almonds, chopped and spread between the layers, ice with plain white icing and decorate with cherries and blanched almonds. This will make three two-layer cakes.

MRS. JOSEPH W. OWEN, Bristol, Tenn.

PINEAPPLE CAKE.

Make a large white cake and slice, take the syrup of one can of grated pineapple and one pint of sugar, boil until it begins to rope, then stir into this the pineapple and spread between the cakes.

MRS H.H. TAYLOR, Knoxville, Tenn.

POTATO CARAMEL CAKE.

Two-thirds of a cup of butter, two cups of sugar, four eggs, one cup of grated chocolate, one cup of hot mashed Irish potatoes, two teaspoons of baking powder, one teaspoon each of cinnamon, cloves, nutmeg, one cup chopped nuts, one-half cup of sweet milk, two cups flour.

Cream sugar, butter and yelks of eggs, add milk, mix potatoes hot and chocolate, which will melt, mix flour, spices and baking powder, sift that in and then the beaten whites, lastly the nuts. Bake in layers and put together with icing. Mexican recipe.

MRS. JOHN M. ALLEN, Knoxville, Tenn.

POUND CAKE.

Seven eggs, whites beaten and yelks creamed with butter and sugar, four cups sifted flour, two cups sugar, one cup butter, one-half cup thick sour cream, one teaspoon Rumford baking powder and about half a teaspoon, scant, of soda. Flavor with nutmeg or lemon as preferred.

MRS. W.N. PATTON, Bristol, Tenn.

PLAIN POUND CAKE.

One pound sugar, one pound flour, three-fourths of a pound of butter, one dozen eggs, flavor with lemon.

MRS. J.A. RAYL, Knoxville, Tenn.

PUFF CAKE.

One cup sugar, one-half cup butter, two-thirds cup sweet milk, two eggs; and a light pint of flour with two teaspoons baking powder sifted in it. Bake in a quick oven about one-half hour and serve with sauce.

MRS. B.J. STEPHENSON, Knoxville, Tenn.

QUEEN'S CAKE.

One pound of white sugar, three-quarters of a pound of butter, a pound of flour, a pound of seeded raisins, one-half a pound of Zante currants, a quarter of a pound of citron, a wineglass of wine, one of French Brandy and one of milk, a teaspoon of soda and six eggs.

Stir the sugar and butter to a cream, beat the eggs to a froth and stirring, add the brandy and wine, then the flour and spices, dissolve the soda in the milk and strain it into the rest of the ingredients when mixed together.

Stir the whole for several minutes, then add the floured fruit gradually, a handful of each alternately; when mixed, line a couple of buttered pans with white paper, butter it, then turn in the cake and bake immediately from an hour and fifteen minutes to an hour and thirty minutes, according to the heat of the oven. If it browns fast, cover it over with thick paper. Be sure and have a good heat at the bottom of the oven. This cake will keep well for a number of months.

MRS. E.C. JONES, Knoxville, Tenn.

QUEEN VICO CAKE.

One pound each of sugar and flour, one-half pound butter, four eggs, one nutmeg, grated, one gill each of wine and brandy, one gill of sweet cream, one pound raisins, two teaspoons baking powder. Beat the butter, sugar and yelks of eggs to a perfect cream, add the cream, then the whites of eggs, and lastly the fruit, which has been rubbed in the flour. Bake one and one-half hours.

MISS ADDIE CARTER, Knoxville, Tenn.

RAILROAD CAKE.

Whites of nine eggs, five cups of flour, one cup of butter, one cup of cream, two teaspoonsful of baking powder, two and one-half cups of sugar.

Divide batter into four parts, leave one white, put one-half pound of raisins in one, one ounce of grated chocolate in another, and English walnuts in another, use as many as you like, no special quantity required. Put together with plain icing or a fruit filling.

MRS. D.F. McCARTY, Bristol, Va.
MRS. L.A. BONHAM.

RAILROAD CAKE.

Make Washington cake batter and divide into two parts. To one-half add two teacups of nice currants or stoned raisins, two teaspoons of molasses, one teaspoon cinnamon, one-half teaspoon each of cloves and allspice. Bake in jelly pans and put alternate layers of dark and light cake with jelly or icing between.

MRS. A.P. WHITE, Knoxville, Tenn.

RAISIN CAKE.

One cup white sugar, whites of four eggs, four tablespoons butter, eight tablespoons of sweet milk, one cup flour, one teaspoon baking powder, flavor with lemon, bake in layers. For filling, add a little water to one cup white sugar, put it on the stove to boil till it strings, take off and pour over the white of one egg, beaten rather stiff, beat till like icing, chop a cup of raisins and add to this icing, and spread on the layers.

MRS. LUCY J. BROWNLEE, Knoxville, Tenn.

RAISIN PUFFS.

Two eggs, one-half cup butter, three teaspoons baking powder, two tablespoons sugar, two cups sifted flour, one cup sweet milk, one cup raisins, chopped very fine.

Put in steamer in small cups and steam one-half hour.

MRS. H.P. WYMAN, Bristol, Tenn.

RIBBON CAKE.

Three cups of sugar, one cup of milk, one cup of butter, five cups of flour, eleven eggs, whites, one teaspoon of baking powder. Take half the batter and color with fruit coloring; bake in jelly pans.

Yellow Part—Yelks of eleven eggs, two cups of sugar, one cup of milk, five cups of flour, one cup of butter, one teaspoon of baking powder. Take half the batter and color with chocolate, grated, bake in jelly pans and put all together with plain white icing.

MISS CORNELIA CROZIER, Avondale Springs, Tenn.

RIBBON CAKE.

Two cups sugar, one cup each of butter and sweet milk, four eggs, three and one-half cups flour with yeast, powder enough for one quart. Divide the dough into four parts, to one part add one cup raisins, one cup currants, one-fourth pound of citron, one teaspoon of cinnamon, one-half teaspoon cloves, one-fourth teaspoon mace. To the three parts add one teaspoon of essence. Bake the fruit part in two pans, the white in four. This makes two cakes, put the fruit in the middle and the white on each side.

MRS. SMILLIE, Atlanta, Ga.

RIBBON CAKE.

Whites of eight eggs, one cup butter, two cups sugar, four cups flour, one teaspoon soda, cup sweet milk, two teaspoons of cream of tartar, bake in jelly tins.

Dark Part—Yelks of eight eggs, two cups sugar, three cups flour, one cup sweet milk, two teaspoons soda, four of cream of tartar, one-half teaspoon each of cloves, cinnamon, and allspice, one grated nutmeg, one-half pound seeded raisins, one-half pound citron cut fine. Bake in jelly tins and spread white and dark alternately with the following icing, made of two pounds of sugar and whites of six eggs, color a deep pink with Price's fruit coloring and add two grated cocoanuts.

MRS. JAMES KENNEDY, Knoxville, Tenn.

ROCKS.

One cup butter, four eggs, one cup sugar, one and one-half tablespoons boiling water, one level teaspoon soda, two and one-fourth cups of flour, one cup English Walnuts, one cup raisins, one-half cup currants, one teaspoon cinnamon, one-half teaspoon cloves. Bake in muffin rings.

MRS. BOYER, Tazewell, Va.

SALEM FANCY CAKE.

Three pints of sifted flour, a pinch of salt, one even teaspoon of baking powder, one pint sugar, one-half pound butter and a piece of lard, size of an egg, five eggs, two nutmegs, grated. Mix as stiff as possible, knead with the hands, roll as thin as a wafer and bake very quickly in a hot oven. Will keep for weeks.

CONTRIBUTED.

SAVOY BISCUIT.

Beat four eggs separately, then beat them together, add half a pound of loaf sugar, season with lemon, lastly quarter of a pound of flour, stirred in slowly, then beat hard, drop the batter on sheets of white paper, greased. Let the cakes be so far apart they will not run together, sprinkle sugar on top, bake quickly, they should be lightly colored.

MRS. J.G.M. RAMSEY, Knoxville, Tenn.

SCRIPTURE CAKE.

Four and one-half cups I Kings IV-22, one cup of Judges V-25, last clause, two cups of Jeremiah VI-20, two cups I Samuel XXX-12, two cups Nahum III-12, two cups Numbers XVII-8, two tablespoons I Samuel XIV-25, a pinch of Leviticus II-13, six Jeremiah XVII-11, one-half cup of Judges IV-19, last clause, two teaspoons Amos IV-5, Season to taste II Chronicles IX-9.

EXPLANATION. Four and one-half cups flour, one cup butter, two cups sugar, two cups raisins, two cups figs, two cups almonds, two tablespoons honey, a pinch of salt, six eggs, one-half cup of milk, two teaspoons baking powder, spice to taste. The cake is delicious.

SCRIPTURE CAKE.

Five cups of I Kings IV-22, two cups Jeremiah VI-20, one cup of Judges V-25, two cups of I Samuel XXX-12, two cups Nahum III-12, one tablespoon of Numbers XVII-8, one large spoonful of I Samuel XIV-25, six tablespoons of Jeremiah XVII-11, a pinch or Leviticus II-13, one-half cup of I Timothy V-23; two tablespoons of Amos IV-5. Season to taste with II Chronicles IX-9. Follow Solomon's prescription for making a good boy, Proverbs XXIII-14, and you will have a good cake.

MRS. W.K. VANCE, Bristol, Tenn.

FRENCH SHORTCAKE.

Make a cottage pudding and bake in a cake pan, when cool, cut out a circle on top, lift it off and take out most of the inside; fill with sugared berries, put on the cover and sprinkle sugar over all; cut down through it as though it were a cake and serve with cream or berry-juice. The next day make a pudding out of the crumbs you took out.

CONTRIBUTED.

STRAWBERRY SHORTCAKE

One quart of flour, two tablespoons of sugar, two teaspoons of baking powder, one teaspoon of salt, one egg, one cup of sweet milk, three ounces of butter, that is three tablespoons rounded. Half this quantity will make a large shortcake. Bake in three jelly cake tins, split and butter and stack, placing the crushed strawberries and sugar on each layer and whole ones on top.

MRS. HUGH W. TAYLOR, Bristol, Tenn.

STRAWBERRY SHORTCAKE.

One quart of flour, two big tablespoons butter, two teaspoons baking powder, no salt, sweet milk enough to make a soft dough, work just enough to mix. Cover the bottom of pan with half the dough, grease with melted butter and place the rest of the dough on. Bake in a moderate oven. When done, open and butter well, pour berries that have been chopped and sweetened between the cake and pour around in the dish, sprinkle with powdered sugar and place a few whole berries over the top. Serve with rich cream.

NEW YORK RECEIPT.

SHREWSBURY CAKE.

Eight eggs, one pound butter, two pounds sugar, three pounds flour, some cinnamon and mace. It may be necessary to use a little more flour. It takes very little working.

MRS. G.W. CHURCHWELL, Knoxville, Tenn.

SILVER AND GOLD CAKE.
Five or six whites, two-thirds of a cup of milk or water, two-thirds cup butter, three cups of flour, one and one-half cups of sugar, teaspoon of baking powder, flavor to taste.

Gold—Yelks of five or six eggs, one cup of sugar, two cups of flour, sifted, one-half cup of butter, one-half cup of water or milk, flavor to taste.
MRS. JOHN H. CALDWELL, Bristol, Tenn.

SNOW CAKE.
One pound sugar, one pound flour, half pound butter, whites of sixteen eggs, and a little soda, flavor.
MRS. J.T. McTEER, Knoxville, Tenn.

SPICE CAKE.
One cup buttermilk, one-half cup butter, two cups sugar, two eggs, one teaspoon soda, flour for medium stiff batter, teaspoon each of cinnamon, allspice, cloves and half a nutmeg, grated.

Bake rather slowly, raisins may be added if liked.
MISS BERTHA PIERCE, Detroit, Mich.

SPICE CAKE.
Six whole eggs, or yelks of twelve, ten ounces butter, one pound sugar, one pound flour, one cup sour milk, one teaspoon soda, one tablespoon each of cloves, cinnamon, nutmeg and allspice.
MRS. WILL HAZEN, Knoxville, Tenn.

SPICE CAKE.
One pound sugar, three-fourths of a pound of butter, one and one-fourth of a pound of flour, cup of molasses, one tablespoon of spice, two tablespoons of ginger, the same of cinnamon, one nutmeg grated, one cup sour cream, one tablespoon soda, five eggs and the juice of two lemons with a teaspoon of vanilla.
MRS. B.J. STEPHENSON, Knoxville, Tenn.

SPICE CAKE.
One and one-half cups sugar, one cup butter, one cup sour milk, three cups flour, five eggs, one teaspoon soda, three teaspoons cinnamon, one teaspoon allspice, two teaspoons cloves. Reserve four of the five whites for icing. Bake in layers.
MRS. RICHARD P. JOHNSON, Knoxville, Tenn.

SPICE CAKE.
Yellows of six eggs, one and one-half cups dark brown sugar, one-fourth pound butter, one cup buttermilk, one teaspoon allspice, two teaspoons cinnamon, one teaspoon soda, sifted with two and one-half cups of flour. Beat all together and bake in muffin tins. Always sift flour before measuring for cakes.
MRS. A.S. BIRDSONG, Knoxville, Tenn.

SPICE CAKE.
Two cups sugar, one cup butter, one cup sour milk, one and one-fourth teaspoons of soda dissolved in the milk, three cups flour, five eggs, leaving out the white of one for icing, spice to color a rich brown.

If one prefers, you can use chocolate instead of spice, this makes three layers. Put together with icing.
MRS. HOWARD ANDERSON, Beverly, Tenn.

SPONGE CAKE.
One pound sugar, three-fourths of a pound of flour, ten eggs. Beat yelks well, add sugar and beat again, then add the whites, beaten to a stiff froth and stir in the flour, flavor to taste.
MRS. CYNTHIA K. BOYD, Knoxville, Tenn.

SPONGE CAKE.
Juice and rind of one lemon, twelve eggs, one pound sugar, ten ounces of flour.

Beat yelks, sugar and lemon to a cream, add whites, beaten to a stiff froth and beat fifteen minutes, stir in flour gently and bake in rather quick oven.
MISS ANN BELL, Knoxville, Tenn.

SPONGE CAKE.

Fourteen eggs, weight of ten in powdered sugar, which is three cups, weight of six in sifted flour, four cups, grated rind and juice of one lemon. Beat the yelks of eight eggs very light, then add the sugar and beat again, put in juice and grated rind of the lemon, and then the whites of fourteen eggs, beaten to a stiff froth, beat all together for fifteen minutes, without cessation, stir in the flour last, barely mixing, do not beat, pour into buttered moulds, bake in hot oven.

A large cake will require fully one hour for baking, if it bakes too fast on top cover with buttered paper. Splendid.

MRS. MARY A. BYARS, Bristol, Va.

SPONGE CAKE.

One cup of flour and one cup of sugar, three eggs, one-half teaspoon of soda, one teaspoon cream of tartar, flavor with vanilla, bake in jelly pans.

MRS. JOE JOUROLMON, Knoxville, Tenn.

BERWICK SPONGE CAKE.

Six eggs, three cups powdered sugar, four even-cups sifted flour, two teaspoons cream of tartar, one teaspoon soda, one cup of cold water, one-half of a lemon. Beat the eggs two minutes, add sugar and beat five minutes more. Stir the cream of tartar into two cups of the flour, add it to the eggs and sugar and beat for one minute. Dissolve the soda in the water and add it also. Wash the lemon, dry it and add both the juice and the rind, grated. Finally add the two remaining cups of flour, and beat all the ingredients together for one minute. Put the dough into two deep tins and bake it in a moderate oven.

WILLIAM BRIGGS, North Berwick, Me.

CHOCOLATE SPONGE CAKE.

Melt four ounces of unsweetened chocolate over hot water, add a cup of powdered sugar, a cup of milk and stir until smooth. Beat the yelks of four eggs and a cup of powdered sugar until very light, using a wire egg-beater, add the hot chocolate mixture and continue beating. Flavor with vanilla, fold in the stiffly beaten whites of eggs and last a heaping cup of flour, mixed with a level tablespoon of baking powder. Bake in a sheet or layers. This is particularly fine made in two layers. Spread the following icing between the layers and on top of the cake. Butter the inside of a granite saucepan, add a cup and a half of sugar and a half cup of rich new milk. Cook to the soft-ball stage, then take from the fire, flavor with vanilla. add a half cup of chopped pecan meats and stir till creamy. The nuts may be omitted for plain icing.

MRS. WILL BEWLAY DUENNER, Bristol, Va.

OLD-FASHIONED SPONGE CAKE.

One pound of sugar, half-pound of flour, ten eggs, grated rind and juice of one lemon.

Beat the yelks very light and mix them well with the sugar, add the lemon and beat well together, then add whites, which have been beaten very stiff, shake in the flour very gently, it should not be stirred after the flour is well mixed. If baked in two pans, one hour and a quarter is sufficient, if in one pan two hours.

MRS. BEN S. BOYD, Knoxville. Tenn.

SPONGE ROLL.

One cup flour, measured after sifting, one cup sugar, four eggs, yelks beaten with the sugar, one-fourth teaspoonful of baking powder and one-half teacup cold water, added after you fold in the whites.

Sauce for the Above—One teacup of sugar into which is stirred the yelk of one egg, two teaspoonsful of cold water, or cream, lump of butter size of a large egg; place in a saucepan on the stove, stirring gently until the butter melts, when it is done. Do not let boil. Flavor with nutmeg.

MRS. MARY BOWEN, Aberdeen, Miss.

SPONGE CAKE ROLL.

The eggs are not beaten separately and the quicker the cake is mixed the better it will be.

Two teacups of coffee, A. sugar, two teacups sifted flour, two heaping teaspoons of baking powder. Bake in stove pan in a quick oven to a light brown. When done, spread with preserves or jelly, roll carefully and wrap in a cloth. Eat with sauce.

Liquid Sauce—Six tablespoons of boiling water, four tablespoons butter, one cup of sugar. Heat the water and sugar very hot, stir in the butter till it is melted, be careful not to let it boil, use very little nutmeg, and flavor with vanilla.

MRS. B. J. STEPHENSON, Knoxville, Tenn.

SODA SPONGE CAKE.

One cup each of sugar and flour, two eggs, one small teaspoon of soda, two of cream of tartar, four tablespoons of milk, flavor.

MRS. E. BOLLI, Knoxville, Tenn.

SUNSHINE SPONGE CAKE.

Six eggs, one cup pastry flour, sifted three times, add a pinch of salt, one cup granulated sugar, sifted, half the grated rind of a lemon, only the yellow part, tablespoon of lemon juice. Beat yelks thoroughly, add sugar a little at a time, then lemon juice, add whites, cut and fold, when whites are nearly blended put in one-half flour, cut and fold and add the rest of the flour. To bake turn heat on at half cock for twenty minutes. Cake is done when it has stopped singing and is elastic to the touch.

ANNA PAULINE DOUGHTY.

VELVET SPONGE CAKE.

Six eggs, leaving out the whites of three for the icing, two cups sugar, three scant cups sifted flour, one cup boiling water, one rounded teaspoon baking powder, in the last cup flour, flavor with lemon. Beat yelks fifteen minutes, add sugar, beat till light, add whites, water and flour, beating very little after the last cup of flour. Bake in a rather quick oven.

Icing and Filling–One-fourth pound sugar to each egg, put sugar on fire with a little hot water and boil till it "strings", then pour over smoothly beaten whites and beat till thick, flavor with vanilla.

MRS. A.P. WHITE, Knoxville, Tenn.

SUGAR CAKES.

One cup sour cream, two cups butter, three cups sugar, four eggs, teaspoon soda, tablespoon powdered mace, flour enough to roll out.

MISS BETTIE ALEXANDER, Lexington, Va.

SUNSHINE CAKE.

Whites of seven eggs, yelks of five eggs, one and one-fourth cups of granulated sugar, one cup of flour, one level teaspoon of cream of tartar, one pinch of salt added to the whites before whipping. Flavor with vanilla. Sift, measure and set aside flour and sugar, separate eggs, beating the whites to a foam, adding cream of tartar and then whip to a stiff foam; add sugar, little at a time, to the whites, whip yelks to a very stiff froth, beat in the whites and sugar, flavor, beat in the flour lightly. Put cake in barely warm oven, do not grease the pan, bake very slow, take from thirty to sixty minutes. When done invert cake pan on the table until cold, before taking the cake out.

MRS. ALLEN S. MEBANE, Knoxville, Tenn.

SWEET CAKES.

Four eggs, one pint sugar, beat well together, one even teaspoon soda dissolved in one tablespoon buttermilk, beat in the eggs and enough for a stiff dough. Make a hole in the flour, stir in the mixture till it is stiff enough to work with the hand, work as little as possible, roll out, cut and bake quickly.

MRS. JOE JOUROLMON, Knoxville, Tenn.

NICEST SWEET CAKES.

Four eggs, one pint sugar, beat them together, one even teaspoon soda, dissolved in one tablespoon of buttermilk, beat in the eggs and sugar, one large spoon of lard worked in the flour, make a soft dough, bake quick, flavor to taste.

MRS. B.J. STEPHENSON, Knoxville, Tenn.

SAND TARTS.

Two cups sugar, one cup butter, three cups flour, two eggs, leaving out the white of one, roll out thin, spread the white of egg on top, press walnut kernel in top and bake.

MISS BRANCH KEEBLER, Bristol, Va.

SAND TARTS.

Two pounds sugar, two pounds flour, one pound butter, three eggs, leaving out the white of one, one-fourth pound of shelled sweet almonds, blanched and chopped coarsely.

Mix flour, sugar, butter and eggs, kneading thoroughly. Roll out in a thin sheet of dough and with a feather moisten it with the white of egg, sift powdered sugar and cinnamon over it. Cut in square cakes and sprinkle or stick almonds on the cakes and brown in a brisk oven.

MRS. W.K. VANCE, Bristol, Tenn.

TEA CAKES.

Five eggs, one pound sugar, three-fourths pound butter, one teaspoon soda, put in dry, flavor with cinnamon and nutmeg, or a fresh lemon, flour enough to make a soft dough.

MRS. JAMES KENNEDY, Knoxville, Tenn.

TEA CAKES.

Four eggs, two good cups sugar, one good cup butter, one teaspoon lemon or vanilla, two heaping teaspoons baking powder, flour for a very soft dough. Roll thin and bake in a quick oven in greased pans.

MRS. A.S. BIRDSONG, Knoxville, Tenn.

TEA CAKES.

One scant cup butter, or three-fourths cup cottolene, two cups sugar, one-half cup milk, three eggs, two teaspoons baking powder, flour to roll, vanilla to taste. Bake in quick oven.

MRS. RICHARD P. JOHNSON, Knoxville; Tenn.

TEA CAKES.

Three cups of sugar, one of butter, one-half cup of sour milk, three to five eggs, level teaspoon of soda, flour enough for a soft dough. Beat well together like pound cake, add more flour, roll out, cut and bake.

MRS. MARGARET BUCKWELL, Knoxville, Tenn.

COCOA TEA CAKES.

Cream a scant half-cup of Cottolene and beat into it gradually one cup of sugar. Then beat in three eggs, singly, until the mixture is light and smooth. Add alternately one-half cup of milk and about a cup and two-thirds of flour, sifted with two teaspoons of baking powder and a quarter of a cupful of Walter Baker's cocoa. Beat well and bake in a moderate oven in muffin tins or a shallow pan. Nuts or fruit may be added, if desired.

MRS. HELEN ARMSTRONG.

ENGLISH TEA CAKE.

Three eggs, nine or ten tablespoons sugar, one-half pint of lukewarm sweet milk. one teacup melted butter, beaten in sugar and eggs, three cakes Fleishman's yeast dissolved in warm water, one-half pound raisins, four tablespoons chopped citron, one nutmeg grated, one teaspoon grated orange peel, flour enough to make a soft dough. Stir all together and let rise four hours, or till light. Make out in rolls or roll out and put in a pie pan and set to rise. When light, bake in a quick oven, watching that it does not burn. Split and butter and sprinkle with pulverized sugar.

MRS. JOHN J. HAGER, Bristol, Tenn.

MONTVALE TEA CAKES.

Three pounds of flour, one and one-half pounds sugar, twelve ounces butter, six eggs, one teaspoon soda, dissolved in a cup of sour cream or fresh buttermilk. After the dough is rolled out pretty thin, sift pulverized sugar over it and cut with a cutter. Very nice.

MISS MARY PLEAS McCLUNG, Knoxville, Tenn.

VANILLA SNAPS.

One cup butter, one and one-half cups sugar, two eggs, two tablespoons milk, three teaspoons vanilla, one teaspoon baking powder in enough flour to make a soft dough. Roll thin and dust with pulverized sugar.

MRS. W.K. VANCE, Bristol, Tenn.

VELVET CAKE.

One cup butter, two cups sugar, four cups flour, five eggs, one teaspoon soda, two of cream of tartar, flavor to taste.

MRS. B.J. STEPHENSON, Knoxville, Tenn.

VELVET CAKE.

One cup butter, two cups sugar, four cups flour, six eggs, one teaspoon of soda, dissolved in cold water, two teaspoons cream tartar, sifted with the flour, flavor with lemon.

MRS. JOE JOUROLMON, Knoxville, Tenn.

WAFERS.

Stir together one-half pound sugar, one-fourth pound butter, add to this six eggs, well-beaten, beat all very light, stir in as much flour as will make a stiff batter, add a teaspoon cinnamon, a little nutmeg and a little lemon, have the batter perfectly smooth, bake on a wafer iron.

MRS. S.B. BOYD, Knoxville, Tenn.

TWELFTH NIGHT WAFERS.

One pound each of butter, powdered sugar and flour, yelks of nine hard boiled eggs, grated or rubbed to a crumb, three raw eggs, two tablespoons whiskey, one grated lemon, entire. Make into a dough, roll thin, cut into little cakes, press an almond or raisin on top and bake. Will keep a long time.

HATTIE KING TAYLOR, Bristol, Tenn.

WASHINGTON CAKE.

Five eggs, one teacup of butter, three cups of flour and one of corn starch, two teaspoons of cream of tartar and one of soda, one teacup of sweet milk, and two cups of sugar, season with lemon.

MRS. JOHN G. KING, "Oakland", Bristol, Tenn.

WHITE CAKE.

Whites of four eggs, three-fourths cup butter, one cup sweet milk, two cups sugar, four cups flour, three heaping teaspoons baking powder, flavor with vanilla.

MRS. ROBERT VESTAL, Knoxville, Tenn.

WHITE CAKE.

Two cups of sugar, two and one-half cups of sifted flour, sift again with one teaspoon of baking powder, a good half cup of butter, after it is creamed, one-half cup of sweet milk, whites of eight eggs.

Beat whites to a stiff froth, pour milk into a larger cup, stir the flour into the milk until it makes a thin batter, beat the creamed butter and sugar together, then add the contents of the cup (flour and milk) beat well, then add a little of the whites, then the flour, lastly the rest of the whites, flavor. Bake in three layers, about fifteen minutes.

Icing—Two cups sugar, whites of two eggs, put sugar on with enough boiling water to dissolve it, when it "strings" pour over the smoothly-beaten whites and beat till cold.

AMERICUS.

WHITE CAKE.

Whites of seven eggs, one-half teacup of sweet milk, four and one-half cups of flour after it is sifted, two and one-half cups of sugar, one and one-half cups of butter, two good teaspoonsful of baking powder, flavor to taste.

ELIZA SMITH, Knoxville, Tenn.

WHITE CAKE.

Twelve eggs, four cups sugar, five cups flour, one cup butter, one and one-fourth cups water, three-fourths of a teaspoon soda, two teaspoons cream of tartar.

MISS RACH DAVIS, Knoxville, Tenn.

WHITE LAYER CAKE.

Whites of ten eggs, one cup of butter, three cups of sugar, four cups of flour, one cup of buttermilk, one-half teaspoon of soda, one and one-half teaspoons of cream of tartar.

Sift cream of tartar thoroughly through the flour, cream butter and sugar, add buttermilk, then a little flour with egg alternately, keeping batter soft, dissolve soda thoroughly in a very little cold water and put in last.

Boiled Icing—Whites of three eggs, three cups of sugar, boil sugar till "stringy", pour slowly over the beaten whites, beating all the time. To make marshmallow cake take half a pound of marshmallows, cut thin, put on the back of the stove in a crock till very soft, mix with the icing and put between the layers, and decorate the top with whole marshmallows.

MISS MARY CROZIER, Knoxville, Tenn.

WHITE OR SILVER CAKE.

One pound sugar, three-fourths of a pound flour, one-half pound butter, whites of fourteen eggs, one lemon, juice only and one teaspoon extract of lemon.

Beat the whites to a stiff froth, add sugar and beat till it looks like icing, stir together the butter and half the flour; add to this half the eggs and sugar and mix thoroughly, then return the mixture to the vessel containing the remainder of the eggs and sugar, add the balance of the flour and lastly the lemon juice.

MRS. HENRY A. CHAMBERS, Chattanooga, Tenn.

VERY DELICATE WHITE CAKE.

Whites twenty eggs, one light pound butter, one pound sugar, three-fourths pound flour, ,one-fourth pound corn starch, cream the butter well, then add the flour and starch (they being well mixed), a spoonful at a time, beat the eggs as light as possible, then beat the sugar into them until you form a nice icing, add to the flour and butter and beat very light, flavor and bake as other white cake.

MRS. O.H.P. ROGAN, Knoxville, Tenn.

WHITE CAKE.

Two cups sugar, three cups of flour, three-fourths of a cup of butter, one cup of milk, one-half teaspoon of soda, one teaspoon of cream of tartar, whites of five eggs, flavor.

YELLOW CAKE.

Yellows of four eggs, one cup of sugar, two cups of flour, half cup of water, half cup of butter, half teaspoon of soda, one teaspoon of cream of tartar, flavor. You can add raisins.

MISS BRANCH KEEBLER.

WHITE CAKE.

Twelve eggs, whites, three cups of sugar, five cups of flour, one cup of butter, one cup of sweet milk, two teaspoons of baking powder, flavor to taste, makes four large layers.

YELLOW CAKE.

Twelve eggs, yellows, three and one-half cups of flour, two cups of sugar, one scant cup of butter, one cup of rich milk, one tablespoon of baking powder, makes three large layers.

MRS. JOSEPH T. KELLY, Bristol, Va.-Tenn.

YELLOW CAKE.

Three eggs, beaten separately, one scant cup butter, two of sugar, three cups sifted flour, one cup sweet milk or water, two teaspoons baking powder.

ELIZA SMITH, Knoxville, Tenn.

YELLOW CAKE.

Yelks of eight eggs, one and one-half cups sugar, two-thirds cup of milk, one-half cup butter, two cups flour, teaspoon baking powder, flavor with vanilla.

Cream butter and sugar, gradually add flour, eggs, milk, lastly baking powder, bake in rather hot oven.

MRS. WALTER McCOY, Knoxville, Tenn.

CANDY

CANDY.

Three things are necessary in making nice candy of any kind; good materials, correct proportions and watchfulness. Coarse, cheap sugar, bad butter, and stale nuts or chocolate foredoom one to failure. Be sure of your receipts. Unless you know a certain candy to be good, make it up the first time in quarter quantities. When you have a receipt, follow it exactly. Weigh or measure, do not guess or trust to the eye. Different kinds of candy need different tests. Fudge, for instance should be taken from the fire when it will just hold together in a ball when dropped into cold water. The reason so much fudge is not creamy, is that it is cooked too long. To test candies that are to be brittle, cook until the mixture snaps when put into cold water.

BUTTER SCOTCH.

Four cups light brown sugar, enough water to dampen, stir until all is wet, boil until it ropes, then add one-half cup melted butter, boil until hard, add one tablespoon vanilla before removing from the fire. Try in cold water, if brittle, it is done.

MISS AMANDA GIBSON, Knoxville, Tenn.

CHOCOLATE CANDY.

Four cups white sugar, one cup milk or cream, one-half cake Walter Baker's chocolate. Butter size of an egg and about one-half teaspoon vanilla added as candy is taken from stove. Put on in kettle over slow fire. Stir thoroughly until sugar and chocolate melts. Do not stir again, as it will grain. Boil until a little cold water forms soft ball. Take from stove and beat until it begins to cream. Pour into buttered pans and when cool mark into squares. Nuts may be added.

MRS. RICHARD P. JOHNSON, Knoxville, Tenn.

CHOCOLATE CARAMEL

One cake Baker's chocolate, three pounds light brown sugar, two teacups of cream or sweet milk, one-fourth of a pound of butter, two tablespoons of vanilla. Put chocolate, milk and sugar together, and when it comes to a boil add butter, boil twenty minutes, or till it forms a soft ball in water, add vanilla, pour off and beat till it resembles cake batter, pour on a dish and when cool, cut in squares.

MRS. HOWELL, Washington, D. C.

CHOCOLATE CREAMS.

Take two cups of granulated or pulverized sugar, half a cup of cream, milk will do, but it needs cream to perfect them, boil first five minutes from the time it begins to boil, not from the time you put it on the stove. After taking from the stove stir till it is stiff, flavor with vanilla, then drop on a buttered plate and let it remain till it is cold. In the meantime have some chocolate broken into little bits in a bowl; have some water boiling in the teakettle, set the bowl over it and the chocolate will soon melt, then take a fork and roll the drops in the melted chocolate and put back on the plate to harden.

MRS. H.H. TAYLOR, Knoxville, Tenn.

CHOCOLATE CREAMS.

To white of one egg add an equal quantity of cold water, stir in one pound or confectioner's sugar, flavor with vanilla and stir till fine, mould into small balls and drop into melted chocolate and set away to cool.

MRS. WATERS, Washington, D. C.

COCOANUT BALLS.

One cocoanut grated, two pounds granulated sugar. Put sugar on the fire with enough water to wet it well, boil till it almost turns to sugar, then pour it on the grated cocoanut, stir till cool and make into balls with the hand. Wet your hand occasionally with a little water. Can be colored with a few drops of fruit coloring.

MRS. R.G. HANSON, Bristol, Tenn.

COCOANUT CANDY BARS.

Two cocoanuts grated, four pounds of granulated sugar, one and one-half pints water, including milk of cocoanut, one and one-half teaspoons of cream of tartar, one tablespoon vanilla. Put sugar and water on the fire, when it boils up nicely stir in a glass of water, then stir in well the cream of tartar, remove from the fire, stir in vanilla, pour on a marble slab and work with paddle until stiff, then with your hand, finally roll out and cut in strips and remove from slab.

MRS. R.G. HANSON, Bristol, Tenn.

COCOANUT CANDY.

One large cocoanut, grated, four pounds sugar, water enough to melt sugar, add two tablespoons of corn starch mixed in a little water. When the sugar threads, let boil up thick again, then add the cocoanut and boil a very few minutes, stirring all the time. When taken from the fire beat hard until it begins to whiten, drop on buttered paper or board in round cakes to harden. Can be made fancy by using fruit coloring.

MRS. J.T. McTEER, Knoxville, Tenn.

CREAM CANDY.

Three cups of sugar, one cup sweet milk. Cook until it turns a light brown, drop in a piece of butter the size of a walnut. Drop in cold water to test. Pull.

MRS. BEAUMONT NORTH. Franklin, Tenn.

CREAM CANDY.

Three cups of white sugar, put enough water to dissolve it and let come to a boil, then add just as much cream of tartar as you can conveniently hold on a point of a teaspoon, dissolved in a little water. Do not stir it, but make a little mop, dip it in water and keep the syrup well mopped from sides of vessel. Boil until it will harden almost immediately when dropped in a glass of cold water. Butter well a tin pan placed in another larger sized one, holding cold water, pour this candy in greased pan and continue turning over the candy until the whole is cool enough to pull. When white, string out and cut with scissors into small chips, place in a covered tureen for a few hours and it will become creamy. Season with a teaspoon of vanilla as you remove from the fire, if you like it.

MRS. L.H. OTEY. Bristol, Tenn.

"SUMMER SCHOOL OF THE SOUTH."

Three cups white sugar, one cup (Karo) corn syrup, three-fourths cup water, boil the above until it begins to rope. Whites of three eggs, well-beaten, when syrup begins to rope pour one cup in eggs and beat well. Cook the remainder of syrup until it pops in a cup of water. Pour altogether and beat until it creams.

W.K. HUNTER, W.H. MAYNARD, Knoxville, Tenn.

CREAMED NUT OR FRUIT CANDY.

Creamed walnuts and dates and figs are all made with the French cream. Open dates carefully and take the stones out, and fill the dates with the cream. For the walnuts, make the cream into a ball and stick the walnuts on the sides of it.

CHRISTIAN OBSERVER.

DIVINITY CANDY.

Whites of three eggs, beaten stiff, teacup sugar, one-half teacup water. Put sugar in water and set on fire. In another pan, three cups sugar, one cup syrup (Karo), one-half cup water. Boil first pan till it "strings' a long string, pour over beaten whites and beat as for icing. Boil the other till it makes a hard ball in water, pour over the other and then beat, add a cup of chopped nuts, flavor with vanilla and beat till very stiff. Pour in pan, and when cold cut in squares.

MISS ISABEL ALLEN, Knoxville, Tenn.

ENGLISH WALNUT CANDY.

Take French cream, mould into balls, large enough to hold half an English Walnut on either side, pressing them into the cream.

MRS. WALTERS, Washington, D. C.

FUDGE.

Two cups of sugar, one cup of sweet milk, butter size of a walnut, a quarter of a cake of chocolate. Stir constantly while cooking. When done it will form a soft ball when dropped in cold water. Add vanilla just before taking from the stove. Stir or beat well after taking from stove until nearly cool, pour into buttered pans, cut off in squares. Nuts, cocoanut or marshmallows can be added before turning into pan.

MRS. H.N. SAXTON, JR., Knoxville, Tenn.

FUDGE.

Three cups granulated sugar, one cup milk, two ounces chocolate, lump of butter size of a walnut, vanilla. Put milk, sugar and butter on fire, let come to a boil, boil two or three minutes, add chocolate and boil five minutes, add vanilla, remove from fire and beat until cool and thick enough to pour out. Pour on buttered dish and when cool enough, cut in squares.

MISS PASCAL HALL, Hagerstown, Md.

FUDGE.

Two cups light brown sugar, one cup rich milk or cream, one-fourth cup of butter, one-fourth cake of chocolate. Put on fire and boil till it makes a soft ball in water, then take off and beat till creamy and pour into pans. The fineness depends on knowing when to take from the fire and how long to beat, which comes with practice.

WOMAN'S HOME COMPANION.

BROWN SUGAR FUDGE.

Three cups brown sugar, one-half cup of butter, one cup of sweet milk, vanilla to taste. Allow to cook until thick, then add one-half pound of marshmallows and one-fourth pound of nuts, chopped fine. Take from the stove and beat, then pour on buttered platters to cool.

MRS. FRANK DAVIS, Bristol, Tenn.

CHOCOLATE FUDGE.

I use a ten cent cake, the bitter chocolate, to fifteen cents worth of brown sugar, a piece of butter, size of an egg, wet all with sweet milk and let boil hard for about twenty minutes, stirring all the time, just before taking off the fire add the flavoring and stir after taking it off until cool. Pour out on a marble table and when cool cut in squares, a few marshmallows added after you remove from the fire improves it.

CONTRIBUTED.

FRUIT BUTTER.

Cup each of raisins, figs, dates, one-half cup nuts. Put through food chopper, orange juice may be added to bind it together. This may be used as a filling for sandwiches or rolled about one-half inch thick and cut into squares, rolled into fondant sugar and wrapped in wax paper and eaten as candy.

MRS. RICHARD P. JOHNSON, Knoxville, Tenn.

PECAN CANDY.

One cup of sugar, melted, two cups of sugar and one cup of sweet milk boiled in another vessel. Pour together and cook until it forms a soft ball when tested in cold water. When you pour the two slowly together stir all the time, as it is apt to boil over. Stir In two cups of Pecan nuts, pour in buttered pan or dish. Cut in squares.

MRS. FRANK MAXWELL, Austin, Texas.

PECAN CANDY.

Three cups brown sugar, one cup sweet milk, butter size of an egg, one teaspoon vanilla. Cook till it makes a soft ball in cold water, then stir into this two cups broken pecans, let cook a little longer, take off and beat till cool and pour in buttered dish.

LAURA LEWIS, Bristol, Tenn.

PEANUT BRITTLE.

One pound sugar, one-half pint shelled peanuts. Put sugar on fire in skillet and stir until melted, add nuts broken up and a little cinnamon. Pour on block to cool.

MRS. RICHARD P. JOHNSON, Knoxville, Tenn.

PEPPERMINT CANDY.

One coffee cup of sugar, one-fourth cup of water. Put on fire and when the bubbles are rising drop in peppermint, take off the stove and beat till light. Drop on marble or greased paper.

MISS RUTH DANIEL, Huntington, W. Va.

PEPPERMINT WAFFERS

One coffee cup of sugar, one-fourth cup water. Put on the fire and when the bubbles are rising drop in a little peppermint, take off the stove and beat till light. Drop on marble or greased paper.

MRS. PARHAM, Chattanooga, Tenn.

PINOCHI.

Four cups light-brown sugar, two cups sweet milk. Cook, stirring constantly, until it hardens when dropped from the spoon in cold water. Take from the fire, add a small lump of butter, one teaspoon vanilla and one and one-half cups of English walnuts or pecans, cut into small pieces. Beat hard for about five minutes, pour into buttered cake pans and cut into squares.

MISS KATHERINE CARSON, Knoxville, Tenn.

POP CORN BALLS.

Cook one cup of molasses and one of sugar till it silks. Pour over one gallon of popped corn, butter your hands and form into balls.

MRS. HUGH TAYLOR, Bristol, Tenn.

PRAULINES.

Three pints nut kernels, two and one-half pints sugar, one-half pint cream. Put the sugar on with just enough water to keep it from burning, and when it begins to boil thick add the cream. Try it by dropping a little in a glass of cold water, and when it can be gathered up in the bottom of the glass, pour over the nuts, which must be put into a bowl. When cool enough to be handled, make into balls.

CHRISTIAN OBSERVER.

SEA FOAM.

Two cups of light-brown sugar, enough water to dissolve and let boil until you think it is done, beat the white of an egg just like you were going to make icing for a cake, pour your syrup in the eggs and beat until cool; dip out with a spoon and put on something to cool.

JOHN HENRY.

SUGAR CANDY.

Three cups of sugar, two cups of water, one cup of vinegar. Boil until tried in cold water, mixture will become brittle. Turn on a buttered plate to cool; pull and cut in small pieces.

MRS. T.W. FLEMING, Knoxville, Tenn.

SUGAR CANDY.

Two pounds sugar, one teacup water, one tablespoon vinegar, two small tablespoons melted butter. Boil hard for fifteen minutes, do not stir, and do not scrape it out of the kettle, or it will grain.

MRS. SMILLIE, Atlanta, Ga.

TURKISH DELIGHT.

One ounce of gelatine and a little more, soak for two hours in one-half cup of cold water, dissolve two cups of granulated sugar in one-half cup cold water and as soon as it boils add the gelatine and cook steadily twenty minutes. Flavor with rind and juice of one orange. After it cools a little, add mixed nuts, turn into tins, wet with cold water, when cold cut into squares and roll in corn starch and confectioner's sugar.

MRS. NATHANIEL TAYLOR, Bristol, Tenn.

CATSUP AND SAUCE

CHILI SAUCE.

One dozen large ripe tomatoes, two red peppers, four onions, two cups of good vinegar, a heaping tablespoon each of sugar and salt. Cook tomatoes by themselves for awhile, also onions and peppers, add a little water to these. Then mix and cook until it is about half as much as when it went on the fire. A little stick of cinnamon may be added.

MRS. McTEER, Knoxville, Tenn.

CUCUMBER SAUCE.

Peel cucumbers and lay in cold water for awhile, then grate and sprinkle with salt, and for every three dozen cucumbers, grate one-half dozen large onions, tie in a bag and let drain all night. Next morning, measure the water and put to the dry cucumbers and onions the same quantity of vinegar as there was water. Season with pepper, mix thoroughly, put in bottles and seal them tight.

MRS. S.B. BOYD, Knoxville, Tenn.

CUCUMBER CATSUP.

Grate one bushel of cucumbers; grate one gallon of onions. Squeeze every particle of water out of both cucumbers and onions, then add good cider vinegar, salt and pepper, grated horseradish, white mustard seed, black mustard seed, celery seed, a little turmeric, cloves, allspice and ground cinnamon, some sugar; all of these ingredients are added to your taste. Put up in pints or half-pints, as it does not keep well after it is opened. Put a clove of garlic in each jar.

CUCUMBER CATSUP.

Take three dozen full grown cucumbers, eight onions, cut them as if for the table, then put them alternately with a layer of salt in a stone jar and draw five hours, drain. Then take half a cup of black mustard seed, half a cup of white mustard seed, one-half cup of black pepper or pods of red pepper, one dozen cloves, a little mace and fill up with strong vinegar.

MISS SARAH K. BOYD, Knoxville, Tenn.

CUCUMBER CATSUP.

Peel and grate one dozen ripe cucumbers, drain them well, measure the water that strains out, then add as much vinegar as water, not using the water, only the same quantity of vinegar. Season to taste with salt and pepper, three teaspoons of celery seed, three onions, chopped fine, mix well and bottle air tight with sealing wax. No cooking.

MRS. R.V. DAVIS, Abingdon, Va.

CURRANT CATSUP.

Four pounds ripe currants, one and one-half pounds white sugar, cook slowly until thick, then add one pint vinegar, one tablespoon ground cinnamon, one teaspoon ground cloves, two teaspoons salt, one-half teaspoon black pepper. Cook twenty minutes and bottle and seal.

CONTRIBUTED.

GREEN CATSUP.

Two heads cabbage, four dozen cucumbers, seven green peppers, one-half peck green tomatoes, one dozen onions. Slice and chop the onions, pour hot water over them and let them stand about ten minutes. Chop the other ingredients, sprinkle salt over them and let it all stand one hour. Drain the water off, pour cold vinegar over it and let it stand twenty-four hours. Pour off the vinegar and to a gallon of the mixture add one-third pound brown sugar. Season with mustard seed, ground cloves and mace to your taste. Put the spices in as much vinegar as will cover the catsup, let it come to a boil, pour over the mixture and bottle closely. Do not boil the mustard seed.

MRS. JOE JOUROLMON, Knoxville, Tenn.

HEINZ'S INDIA RELISH.

One gallon of green tomatoes, one large head of cabbage, four hot green peppers, a teacup of salt; let stand for half an hour and drain. Make a mixture of three pounds of brown sugar, one-half ounce of turmeric, one-half ounce of celery seed, one-fourth of a pound of mustard. Add to the tomatoes, cabbage and peppers and cover with apple vinegar, cook slowly for two hours.

MRS. NEWT. R. HALL, Knoxville, Tenn.

HYDEN SALAD.

One gallon cabbage, one gallon green tomatoes, one pint green pepper, one quart onions, chop fine and salt down. Drain off next day, or in a few hours, add five tablespoons of mixed mustard, two tablespoons of ginger, one tablespoon of cinnamon, one each of cloves and mace, three ounces of turmeric, one ounce celery seed, three pounds sugar, mix well and cover with vinegar and boil until tender.

MRS. C. PEPPER, Rural Retreat, Va.

LOTUS CLUB SAUCE.

To one quart bottle of tomato catsup, allow ten shalots, one bunch of chervil, a small bunch of chives, a teaspoon of Worcestershire sauce, a dash of tobasco sauce and one-half pint of vinegar. Chop the shalots, the chervil and the chives very fine; then add them to the other ingredients and beat all well together until you have a smooth mixture. Pour into bottles and seal. To be served with fish or cold meat.

"THE LOTUS CLUB." New York.

PEPPER RELISH.

Twenty-four green peppers, fifteen medium onions, two and one-half cups sugar, three tablespoons salt, one quart vinegar. Seed peppers and chop onions and peppers together fine. Pour over them boiling water to cover and then drain. Scald the vinegar, salt and sugar until the latter has dissolved, and then add onions and peppers and boil one-half hour. This rule makes two quarts.

MRS. E.V. FISH, Providence, R. I.

PEPPER SAUCE.

One dozen sweet peppers, green, and one dozen sweet peppers, ripe, one dozen nice onions, one quart vinegar, one cup sugar, one tablespoon salt. Grind peppers and onions in meat grinder, then pour boiling water over and let stand five minutes, drain, pour boiling water over again, and let stand ten minutes. Drain thoroughly, put on sugar, salt and vinegar and boil twenty minutes. Put in bottles and seal.

MISS JENNIE M. ANDREWS, Chattanooga, Tenn.

RUSSIAN SAUCE.

One-half peck of firm, ripe tomatoes, scald and skin. Cut into pieces the size of dice, then put them in a colander for four or five hours to drain. Three large bunches celery, cut near the size of the tomatoes, one large cup granulated sugar, one small cup of salt, one tablespoon ground black pepper, one-half spoon of cayenne pepper, two ounces white mustard seed, one ounce celery seed, one large root horseradish, grated. Mix together and add quart good cider vinegar. Now add tomatoes and celery and put away in air tight jars and keep in a cool place. It must not be heated in making, and if the vinegar is good it will keep as long as there is any of it. It is ready for use in a few days.

MRS. SPENCER MUNSON, Mentor, Ohio.

TOMATO CATSUP.

One peck tomatoes, boil until soft, then mash through a wire sieve, add one pint vinegar, one and one-half gills salt, half ounce cloves, one ounce allspice, three-fourths ounce cinnamon, one tablespoon pepper, one head garlic, skinned and separated, one teacup brown sugar. Mix all together and boil till reduced one-half, then bottle and seal.

MRS. SOPHIE K. HUNTER, Knoxville, Tenn.

TOMATO CATSUP.

Slice tomatoes, put in a preserving kettle, boil until all the juice is extracted, stirring constantly to prevent scorching, strain first through a colander, then through a sifter, pressing the pulp through. To two pints of this juice take one pint best cider vinegar, have kettle cleaned and return this mixture to it, adding black and white mustard seed, black pepper, cloves, grated nutmeg, horseradish, celery seed, mixed mustard, red pepper and sugar. Add all these things to suit taste, boil until quite thick, just before done add chopped onion, a little garlic and salt, bottle, seal and keep in a cool, dry place.

MRS. MARY McCLUNG, Knoxville, Tenn.

TOMATO CATSUP.

One gallon sliced tomatoes, four tablespoons salt, three tablespoons black pepper, four tablespoons mustard seed, three pods red pepper, two teaspoons cloves, one-half ounce cinnamon, one pint onions, two tablespoons allspice. Put all this in a kettle and boil till half the quantity, then strain and bottle very tight with sealing wax and keep in a cool place.

M.C. CUSTER.

TOMATO CATSUP.

One peck ripe tomatoes, one dozen good-sized onions, sliced or chopped fine, one-half dozen green peppers. Cook till perfectly tender, run through a coarse sieve, cook again until thick, with the following spices pounded coarsely and put in a muslin bag. One tablespoon cloves, two tablespoons spice, two tablespoons white mustard seed. At the same time, add two heaping tablespoons of sugar and salt to taste. If wanted hotter put in one-half teaspoon red pepper. Thin with good cider vinegar, until like thick cream, and seal in bottles.

MRS. V. DORIOT, Bristol, Tenn.

TOMATO CATSUP.

To one gallon tomato pulp, add one-half gallon strong vinegar, one pound brown sugar, four onions, chopped fine, three tablespoons each of salt, ginger, horseradish, mustard, one tablespoon black pepper, two tablespoons cloves, one tablespoon celery seed. Boil thirty minutes after spices are added.

MRS. ARCHER A. PHELEGAR, Bristol, Va.-Tenn.

TOMATO CATSUP.

One bushel ripe tomatoes, twelve onions, cut fine, boil two hours, then strain through a sieve, pour the liquid into the kettle and add three quarts of good strong cider vinegar; add two ounces ground spice, one ounce ground mustard, one ounce cloves, three pounds light brown sugar, one pint salt: mix these ingredients well together before putting in the boiler; add cayenne pepper to taste, leaving out black pepper, as it will darken the catsup. Boil till thick enough to bottle, stirring continually to prevent burning; when cool, fill bottles, cork and seal with bottle wax, so as to exclude the air.

MRS. F.B. McDANNEL, Knoxville, Tenn.

GREEN TOMATO SAUCE.

One peck green tomatoes, one dozen large onions sliced, boil until very soft in a quart of good strong vinegar, pass through a sieve, put on fire again and boil till very thick, add one ounce each of white ginger, mace and cinnamon, one-half ounce cloves, a tablespoon of celery seed, sift the spices. Add one pound brown sugar, and vinegar till of a proper thickness.

MRS. JAMES S. BOYD, Knoxville, Tenn.

GREEN TOMATO CATSUP.

Chop or grind one quart of green tomatoes, one large green pepper, one large onion, then add one cup of vinegar, one cup sugar, salt, pepper and spice to taste. Cook till done. It is ready for use immediately.

MRS. CARRINGTON, Knoxville, Tenn.

CHEESE

CHEESE BALLS.

One cup grated cheese, pinch red pepper, pinch salt, well-beaten white of one egg, mix, mould in small balls and drop in boiling lard, plenty of it. Will brown almost instantly.

MRS. JERRY FICKLIN, Washington, D. C.

CHEESE BALLS.

Mix together thoroughly one and one-half cups grated cheese, or the same quantity of cottage cheese, one-fourth of a teaspoon of salt and a few grains of cayenne; then add the whites of three eggs beaten stiff, shape in small balls, roll in cracker crumbs sifted or crushed to a fine meal, fry in deep fat, drain on brown paper, serve with a simple vegetable salad.

CONTRIBUTED.

CHEESE CUSTARD.

One-half small loaf bread, one cup grated or chopped cheese, two eggs, one pint milk, butter, salt and white pepper. Remove crumb from bread, slice and spread lightly with butter and cut in small squares, put a layer of the prepared bread in a baking dish and sprinkle with cheese, salt and a very little pepper, continue this until all the materials are used, beat the eggs, add the milk and pour over the other ingredients. Bake about half an hour in moderate oven and serve.

MRS. L.H. OTEY, Bristol, Va

EGGS WITH CHEESE.

Melt a lump of butter in each shirred egg dish. When hot break in egg, season with salt and pepper and place in oven until partly cooked, then pour over a thick cream tomato sauce, sprinkle the whole with grated Parmesan cheese and return to oven until egg is cooked.

CONTRIBUTED.

FRENCH CREAM CHEESE.

One quart of cream. Let it stand two days. On the second day add a heaping tablespoon of salt and mix well. Then put in a cheese cloth and let it drain one day, laid in a colander. On the third day change the cloth and let it drain another day. On the fourth day change the cloth again and put on a plate covered by another plate. On the fifth day, put one flat iron on it over night and on the sixth day add another flat iron.

MRS. DUNDAS LIPPINCOTT, Philadelphia, Pa.

GOLDEN BUCK. (FOR CHAFING DISH)

Cut a pound of fresh American cheese into small pieces, put into pan with small piece of butter and have ready six eggs well beaten and seasoned with salt, black pepper, cayenne and a tiny bit of minced onion. When cheese is creamy add a tablespoon of milk, then pour in the eggs. Stir constantly until about the consistency of scrambled eggs.

MRS. H.M. SIMMONDS, Knoxville, Tenn.

CHEESE OMELET.

Beat up three eggs and add to them a tablespoon of milk and a tablespoon of grated cheese; add a little more cheese before folding; turn the omelet cut on a hot dish and grate a little cheese over it before serving.

WHITE HOUSE COOK BOOK.

CHEESE PUDDING.

Soak small squares of stale bread in a batter made of milk and well beaten egg. Place a layer in the bottom of a pudding dish, add a generous covering of grated cheese, then a layer of the moistened bread and another covering of cheese, and so on until the baking dish is filled. Pour over all a cup of milk, in which an egg has been beaten and bake in a moderate oven until a rich brown. This may be seasoned with paprika and a little dry mustard.

MRS. WILL BEWLAY DUENNER, Bristol, Va.-Tenn.

"RINK-TUM-DIDDY."

Four medium sized onions, chopped fine, two tablespoons butter, one and one-half pounds cheese, kind used for Welsh rarebit (American cheese), two eggs well-beaten, two tablespoons Worchestershire sauce, two tablespoons vinegar, a little tobasco, one teaspoon salt, a little pepper, one teaspoon mustard, one can Campbell's tomato soup.

Put chopped onions and butter in pan and cook, stirring constantly until onions are tender and brownish. Add cheese, which has been cut into small pieces, stir and mash lumps until smooth, then add eggs and then the condiments that have been mixed together in a cup, and then after a little stirring, add the soup and stir until it boils. Serve on crackers.

MRS. C.S. NEWMAN, Knoxville, Tenn.

CHEESE SALAD.

Two large heads of lettuce coarsely minced, with two cups grated cheese, a small teacup of rich, sweet cream, or two tablespoons of "Salad Oil", vinegar, mustard, pepper and salt to taste.

MRS. H.H. TAYLOR, Knoxville, Tenn.

CHEESE STRAWS.

Cream two cups cheese with one cup of butter and one-half cup of cold water, season with red pepper and salt, add flour enough to make a stiff dough. Roll thin, cut in strips and bake in a quick oven, top rack of oven usually.

MRS. B.B. BURNS, Bristol, Va.-Tenn.

CHEESE STRAWS.

Twelve tablespoons cheese, three tablespoons butter, enough flour to make like tea cake dough. Roll out thin, cut in strips about one inch wide and three inches long, or different lengths, as you please. Put on buttered paper and bake.

MISS LAURA JONES, Marion, Ala.

CHEESE SOUFFLE.

Stir into one cup sweet milk, one teaspoon Kingsford corn starch and let come to a boil. Stir in one-half cup grated biscuit. Beat well the yelks of three eggs and stir into one cup grated cheese. Add this to milk and biscuit. Season to taste. Add whites of eggs, beaten to a stiff froth and bake at once, also serve at once.

EMMA CHURCHMAN HEWITT.

CHEESE SOUFFLE.

One tablespoon flour, one tablespoon butter, two tablespoons cheese, two eggs, a little salt, one-half cup sweet milk. Boil until thickens, then add the cheese and salt. Take from the fire, add the well-beaten yelks, last stir in the well-beaten whites, which have been beaten stiff. Pour into a buttered pudding dish and set in oven to brown. Serve immediately.

MRS. JOHN PEYTON MOFFETT.

WELSH RAREBIT.

Cut one-half pound of good cheese in small pieces, add pepper and salt, or not, as preferred, then pour over the cheese a half cup of sweet milk, let it slowly melt until it comes to a boil. Beat an egg light and when the cheese is all melted and boiling, take it off the fire and add immediately the beaten egg. Brown nicely slices of bread, butter if preferred and cover each slice with the mixture and send to the table hot.

MRS. J.G.M. RAMSEY, Knoxville, Tenn.

WELSH RAREBIT.

Enough for six. One-half pound of soft cheese, run through a food chopper. Put butter size of a walnut in the blazer, add the cheese, when thoroughly melted add one-half cup of cream or sweet milk and stir again, put in salt, a little paprika, beat one egg, enough to mix it thoroughly, add egg, and stir constantly for a minute or two.

Remove from blazer and place in water pan filled with hot water. Serve on toast.

MRS. H.P. WYMAN, Bristol, Tenn.

DESSERTS

AMBROSIA.

Peel, slice and seed six sweet oranges, peel and shred a pineapple and grate a large cocoanut. Arrange in alternate layers, sprinkling each layer well with powdered sugar and having the last layer of cocoanut and sugar. Serve cold.

CONTRIBUTED.

AMBROSIA.

One-half dozen oranges, sliced, one can grated pineapple, sugar well and grate cocoanut over the mixture.

CONTRIBUTED.

AMERICAN CREAM.

Dissolve one-half box of gelatine in one quart of milk, set on fire and stir all the time; just before it boils stir in the yelks of four eggs, with four tablespoons of sugar. Put on the fire until it reaches the boiling point, take off and stir in whites of four eggs well beaten with four tablespoons of sugar, flavor with vanilla and pour into mould.

MRS. C.H. ALLEN, Knoxville, Tenn.

APPLE COMPOTE.

Choose six large tart apples, with a sharp knife dig out the core, leaving the skin at the bottom of the cavity unbroken, chop nut meats, (pecans, English walnuts or hickory nuts), mix with them as much sugar as nut meats, mince and stuff apples with them. Arrange the filled apples in a bake dish; pour in enough water to come up half-way to the top of the apples, cover closely and bake in a good oven until a straw will pierce the apples. Leave covered until the apples are perfectly cold. Set on ice and serve with cream.

MRS. CHARLES LEONHARDT, Knoxville, Tenn.

APPLE MERINGUE.

Sweeten and spice a quart of apple sauce, add the yelks of three eggs, pour into buttered baking dish and set in stove until piping hot. When well rusted over, cover with meringue of the three whites, whipped with three tablespoons of sugar. Brown quickly and serve hot with cream.

MRS. RICHARD P. JOHNSON, Knoxville, Tenn.

APPLE SNOW.

In the bottom of a fancy glass dish place a layer of fine, well-sweetened apple sauce, then a very scant layer of fine, dry bread crumbs, or cracker crumbs and a few tiny lumps of jelly, over this spread a generous layer of sweetened whipped cream, then another layer of apple sauce, one of bread crumbs and jelly and another of whipped cream, and so on till the dish is sufficiently full, having the whipped cream on top, over which place a few tiny lumps of the bright jelly and one has a delightful dessert, easily prepared, and as attractive to the eye as it is to the palate.

"FARM AND HOME".

BAKED APPLES.

Baked apples are never more delicious than when the fruit is fresh from the trees. Wipe the apples clean, core them, put a little sugar in the cavity, together with a clove, pour a cup of hot water in the baking pan and bake in a hot oven with frequent bastings. Sour apples will bake in from twenty to thirty minutes. Sweet apples take much longer and should be covered during the baking process. Served with sweet, thick cream, they are like Walton's fish, "too good for any but very honest folks". For a high tea, or some other festive occasion, apples steamed tender and their core cavities filled with candied fruits are very nice.

CONTRIBUTED.

JELLIED APPLES.

One and one-half pounds apples pared and cored, one pound sugar, put on the fire with enough water to keep from burning, cook till the apples are clear, then take out of the syrup and slice one large lemon in the syrup on the fire, then put in one ounce of gelatine dissolved in water and let it mix well and pour over the apples. A little wine or brandy is an improvement.

MRS. BARNETT, Atlanta, Ga.

JELLIED APPLES.

For six large apples, peeled and cored and quartered, make a syrup with a cup each of sugar and water to which is added the juice and a little of the yellow rind of a lemon; bring to the boiling point, skim and remove the rind. Have a flat pan, broad bottomed enough to allow the quarters to lie singly in the syrup, when the pieces are tender remove carefully from the syrup into a flat glass dish, first tempered with hot water, then add a tablespoon of granulated gelatine, dissolved in a little cold water; stir and pour over the fruit, stand in a cool place and when cold each piece of fruit may be dished out, surrounded by a jelly of just the right solidity. You can use whole apples and place on each apple a slice of lemon, topped by a red or green cherry, or you can frost the apple and put on top a bit of bright jelly.

CONTRIBUTED.

BANANAS.

Slice fruit length wise, sprinkle with powdered sugar and squeeze lemon juice over this and chill.

MRS. H.M. SIMMONDS, Knoxville. Tenn.

BAVARIAN CREAM.

One pint cream, sweetened, flavored and whipped, one-fourth of a box of gelatine, soaked in one pint of cream two hours, then heat slowly, stirring all the time, when it boils pour it over the whipped cream, stir well and let it congeal. Fill your stand with whipped cream.

MRS. SOPHIE K. HUNTER. Knoxville, Tenn.

PEACH BAVARIAN CREAM.

Cover one-half box of gelatine with cold water and let it stand half an hour. Take eighteen halves of canned peaches and a cupful of juice, sweeten and strain. Stir the gelatine over boiling water till dissolved, whip a pint of cream, add gelatine to peaches, mix and put in a tin pan and set on ice and stir till it begins to thicken, then add the whipped cream, stir well, turn in a mould and stand in a cool place to harden, serve with whipped cream. Strawberries are delicious used instead of peaches.

MRS. J.H. McCUE.

BLANC MANGE.

Wash a teacup of Irish moss in three tepid waters, letting it stand in the last water until it has dobled its size. Let three quarts of new milk come to a boil, add moss, two cups of sugar and a little stick cinnamon. Boil until it thickens, stirring to prevent sticking. Strain away into moulds and when cold serve with whipped cream, flavored and sweetened to taste.

MRS. JAMES PARK, Knoxville, Tenn.

BLANC MANGE.

One box Cox's gelatine, rinse in cold water, put on the fire in two quarts of milk till melted. Take off fire and add two cups of sugar, a very little stick of cinnamon, boil ten or fifteen minutes. Take off and add one teaspoon of lemon and two of vanilla and brandy to taste. Put in a mould.

MRS. ROCK, Newark, N. J.

BLANC MANGE.

Wash one-half teacup of Irish moss in a teacup of water which has had one-half teaspoon of soda dissolved in it, then wash the moss through several waters. Put the moss into a double boiler with one-half gallon of new milk, flavored with vanilla and sweetened to taste. Boil a few minutes and when it "sets" in a spoon, take off and strain into a bowl or small moulds. Eat with cream and an acid jelly or preserve.

MRS. S.B. BOYD, Knoxville, Tenn.

BOILED CUSTARD.

Yelks of sixteen eggs, nearly a pint of sugar, four pints of morning's milk. Let it come to a hard boil and pour it over the sugar and eggs, stirring all the time, put on whipped cream when cold.

MRS. JAMES KENNEDY, Knoxville, Tenn.

CONFEDERATE BOILED CUSTARD.

Twelve eggs, one-half gallon milk, beat the yellows with one teacup of molasses and just before stirring it in the hot milk add one teaspoon of soda.

REBECCA E. DAVIS, Virginia.

BROWN BETTY.

Two cups tart apples chopped, one-half cup brown sugar, one cup bread crumbs, two tablespoons butter, cinnamon, ground. Put a layer of apples in buttered baking dish. Sprinkle well with sugar, add bits of butter and a little cinnamon. Then a layer of crumbs, then apples, etc., with crumbs on top. Cover and cook about an hour in moderate oven, then brown quickly. Hard sauce if served hot, and cream and sugar if served warm.

MRS. RICHARD P. JOHNSON, Knoxville, Tenn.

CHARLOTTE DE RUSSE.

One box of gelatine, four eggs, six ounces of sugar, three pints of cream, vanilla to taste. Dissolve the gelatine in half a pint of fresh sweet milk, whip the cream to a stiff froth, beat the eggs separately, Stir the gelatine till dissolved, it must not boil, and then set aside till luke warm. Beat the yelks, then add the sugar and beat well, fold in the whites and add flavoring. Pour the lukewarm gelatine into this, stirring all the time and at once add the whips, stir, but do not beat, pour into a glass dish or small glasses as it sets at once.

MRS. S.B. BOYD, Knoxville, Tenn.

CHARLOTTE DE RUSSE.

One quart sweet rich cream, one pound white sugar, one box gelatine, vanilla. Dissolve the gelatine in a pint of water; boil it down one-half, cool, and when about blood heat stir it very quickly into the cream, well whipped, sweetened and flavored. When the consistency of clabber pour immediately into the mould, which should be ready, lined with lady fingers or sponge cake. Set in a cool place to congeal.

MRS. T.W. FLEMING, Knoxville, Tenn.

CHARLOTTE DE RUSSE.

Boil one ounce of gelatine in one pint of water until it is reduced one-half. Put one-half pint sweet milk on fire, beat the yellows of four eggs light with four ounces white sugar; when the milk boils pour over the eggs and sugar, then return to the fire, let it come to a boil, but not boil, set this aside to get cool. Whip one quart of rich cream, as you whip it pile on a sifter to drain. Put your custard that is now cold into a bowl, add the gelatine that has cooled, put into this a teaspoon of vanilla, then add the whips. Mix well. Have a bowl lined with sponge cake, pour in your russe, lay a few slices of cake on top. When you serve this, whipped cream piled on top is a great improvement to the looks of the dish.

MRS. E.S. McCLUNG, Knoxville. Tenn.

CHARLOTTE DE RUSSE.

One quart cream, one box gelatine, flavoring of vanilla, rose or wine, four eggs, whites only. Pour a little cold water on the gelatine, then set it on the stove and stir till it melts, set it where it will cool, not congeal. Sweeten and flavor the cream to taste, beat to a stiff froth, add the whites well-beaten, then the gelatine. Have the sponge cake ready to line the moulds. Be careful to scald the mould well then cool thoroughly, let it stand with cold water in it. Just before using pour out the water but do not wipe it, then arrange the cake and set aside to congeal.

MRS. T.W. FLEMING, Knoxville, Tenn.

CHARLOTTE DE RUSSE.

One pint of sweet milk, one small cup of sugar in it, one-half ounce or gelatine dissolved in it. Mix all and boil until thick as boiled custard. One pint of whipped cream measured before whipping whites of four eggs, cook with boiling water. When the first mixture is nearly cold mix all by beating. A box of Cox's gelatine holds one and one-half ounces of gelatine.

CONTRIBUTED.

CHARLOTTE DE RUSSE.

One pint cream, whites three eggs, heaping tablespoon gelatin dissolved in two-thirds cup of milk. Put gelatine in a vessel of hot water till dissolved, when tepid pour into the whips, add eggs and one-half cup of sugar, beating all the time, flavor.

MRS. PARHAM, Chattanooga, Tenn.

CHARLOTTE DE RUSSE.

One pint thick cream, two eggs, beaten separately. Add to the yellows three tablespoons of sugar, then one-fourth of a pint of hot milk in which one-third (scant) box of Cox's gelatine has been dissolved, flavor with sherry. Then add beaten whites and whipped cream, beating constantly until the mixture is cool. Line a bowl with lady fingers, pour this in and set in a cool place.

MRS. ERNEST BRISCOE, Knoxville, Tenn.

CHARLOTTE RUSSE.

Whip light one pint of cream to which has been added three-fourths cup of powdered sugar and two teaspoons vanilla, stir lightly into this the beaten whites of two eggs. Line a bowl with slices of sponge cake or lady fingers, and pour over it the cream. This may be varied by adding chopped marshmallows, pecans and candied cherries to the cream.

MISS KATHERINE CARSON, Knoxville, Tenn.

ANGEL CHARLOTTE RUSSE.

One tablespoon Knox's gelatine, one-fourth cup cold water, one-fourth cup boiling water, one cup sugar, one pint heavy cream, one-half a dozen rolled stale macaroons, one dozen marshmallows, cut in small pieces, two tablespoons chopped candied cherries, vanilla or sherry, one-fourth round blanched and chopped almonds. Soak gelatine in cold water, dissolve in boiling water, add sugar, when mixture is cold, add cream beaten until stiff, almonds, macaroons, marshmallows and candied cherries. Flavor and turn into a mold first dipped in cold water and chill. Remove from mold and serve with Angel cake. This dessert may be made more elaborate by cutting the top from an angel or sponge cake and removing some of the inside, leaving a case with three-fourths inch walls, then filling case with mixture, replacing top of cake, covering with frosting, and garnishing with candied cherries and blanched almonds.

MRS. J.E. RANDAL, Cleveland, Ohio.
First Prize Winner.

AN EASY CHARLOTTE DE RUSSE.

One quart of cream sweetened and flavored with vanilla, whip the cream till stiff and put into this the whites of three eggs well-beaten. Put one-third of a box of gelatine in a small teacup of fresh milk. After the gelatine stands in the milk a little while you dissolve it on the fire. When it begins to cool beat it into the cream.

MRS. H.H. TAYLOR, Knoxville, Tenn.

CHARLOTTE POLONAISE.

Boil over a slow fire a pint and a half of milk, cream is better, and while it is boiling have ready yelks of six eggs beaten with two tablespoons of powdered arrowroot or fine flour, stir this gradually into the boiling cream, take care to have it perfectly smooth; ten minutes will suffice for the egg and cream to simmer together. Divide the mixture by putting into two separate saucepans; add to one of the pans six ounces of Baker's chocolate, grated fine, two ounces powdered sugar, let it simmer a few minutes, then take off the fire to cool. Have ready for the other saucepan of cream and egg a dozen bitter almonds and four ounces of sweet almonds, all blanched and pounded in a mortar with enough rosewater to make a smooth paste, mix with an ounce of citron chopped very fine and four ounces powdered sugar, stir in this mixture, let it simmer a few moments and set aside to cool, add vanilla. Cut a large sponge cake into slices half an inch thick, spread one slice thickly with the chocolate cream, putting another slice on top of this and cover with the almond cream; do this alternately, piling them evenly on a china dish till all the ingredients are used. You may arrange it in the original form of the cake before it was cut. Have ready the whites of six eggs, whipped to a stiff froth, gradually mix in it six ounces of powdered sugar, and with a spoon heap this all over the top and sides of the cake, then sift sugar over it, place in a slow oven till of a light brown.

MRS. H.H. TAYLOR, Knoxville, Tenn.

DELICATE DISH.

One-half dozen sliced bananas, one-half dozen sliced oranges, one can of pineapple, juice of one lemon. Place the fruits in the dish alternately, over which pour the lemon juice and one grated cocoanut; serve with cream.

CONTRIBUTED.

FLOAT.

One pint or quart of rich cream, according to needs, sweeten and season with sherrywine to taste, whip and place in glass bowl. Whites of four or six eggs, add to them, without beating, for each egg one tablespoon of granulated sugar and one tablespoon of acid jelly, plum preferred. Beat these ingredients until perfectly firm and stiff, then stand in spoonsful over the bowl of whipped cream.

MRS. E.S. McCLUNG, Knoxville, Tenn.

FLOAT.

One quart or cream, flavored with wine and sweetened. Take the whites of five eggs, a small tablespoon of sugar to each egg and the same of any acid jelly, beat all well together until very light and stiff, then drop upon the cream.

MRS. H.H. TAYLOR, Knoxville, Tenn.

APPLE FLOAT.

Cook one-half gallon of apples and run them through a colander, add one cup sugar, when cool, place on ice. Beat whites of two eggs until stiff, add one teaspoon of vanilla, by dropping it slowly into the eggs while beating them briskly. Stir in apples and place on ice until time to serve.

ALBERTINE LUTTRELL VANCE, Knoxville, Tenn.

FLUFFTE RUFFLES.

The whites of four eggs, one large teaspoon of Knox's gelatine, one-fourth pound sugar, candied cherries and nuts. Beat the eggs to a stiff froth, dissolve the gelatine first in a little cold water, then fill the cup with boiling water, pour over the eggs and sugar, beating them all the time till well mixed and cool. Divide in two parts, coloring one with fruit coloring. Put in a glass dish or bowl, first one then the other, using cherries and nuts on the top of each layer. This is a lovely winter dish. Flavor to suit taste.

MRS. J.T. McTEER, Knoxville, Tenn.

GELATINE.

One box Cox's gelatine, one pint boiling water, one lemon, one orange, one-fourth pound white sugar, one pint sherry wine. Pour water over the gelatine, when dissolved add sugar, fruit and wine, add one pint cold water, then strain and set in moulds to cool.

MRS. H.H. TAYLOR, Knoxville, Tenn.

"HIGHLAND" TRIFLE.

One quart whipped cream, one pound lady fingers, one pound macaroons, one dozen bananas, sliced. Mix the lady fingers, macaroons and bananas alternately, pour over the whole one wine glass of wine. Cover the top with whipped cream.

CONTRIBUTED.

ITALIAN CREAM.

One quart cream, sweetened and flavored to taste, one-half ounce Cox's sparkling gelatine, dissolved in one-half pint sweet milk whites of three eggs, beaten well. Whip the cream until very light, add the gelatine and whip again, then add the whites and pour into a bowl or forms to harden.

MRS. C.H. ALLEN, Knoxville, Tenn.

MARSHMALLOW CREAM.

One tablespoon gelatine, one cup sugar, one-fourth cup cold water, one-fourth cup hot water, four eggs (whites only). Soak gelatine in cold water until soft, pour boiling water on gradually to dissolve, heat eggs stiff and sift sugar into them, beat in dissolved gelatine and flavoring. Divide the mass into two equal parts, color one part pink or chocolate. Put layer of white into deep round dish, layer of colored, layer of white, another layer of colored. Let it get hard. Turn out on pretty plate and garnish with whipped cream, or custard made from yelks; or cherries, or whatever you wish. It is delicious with nuts in it.

CONTRIBUTED.

ORANGE CHARLOTTE.

One-third box gelatine, one-third cup cold water, one-third cup boiling water, one cup sugar, three tablespoons lemon juice, one cup orange juice and pulp, whites of three eggs, whips from three cups of cream. Soak gelatine in little water, add remaining water and sugar and juice. Chill mixture in pan of ice water, when quite thick beat with wire spoon till frothy, add whites of eggs, beaten stiff and fold in whipped cream. Take a mold and line with sections of orange. Turn in mixture, smooth evenly and chill. Serve with whipped cream.

PEACH MELBA.

Three eggs, three-fourths cup sugar, three-fourths cup flour, three tablespoons boiling water, one and one-half teaspoons baking powder, flavor with vanilla. Beat yelks and sugar first, add boiling water, flour, baking powder and the beaten whites. Grease a large shallow pan, pour in the mixture, cover with sliced peaches, either fresh or canned, sprinkle with granulated sugar, bake in a moderate oven, serve hot with whipped cream, sweetened and flavored.

MRS. BENJAMIN D. BRABSON, Knoxville, Tenn.

QUEEN OF TRIFLES.

One-half pound each of lady fingers, macaroons, sweet almonds, blanched, crystalized fruit, one cup sweet jelly, one glass brandy, one glass wine, one pint milk, one pint cream, whipped, four eggs, whites and yelks beaten separately; one tablespoon corn starch, one cup of sugar for the custard. Put lady fingers in bottom of a glass dish, wet with brandy, and cover with jelly, strew the fruit thickly over this, then the macaroons wet with the wine and jelly, set the dish in a cool place while you prepare the custard. Make a custard of the milk, eggs, sugar and corn starch, put in the almonds after they are beaten smooth, and when the custard is cold stir in the whipped cream and whites, give all a good stir-up and set it away to thicken. Then pour over the cake and fruit.

MISS ANN BELL, Knoxville, Tenn.

RAINBOW CREAM.

Whites of four eggs and three-fourths cup granulated sugar, beaten together until very dry, one tablespoon powdered gelatine, dissolved in one-half cup cold water; if gelatine does not dissolve thoroughly, hold over steam, then add one-half cup more of cold water. Beat this dissolved gelatine gradually into the eggs. Divide into three parts; color one part green and flavor with mint; color the second part pink and flavor with vanilla; leave the third part white and flavor with lemon. Line a deep, square pan with oiled paper, put pink layer first, then the green, and then the white. Set on ice to cool. Serve with whipped cream which has been sweetened and flavored and colored lavender.

MISS KATHERINE CARSON, Knoxville, Tenn.

GRANDMOTHER'S RICE AND MILK.

Two-thirds of a cup of rice, two quarts milk, two eggs and a little salt. Boil the rice dry in water, then put the milk and the rice into another pot and boil for twenty minutes, or half an hour. Mix the eggs with one-half teacup of cold milk, add this to the boiled rice and milk, stirring it all the time. Let this come to a boil again. Remove from the fire, add salt. Eat cold.

C.C.

SNOW CREAM.

Beat the whites of four eggs till foamy, then add gradually four tablespoons of powdered sugar, beating all the while, beat till stiff enough to stand alone, add one tablespoon of sherry and a teaspoon of vanilla, stir in carefully one pint of cream, whipped. Serve in small glasses with a few maraschino cherries.

MRS. BARNETT, Atlanta, Ga.

SNOW CREAM.

One pint thick cream, whites four eggs, beaten to a stiff froth, two heaping tablespoons of white sugar. Beat eggs first, add sugar, and beat as for icing, mix with the cream and whip in a cool place till stiff, flavor to taste.

MISS MARY PLEAS McCLUNG, Knoxville, Tenn.

SNOW CUSTARD.

One-half package of gelatine, three eggs, one pint milk, two cups sugar, juice of one lemon, one large cup boiling water. Soak the gelatine one hour in a teacupful of cold water, then stir in two-thirds of the sugar, the lemon juice and boiling water. Beat the whites of the eggs to a stiff froth and when the strained gelatine is quite cold, whip it into the whites a spoonful at a time, for half an hour at least. When all is white and stiff pour into a wet mould and set in a cold place. Make a custard of the milk, eggs and rest of the sugar, flavoring with vanilla, boil until it begins to thicken. When the meringue is turned into the dish, pour this custard cold about the base.

MISS ANN BELL, Knoxville, Tenn.

SNOW CUSTARD.

One-half box Cox's gelatine, one pint boiling water, two cups white sugar, three eggs, two lemons, grate the rind of one. Pour the boiling water over the gelatine and stir until dissolved, add the sugar and juice of the lemons, when nearly cool add the whites of the eggs, beaten to a stiff froth, beat thoroughly together all the ingredients and pour into a dish to harden.

Custard for the above—Take the yelks of the eggs, one pint of milk, sweeten to taste, put into a tin pail or pitcher and set in a kettle of boiling water and stir constantly until done, when nearly done add a little salt, flavor with vanilla and pour over the "snow".

MRS. H.H. TAYLOR, Knoxville, Tenn.

SNOW PUDDING.

One-half box of gelatine, pour on it one-half pint cold water, when almost dissolved add one-half pint boiling water, two cups white sugar, juice of two large lemons, or four small ones, let this cool till almost jellied, then put in the whites of two eggs and beat them to a stiff froth-have the whites of the eggs as cold as possible-it takes quite a long time to beat it. It must look perfectly white and frothy all through. Serve the pudding with the following soft custard poured over it: One even large spoon of corn starch, beaten with the yelks of two eggs, two large spoons of white sugar, one pint of milk. Put the milk on to boil and thicken with the other ingredients. Flavor as you like.

MRS. JOE JOUROLMON, Knoxville, Tenn.

PRUNE SOUFFLE.

One pound of French prunes, stew and chop fine and strain off the juice, whites of eight eggs, sweeten to taste, bake chopped prunes and eggs together and serve with whipped cream. You do not use the juice in this dish, save it for something else.

CONTRIBUTED.

SPANISH CREAM.

Dissolve half a box of gelatine in half a pint of sweet milk, boil one quart of sweet milk and while boiling beat six eggs separately and very light, mix the yelks with the boiling milk, and when it thickens add the gelatine, sweeten and season to taste, pour all while hot on whites of eggs, pour in moulds and cool on ice.

MRS. MARY A. BYARS, Bristol, Va.

TIPSY PARSON.

Slice sponge cake rather thin and put in bowl, then a layer of chopped, blanched almonds on this, then continue layer cake and almonds until bowl is almost full, over this pour sherry wine. Just before serving pour over this boiled custard and ornament top with whipped cream.

MRS. JAMES A. HENSLEY, Knoxville, Tenn.

WHIPPED CREAM.

One pint of rich cream sweetened to taste and whipped to a stiff froth, whites of six eggs whipped to a stiff froth, add vanilla to the cream, them put together and beat well.

MRS. H.H. TAYLOR, Knoxville, Tenn.

WHIPPED CREAM.

Three pints of cream, the juice of two lemons and rind of one, one teacup of wine and one and one-half cups of powdered sugar, whip till stiff. Line the bottom and sides of a bowl with sponge cake and pour in the whips.

MRS. A.P. WHITE, Knoxville, Tenn.

MENUS FOR BANQUETS

MENU FOR BANQUET.
Minced Oysters, Long Branch Crackers
Pickles
Roast Turkey, Cranberry Jelly
Celery
Mashed Potatoes, Green Peas
Finger Rolls
Charlotte de Russe Pound Cake
Mints, Almonds
Coffee, Crackers, Cheese

DINNER FOR A WEEK.

MONDAY.
Soup, stuffed veal, potatoes, rice, asparagus, peach ice cream, coffee.

TUESDAY.
Vegetable soup, lamb chops, beets, rice, potatoes, fried egg plant, sliced tomatoes, lettuce, blackberry pie,
sweet milk, coffee.

WEDNESDAY.
Corn soup, broiled chicken, cream gravy, tomatoes, rice, beets, red raspberries, coffee.

THURSDAY.
Asparagus soup, breaded veal cutlets, brown potatoes, lettuce, beets, asparagus on toast, string beans,
rice, red raspberries, coffee.

FRIDAY.
Gumbo, broiled ham, potatoes, sliced tomatoes, beets, rice, squash corn, cantaloupe, coffee.

SATURDAY.

Vegetable soup, lamb with mint sauce, rice, potatoes, fried egg plant, stewed corn, lettuce, vanilla ice cream, coffee.

SUNDAY LUNCH.

Salmon salad, bread, toasted crackers, jelly, coffee, berries.

SUNDAY TEA.

Chicken salad, hot muffins, potato chips, ham sandwiches, tomatoes, broiled chicken, peach ice cream, cake, coffee, iced tea.

DINNER FOR A WEEK.

SUNDAY LUNCH.

Broiled ham, minced potatoes, honey, toast, crackers, biscuit, red raspberries, coffee.

SUNDAY TEA.

Jellied chicken, potato salad in a bed of lettuce and garnished with stuffed olives, bread, toasted crackers with grated cheese, iced tea with lemon, soft peaches, coffee.

MONDAY.

Clear tomato soup, lamb with mint sauce, potatoes, rice, corn, beets, lemon meringue pie, coffee.

TUESDAY.

Vegetable soup, croquettes, lamb and chicken (left-overs), green peas, potatoes, rice, asparagus, tomatoes and lettuce, sliced pineapple, coffee.

WEDNESDAY.

Cream of celery soup, roast beef, potatoes, rice, slaw, beets, boiled corn, peach ice cream, cake, coffee.

THURSDAY.

Cream of potato soup, roast veal, whole tomatoes, french dressing, peas, potatoes, cream dressing, rice, beets, radishes, bread and butter, black raspberries, ice cream, coffee.

FRIDAY.

Gumbo, broiled chicken with parsley, boiled potatoes, butter beans, rice, cucumbers, fried egg plant, cantaloupe, coffee.

SATURDAY.

Tomato soup, steak, lettuce, rice, squash, potatoes, watermelon, coffee.

DINNER FOR A WEEK.

SUNDAY TEA.

Chipped Beef and Eggs, sliced ham, lettuce and tomatoes, bread, muffins, peaches and cake, coffee.

MONDAY.

Smothered chicken, hamburg steak, boiled corn, stewed tomatoes, rice, squash, apple pudding,

TUESDAY.

Steak, beets, sliced tomatoes, mashed potatoes, stewed corn, peach cake, coffee.

WEDNESDAY.

Lamb, corn pudding, stewed tomatoes, boiled potatoes, rice, cantaloupe, coffee.

THURSDAY.

Steak, rice, sliced tomatoes, cucumbers, mashed potatoes, string bean salad, peaches and cream, coffee.

FRIDAY.

Smothered chicken, hamburg steak, mashed potatoes, stewed tomatoes, rice, squash, sliced sweet potatoes, peaches and cream, coffee.

SATURDAY.

Steak, boiled ham, cabbage, succotash, rice, tomatoes, potato cakes, apple float, cake, coffee.

MENU FOR FIFTY.

Grape Fruit, Pickles
Escalloped Oysters
Green Peas, Mashed Irish Potatoes
Sandwiches
Charlotte de Russe
Coffee
Twenty-five grape fruit.

Ten loaves white bread; ten loaves brown bread for sandwiches.
One peck of Irish potatoes for mashed potatoes.
One and one-half gallon oysters for escalloped oysters.
One-half gallon pickles.
Seven cans of peas.
One and one-half pound coffee.
One and one-half quantities Charlotte de Russe.

MRS. JOHN M. ALLEN, Knoxville, Tenn.

LUNCH FOR ONE HUNDRED.

Eight chickens and three pounds chopped veal for salad.
Eight dozen eggs, stuffed.
Eight dozen beaten biscuit, six loaves cream bread, generally thirty slices to the loaf.
Twelve quarts of oysters, ten loaves of stale bread makes one gallon of bread crumbs.
Two hams, one-half bushel Irish potatoes.
One bunch of celery, meaning one composed of twelve small bunches, use the nicest on the plates and the rest in the salad.
Three gallons of ice cream, if served in glasses, five average cakes.
Three pounds of coffee.
You can mash and brown the potatoes and serve hot with the lunch, or make potato salad.

MENU FOR TWO-HUNDRED PEOPLE.

Chicken Salad—Twenty chickens, fifteen pounds cooked veal, three bunches or bundles of celery, two gallons salad dressing. Escalloped Oysters—Eight gallons of oysters, twelve loaves bread for crumbs. Ham—Two or three hams, if quite small. Beaten Biscuit—Forty dozen biscuit. Buttered Bread—Twenty-six loaves of bread. Ice Cream and Sherbet—Five gallons cream, three gallons sherbet. Cake—Twelve cakes. Tea—One-half pound. Coffee—Three pounds. Milk to Drink and Use in Cooking—Three gallons of milk. Sugar—Five pounds loaf sugar.

SEVERAL MENUS.

Minced Oysters, Bread
Olives
Sliced Ham, Biscuit
Mashed Potatoes
Ice Cream, Cake
Coffee
Chicken Salad, Sliced Bread

Olives
Sliced Ham, Beaten Biscuit
Browned Potatoes
Ice Cream, Assorted Cake
Coffee
Salmon, Salad, Rolls
Pickles
Veal, Croquettes, Sliced Bread
Stuffed Eggs
Ice Cream or Sherbet Cake
Coffee

THANKSGIVING MENU.

Blue Points on Half Shell, Cream of Tomato Soup, Salted Almonds, Olives, Roast Turkey, Cranberry Sauce or Currant Jelly, Mashed Potatoes, Glazed Sweet Potatoes, Succotash, Onions with Cream Sauce, Mayonnaise of Celery, Wafers, Cheese, Pumpkin Pie, Mince Pie, Apples, Oranges, Grapes, Coffee

POOR MAN'S FEAST (THANKSGIVING).
Consomme
Roast Turkey, Cranberry Sauce
Potatoes, Beets, Celery, Plum Pudding, Hot Sauce
Nuts, Candy
Coffee, Cheese, Crackers

EGGS

EGG CROQUETTES.

B oil eggs hard, drop in cold water, squeeze through a potato masher. For six croquettes take six eggs, one-half pint sweet milk, one tablespoon butter, two ounces flour, one tablespoon chopped parsley, ten drops onion, one tablespoon each of pepper and salt. Make a thick sauce of butter, flour and milk, then add the other ingredients. Turn in a plate to cool and let the mixture stand three hours. Shape and drop in beaten eggs, then roll in bread crumbs and fry in boiling lard.

MRS. WM. J. BROWN, Bristol, Va.

EGG PIE.

Make pastry as you would for chicken pie. Line a pan with it and break six or eight eggs into it, being careful not to break the yelks, season with butter, pepper, etc., as you would a chicken pie and add a little milk or water to keep it from being dry. This is a good substitute for chicken pie in the early spring before chickens come in.

MRS. EDWIN H. FAY, Knoxville, Tenn.

BAKED EGGS.

Slice one dozen hard-boiled eggs, put in a baking dish alternately a layer of cracker crumbs, with pepper and salt and sliced eggs, the last layer being cracker crumbs and bits of butter. Pour over all one-half cup sweet milk or cream. Brown in oven and serve immediately.

MRS. BARNETT, Atlanta, Ga.

BAKED EGGS.

Eight hard-boiled eggs, cut lengthwise, sprinkle in bottom of baking dish browned bread crumbs, then a layer of eggs, butter, cheese and crumbs, then another layer, having crumbs on top, pour enough cream or sweet milk to moisten real well. Bake for a few minutes. Serve very hot.

MRS. HOWARD ANDERSON, Beverly, Tenn.

EGG A LA REINE.

Cover toasted rounds of bread with foie gras, or as variation, anchovy paste, place a poached egg on top of each, pour cream sauce over and serve hot.

CONTRIBUTED.

EGGS IN BREAD CUPS.

Thick squares of bread are scooped out, dipped in melted butter and baked in the oven. When nearly brown an egg is broken into each cup, which is returned to the oven until the eggs are set. Season well with salt and pepper and put a bit of butter on each egg.

CONTRIBUTED.

EGGS WITH CREAM SAUCE.

Hard boil as many eggs as needed, slice and place on a dish. Then make a cream sauce of sweet milk, flour and butter, while the sauce is hot, pour over the eggs and serve.

MRS. W.M. HOUSE, Knoxville, Tenn.

FRIED EGGS.

Melt a sufficient quantity of ham drippings; when hot, break four eggs in a saucer and put them gently into a dish. Dip the fat over them, cooking them on top. Serve when the white is done.

CONTRIBUTED.

POACHED EGGS.

Take one pint of sweet milk, just before it boils stir in one tablespoon of butter and one teaspoon of salt. Beat six eggs to a froth and pour in until the whole thickens, say about two minutes. Put out the lamp and stir half a minute or so. Pour over the toast.

CONTRIBUTED.

POACHED EGGS.

Place buttered muffin rings in a pan of hot salted water, underneath which is an asbestos plate, or another pan of hot water, that it may not come in direct contact with the fire. Drop an egg into each ring, and if they do not cook quickly enough, put some hot water on top of them. Use a griddle cake turner to take up the eggs when done. Eggs poached in milk are very nice. Put an egg on a slice of toast and pour some of the hot seasoned milk over it.

CONTRIBUTED.

SCALLOPED EGGS.

Boil four eggs hard and cut in fairly thin slices and put in baking pan, one layer of eggs sliced with one alternate layer of browned bread crumbs spread with butter, pepper and salt, then fill the pan with sweet milk.

MRS. FRANK DAVIS, Bristol, Tenn.

EGGS WITH SPINACH.

Butter individual shirred egg dishes and cover bottom with a layer of well seasoned, chopped spinach. On this break one or two eggs to suit, cover whole with well seasoned cream sauce and bake in a hot oven until egg is set. Asparagus tips, chopped chicken or mushrooms may also be used.

CONTRIBUTED.

SHIRRED EGGS.

Butter a deep plate and break into it some eggs carefully that they may not lose their shape. Sprinkle with a little salt and set them in the oven till the whites become set. When the whites are set they are sufficiently cooked.

MRS. W.K. VANCE, Bristol, Tenn.

HAM IN RAMEKINS WITH SHIRRED EGGS.

Line small ramekins with a thin layer of minced ham and parsley. Whip the whites of four eggs to a stiff froth, adding a pinch of salt; fill the ramekins with this, making a slight depression in the centre of each; into these slip the yelks of the eggs, being careful that they are not broken. Bake in a moderate oven just long enough to set the egg, and serve immediately.

MRS. WILL BEWLAY DUENNER, Bristol, Va.

STUFFED EGGS.

Boil hard one dozen eggs, halve and take out the yellows, mash the yellows together until perfectly smooth, season with one teaspoon of celery seed, lump of butter size of an egg, pepper, salt and one slice of onion chopped very fine, mix well, stirring until smooth.

Fill each half of the whites and stand them upon a dish, piling up to suit the fancy, add a bit of butter to each egg when you put in the stove, placing it upon the top that it may melt and run through. Bake slowly about half an hour. A little cream added to the paste is an improvement.

MRS. E.S. McCLUNG, Knoxville, Tenn.

EGGS AND TOMATOES.

Cut a circle out of the stem end of medium tomatoes. Drain seeds and juice and take middle divisions out. Break an egg into each tomato, add salt, butter and a few bread crumbs. Set in stove until egg is set and tomato baked.

MRS. RICHARD P. JOHNSON, Knoxville, Tenn.

EGGS IN TOMATOES FOR BREAKFAST.

Take ripe, firm tomatoes, scoop out heart and drop into each a raw egg, season with salt, pepper, paprika and a dash of Worcestershire sauce, next add a teaspoon each of chopped onion and ham. Bake until eggs are firm. Serve with toast.

MRS. H.M. SIMMONDS, Knoxville, Tenn.

EGGS ON TOAST.

One tablespoon of butter, with pepper and salt, put in chafing dish, and when hot add one gill of cream and six eggs. Stir constantly for two or three minutes, serve on hot toast.

CONTRIBUTED.

FISH SAUCES & FISH

CREAM SAUCE.
One tablespoon each of flour and butter, mixed smooth, one cup of milk with salt and white pepper to taste. Cook till rather thick.

MRS. HUGH INMAN.

FISH SAUCE.
One-half cup butter, yelks three eggs, one and one-half tablespoons lemon juice, one-fourth teaspoon salt, a pinch of pepper, one-third cup boiling water, cream butter and yelks together and cook like a custard.

CONTRIBUTED.

FISH SAUCE.
Make a pint of drawn butter, add one tablespoon of pepper sauce or Worcestershire sauce, a little salt and six hard boiled eggs, chopped fine. Pour over boiled fish and garnish with sliced lemon.

WHITE HOUSE COOKBOOK.

FISH SAUCE.
To two yelks of eggs beaten with even tablespoon of flour, add a cup of milk and stir until it comes to a boil, then stir in one tablespoon of butter, two tablespoons of vinegar and one after dinner coffee spoon each of salt, pepper and ground mustard.

MRS. C.J. McCLUNG, Knoxville, Tenn.

CHAFING DISH-SAUCE SUPREME.
Put a tablespoon of melted butter into a quart of milk, add flour and water for thickening, two tablespoons chopped parsley, boil one-half hour in double boiler.

MRS. H.P. WYMAN, Bristol, Tenn.

TARTARE SAUCE.
To a pint of mayonnaise add one tablespoon of the flower heads of Cross and Blackwell's mustard cauliflower pickle, one teaspoon of finely chopped or scraped onion, one teaspoon of capers.

MRS. W.B. LOCKETT, Knoxville, Tenn.

A COLD FISH SUPPER.

Boil carefully a large trout or any good white fish in salted water, seasoned with a bay leaf, an onion, a carrot, a piece of celery, and some whole peppers. When tender, take out without breaking, place on a very large meat dish and peel off the skin from the upper side. When cold the fish is covered with slices of hard boiled eggs, lemon, bits of sweet red peppers and spoonful of mayonnaise. Boil in salted water separately a few carrots, beets and Irish potatoes, also some string beans, asparagus tips or peas, if convenient. Cut the vegetables, when cold in tiny cubes and place in little heaps on the meat dish around the fish, alternating the different colors. Fresh cucumbers and green peppers are also used. Any cold vegetables are suitable, if cut up small in regular shapes. The whole dish is then decorated with plenty of parsley and lemon points. Serve with mayonnaise and bread and butter. This dish can be prepared with whatever vegetables are on hand, even white turnips being used and an endless variety of decoration is possible.

MRS. D.B. MACGOWAN, Knoxville, Tenn.

TO BAKE FISH.

Rub the fish with salt and pepper and a very small quantity of cayenne pepper, inside and out, prepare a stuffing of bread, seasoned with pepper, salt, thyme or parsley, sew or tie with a string; put, in a pan and to a good-sized fish allow a pint of water, sprinkle with flour and add some butter, baste well; bake slowly one and one-half hours.

MRS. C.H. ALLEN, Knoxville, Tenn.

BAKED FISH.

Dress as for baked chicken, then put strips of fat meat over the flesh, put in the stove and baste as you would a chicken while cooking.

MRS. B.J. STEPHENSON, Knoxville, Tenn.

BAKED HALIBUT.

Take a piece of halibut, weighing five or six pounds, and lay in salt and water for two hours. Wipe dry and score the outer skin. Set in the baking-pan in a tolerably hot oven, and bake an hour, basting often with butter and water heated together in a saucepan. When a fork will penetrate it easily it is done. Take the gravy in the dripping-pan, add a little boiling water, if necessary, stir in a tablespoon of Worcestershire sauce a tablespoon of walnut catsup, the juice of a lemon, thicken with browned flour, previously wet with cold water. Boil up once, and serve.

MRS. C.R. McILWAINE, Knoxville, Tenn.

TO BOIL FISH.

Clean well, rub with pepper and salt and sew it in a towel and drop in boiling water, keep it boiling fast. A large fish will take three-quarters of an hour, a small one less time. When done put in a dish and dress with hard boiled eggs and drawn butter sauce and parsley. Walnut and mushroom catsup are good with boiled fish.

MRS. C.H. ALLEN, Knoxville, Tenn.

STEWED CODFISH WITH POTATOES.

Soak codfish thoroughly in tepid water from an hour and a half to two hours. Boil and pick it into shreds. Take one cup mashed potatoes, one large tablespoon butter, milk enough to make the mixture moist. Put enough boiling water into chafing dish to keep from scorching. Stir until very hot, add pepper and salt and serve.

CONTRIBUTED.

FRESH CODFISH STEAK.

Have the butter hot; put on steak, cover blazing pan, cook fifteen minutes, sprinkle with paprika, pour over sauce supreme, when the sauce is thoroughly hot, turn out fire and serve from chafing dish. Great.

MRS. H.P. WYMAN, Bristol, Tenn.

COLD CRAB RAVIGOTTE.

One pint best crab meat, two large fresh ripe tomatoes, one large green pepper, one large red pepper. Chop the tomatoes and peppers fine (be sure to remove seeds from peppers), add a tablespoon of chopped parsley; mix all together with mayonnaise, enough to have them quite wet and moist, season to taste with salt and a dash of paprika; fill each shell heaping full of the mixture and garnish the top with two anchovies, a small piece of cut pickle and slices of lemon. Serve in six shells.

MRS. C.R. McILWAINE, Knoxville, Tenn.

STUFFED CRABS.

Boil crabs half an hour, when cold pick meat carefully from the shells; to this add one-third as much fine bread crumbs and season with salt, pepper and parsley. Brown a small piece of onion in a large spoonful of butter, to which add the mixture and fry a few minutes. Carefully wash and scrub the shells and when wiped, fill with the crab meat. Dust the tops with pulverized toasted bread and brown a few moments in a hot oven.

MISS OLIVE MOODY, New Orleans, La.

CREAMED SHRIMPS IN CASES.

For one pint shrimps, broken in small pieces, make sauce with two tablespoons butter, three flour and a scant pint cream. Season with salt, pepper and lemon juice, add shrimps, stir gently and when very hot, pour in cases.

MRS. PARHAM. Chattanooga, Tenn.

CREOLE SHRIMP STEW.

Heat one large tablespoonful of lard, add one tablespoon of flour, one onion, sliced fine, also parsley and thyme and brown all together. Add one pint of boiling water and drop in shrimps, which have previously been boiled five or ten minutes, then add salt and cook slowly for twenty minutes.

MISS OLIVE MOODY, New Orleans, La.

CREAMED SALMON.

One can salmon, minced fine, drain off the liquor and throw away. For the dressing boil one pint of milk, two tablespoons butter, salt and pepper to taste. Have ready one pint of fine bread crumbs, place a layer in the bottom of the dish, then a layer of fish, then a layer of dressing and so on, having crumbs for the last layer. Bake until brown.

MRS. C.R. McILWAINE, Knoxville, Tenn.

LOBSTER CROQUETTES.

To the meat of a well-boiled lobster chopped fine, add pepper, salt and powdered mace. Mix with this, one-quarter as much bread crumbs as you have meat, make into ovates or pointed balls, with two tablespoons melted butter. Roll these in beaten egg, then in cracker crumbs and fry in butter or lard. Serve dry and hot, and garnish with crisp parsley.

MRS. C.R. McILWAINE, Knoxville, Tenn.

SALMON CROQUETTES.

One can salmon, same quantity of hot mashed potatoes, yelks of two eggs, beaten, pulverized crackers. Mix salmon and potatoes, season highly with pepper and salt, form in any shape you may fancy, dip first in the egg and then cover with crumbs. Drop them into boiling lard and fry until light brown.

MRS. H.H. TAYLOR, Knoxville, Tenn.

DRESSING FOR CANNED SALMON.

To one can of salmon, boil hard, six eggs, mash smoothly the yellows of four, to this paste add butter size of an egg, pepper, salt, celery seed and one teaspoon of Durkee's Salad Dressing. Heat the salmon in the can, also beat the dressing separately and pour over the salmon before serving. Slice the other hard eggs over the top.

MRS. A.P. WHITE, Knoxville, Tenn.

FISH PUFF.

A delicious way of using remnants of cold cooked fish. Chop fish and mix with it an equal part of mashed potatoes. Season with salt and pepper and an ounce of melted butter. Stir into it two well beaten eggs. Form into a roll and place on buttered tin. Brush over with a beaten egg. Roll in bread crumbs and bake one-half hour in hot oven.

MRS. WILL BEWLAY DUENNER, Bristol, Va.

NEWBURY MIXTURE.

One cup cream, the beaten yelks of three eggs, salt and pepper. Cook till it is creamy, add two tablespoons sherry, put in the crab meat, heat well and serve hot.

MRS. A.P. WHITE, Knoxville, Tenn.

PLANKED SHAD.

Planking is an old, new way of cooking fish, and it is said to have a more delicious flavor when "planked" than when cooked in any other way. Have a two-inch plank made from hard wood, oak is the best, about the size of a large platter. Several sizes can be prepared for convenience. When ready for use, put in the bottom of the oven and heat very hot. Have the fish well cleaned; wipe with a dry cloth, split down the back and put it skin down on the hot plank and keep the oven quite hot for ten minutes; then baste from sauce as follows: Two tablespoons of butter, one of water, two of vinegar, one teaspoon of salt, a pinch of red pepper. After basting it may bake more moderately about thirty minutes, basting at intervals of ten minutes, putting on very little at a time. To prevent waste by running from the plank, place in a large dripping pan, or, better, fashion a narrow tin about the plank which may be placed on a large platter or tray, and garnished with lemon, parsley or lettuce. It will add to the looks of the dish if the planks rest on a bed of oak leaves, if in season for them, the leaves to be placed on the platter or tray.

CONTRIBUTED.

TOMATO SAUCE FOR BAKED FISH.

One can tomatoes, one bottle olives (twenty cent size), two lemons: Put tomatoes in pan and heat to a boiling point with a half level teaspoon of soda. Strain, add olives and juice, also the two lemons, sliced. Then cook fifteen minutes. Thicken as for gravy with a little flour and water, stirred smooth. Serve hot on baked fish.

MRS. JOHN B. KING, Bristol, Tenn.

FILLING

ICING.

One cup granulated sugar and four tablespoons cold water, boiled till it "threads"; then add the well-beaten white of one egg and beat till it is thick and smooth.

Another way is this: Two cupsful powdered sugar, two-thirds cup sweet milk and butter size of an egg, boiled together ten minutes and then stirred till cool enough to spread on the cake. Add flavoring.

CONTRIBUTED.

ICING.

Two tablespoons of powdered sugar to each egg, using as many as you wish. Put a vessel of tepid water on the fire and place your bowl for making the icing in, in the water and break the whites on the sugar. Beat it until the water boils, then remove from the fire, but continue to beat until stiff enough to pour. Flavor with lemon juice instead of extract.

MRS. HENRY A. CHAMBERS, Chattanooga, Tenn.

ICING.

Three eggs, one pound and five ounces of sugar. Put sugar on the fire with a small teacup of water, when it ropes well pour it very slowly into your eggs, which you must beat to stiff froth; first add a pinch of citric acid and vanilla, beat until stiff.

MRS. E.S. McCLUNG, Knoxville, Tenn.

ICING.

For large cake. Four eggs, their weight in sugar, break the whites in a tin can, put the sugar in, mixing well, set this can in a vessel of hot water on the stove, stir constantly to prevent lumping, let it get as hot as you can bear your finger in, then pour in a bowl, add one-fourth teaspoon tartaric acid, flavor, beat until thick enough to spread on the cake.

MRS. JOSEPH L. KING, Knoxville, Tenn.

ICING.

Two whites to each cup of sugar, cream of tartar size of a pea, water to moisten. Cook sugar and water and cream of tartar till it "threads", pour over beaten whites and beat a long time.

MRS. JOHN I. COX, Bristol, Tenn.

ICING.

Four cups sugar, seven tablespoons boiling water, one and one-half teaspoons apple vinegar. Boil till it just "flies a silk", pour over the whites of two eggs, beat till it stiffens.

MISS ELLA McNEIL, Bristol, Va.

CARAMEL ICING.

One pound brown sugar, one cup sweet milk, lump butter size of an egg, half teaspoon vanilla. Boil milk and sugar fifteen minutes, stirring constantly, take from fire, drop in butter and vanilla and beat till quite thick.

MRS. H.N. SAXTON, JR., Knoxville, Tenn.

CARAMEL FILLING.

One-half cup of Baker's cocoa, one and one-half pounds sugar, a lump of butter the size of an egg, and one cup milk. Stir together and set in a warm place to melt. Place over the fire and boil for twenty minutes, stirring constantly. Test by dropping a little bit in cold water, if it hardens quickly, it is done. Flavor with vanilla.

MRS. W.K. VANCE, Bristol, Tenn.

CARAMEL FILLING.

One pound brown sugar, one-half teacup butter, one-half teacup sweet milk, one-fourth teaspoon vanilla. Put in saucepan and cook until it forms a soft ball in water. Then beat til creamy and spread on cake.

MISS BRANCH KEEBLER, Bristol, Va.

CARAMEL FILLING FOR CAKE.

One-half cake of chocolate, one and one-half pounds sugar, butter size of an egg, one cup milk. Set chocolate in a warm place to melt, then put all over fire and boil twenty minutes, stirring constantly. When it hardens when dropped in cold water take off and flavor with one tablespoon of vanilla, beat till thick, then spread on cake.

MRS. W.K. VANCE, Bristol, Tenn.

CHOCOLATE FILLING.

Butter size of an egg, one pint sugar, one-half cup water or milk, one-half cake chocolate. Put all together and boil till thick, stirring occasionally.

MISS LUCY HUGHES, Lea's Springs, Tenn.

FRUIT FILLING.

Four tablespoons very finely chopped citron, four tablespoons seeded raisins, half a cup of blanched almonds, chopped fine, also one-fourth of a pound of finely chopped figs.

Beat the whites of three eggs to a stiff froth, adding a half cup of sugar, then mix thoroughly into this the whole of the chopped ingredients. Put it between the layers of cake when the cake is hot, so that it will cook the egg a little. This will be found delicious.

WHITE HOUSE COOKBOOK.

LEMON CAKE FILLING.

One scant tablespoon butter, two cups sugar, four eggs, one tablespoon corn starch, juice of two lemons. Boil until it thickens and spread warm.

C. C.

LEMON JELLY.

One coffee cup of sugar, two tablespoons butter, two eggs, juice of two lemons. Beat all together and boil until the consistency of jelly.

MRS. JOS. S. DONNELLY, Shoun's, Tenn.

LEMON JELLY.

One cup sugar, juice and grated rind of one lemon, one egg.

Cook lemon and sugar together until well blended, then add beaten egg and cook, stirring constantly until thick. Nice for either layer cake, roll, jelly cake or tarts.

MISS BERTHA PIERCE, Detroit, Mich.

ORANGE FILLING FOR CAKE.

Stir the whites of two eggs and one pound powdered sugar as for icing. Add the grated rind and juice of half a lemon and two grated oranges, having first pared them. When thoroughly mixed, spread between layers.

Another way, and an easier way of preparing a jelly is to pare two good-sized oranges and grate them into a pound of powdered sugar. Mix and spread between the layers. You can ice the cake smoothly on the outside with plain white icing.

MRS. W.K. VANCE, Bristol, Tenn.

FILLING FOR R. E. LEE CAKE.

One orange grated, peel and all, two bananas, small can grated pineapple, (do not use all the juice), the juice of one lemon and a little of the peel grated and enough sugar to make thick enough to spread. Use a sponge cake made in this way: Ten eggs, one pound sugar, cake three-quarters pound flour, bake in a loaf and cut, or in jelly pans.

CONTRIBUTED.

MISCELLENOUS & HINTS

SALTED ALMONDS.

Shell and blanch the almonds, put them in a baking pan, with an even teaspoon of butter to each pound of almonds. Bake slowly until a light brown and thoroughly dried. Stir them frequently until every almond is nicely oiled with the butter, take from the oven and dust thickly with salt. Turn on a cold dish and place in a cool, dry place until wanted.

CHRISTIAN OBSERVER.

TO CLEAN ALUMINUM VESSELS.

Clean aluminum vessels with plenty of soap suds and hot water, rinse, and dry with a cloth and place empty upon a hot stove for a few seconds to dry quickly and thoroughly. If anything sticks to the bottom scrape with the edge of a wooden paddle-if hard to remove, pour boiling water in the vessel and let it stand to soak.

TO WASH BLANKETS OR FLANNELS.

Soak over night in cold water, in which two teaspoons of powdered borax to each gallon of water has been dissolved. Next morning rub through two cold suds and rinse through blue water in which there is a little soap. Drain rather than wring and shake well before hanging on the line. Flannels must be ironed before they are thoroughly dry, but not sprinkled.

MRS. HENRY A. CHAMBERS, Chattanooga, Tenn.

BLUEING.

One ounce of Oxalic Acid, one ounce of Chinese or Prussian Blue, either will do, one quart of soft water, put in bottle and shake well several times after mixing; then do not shake at all.

If any settles in the bottle, after using the first water, can fill again. If when you buy, it is not powdered, ask the druggist to powder it for you.

Be sure to have Chinese or Prussian blue. This quantity will last a family of six or eight persons a year, and will not injure the finest clothes.

MRS. JACOB THOMAS, Bristol, Tenn.

BORAX.

Lady readers who have not tested the magic properties of borax; have been losing a great help and comfort. If once used you will never be without a bottle on your toilet table.

It removes stains and dirt from the hands better than soap, and at the same time softens and smooths the skin. It is splendid for washing the hair and will, without injury cleanse brushes and combs in a few moments. For washing purposes it saves both soap and labor. It will extract the dirt from articles of delicate texture without rubbing, it being only necessary to put the articles to soak with a solution of borax over night and need only to be rinsed in the morning. Two tablespoons of pulverized, borax, dissolved in a quart of water, to which water enough is added to cover a pair of blankets, will cleanse them beautifully. It also saves great labor in washing paint. It is said to drive away ants and roaches if sprinkled on the shelves of safe and pantries.

MRS. B.J. STEPHENSON, Knoxville, Tenn.

BURNS AND SCALDS.

Cover with cooking soda and lay wet cloths over it. Whites of eggs and olive oil. Olive oil or linseed oil, plain or mixed with chalk or whiting. Sweet or olive oil and limewater.

BURN SALVE.

One pint linseed oil, a piece of beeswax size of a walnut, melt together, remove from the fire and stir in one-half cup of sweet cream, stir until it congeals.

MRS. B.J. STEPHENSON, Knoxville, Tenn

FIRM BUTTER WITHOUT ICE.

In families, or where the dairy is small, a good plan to have butter cool and firm without ice, is by the process of evaporation, as practiced in India and other warm countries. A cheap plan is to get a very large-sized, porous, earthern flower pot, with an extra large saucer; half fill the saucer with water; set in it a trivet or light stand, such as used for holding hot irons will do; upon this set your butter; over the whole invert the flower-pot. letting the top rim of it rest in and be covered by water; then close the hole in the bottom of the flower-pot with a cork; then dash water over the flower-pot, and repeat the process several times a day, or whenever it looks dry. If set in a cool place or where the wind can blow on it, it will rapidly evaporate the water from the pot, and the butter will be as firm and cool as from an ice house.

MRS. JOSEPH McTEER, Knoxville, Tenn.

MELTED BUTTER.

This simple luxury, owing to ignorance or carelessness in making, is often anything but a luxury.

First be careful to have an exceedingly clean saucepan, put into it, in the proportions of a small teacup of water, two ounces of butter and a large teaspoon of flour. The flour should be mixed smoothly with the cold liquid before it is put near the fire, and if the mixture is allowed to stand an hour before melting, so much the better, but it must not be put near the fire until ready to be melted. When once on the fire, keep it stirred or move it about by occasional shaking the saucepan the same way. If it sometimes moves to the right and then to the left it will be oily and fit for nothing. A little cream or good milk may be used instead of part water, and will be found an improvement.

MRS. M. McCLUNG, Knoxville, Tenn.

PRESERVING BUTTER.

The farmers of Aberdeen, Scotland, are said to practice the following method of curing their butter, which gives it a great superiority over that of their neighbors. Take two quarts of the best common salt, one ounce of white sugar and one ounce of common saltpetre, mix, and to one pound of butter add one ounce of the composition work it well into the mass and close it up for use.

ANOTHER METHOD.

Make a strong brine, into which the butter prepared as directed above is placed. But the butter must be made into rolls and each roll enclosed in a piece of cloth.

MRS. HENRY A. CHAMBERS, Chattanooga, Tenn.

HOW TO PURIFY STRONG BUTTER.

Melt the butter gradually, and while it is melting add two ounces of pulverized alum to every five pounds of butter and stir slowly, when all is melted strain through a finer strainer into some cold water. When the butter is cool enough to work, take out and for every five pounds of butter add three ounces of salt, one ounce of clean saltpetre and one ounce of pulverized sugar. Make up into rolls or balls, wrap up in thin cloth separately and cover with strong brine and keep in a cool place and it will keep sweet a long time.

MR. HOLMDEN, London, England.

WASHING CALICOES.

To wash calico or muslin without fading, soak twenty or thirty minutes in a pint of water in which two ounces of sugar of lead has been dissolved, then wash as usual, if they soak longer it will do no harm.

MRS. HENRY A. CHAMBERS, Knoxville, Tenn.

CINDERS IN THE EYE.

Roll soft paper up like a lamp lighter, and wet the tip to remove or use a medicine dropper to draw it out. Rub the other eye.

CLEANING FLUID.

One-eighth pound white Castile soap dissolved in one pint boiling rain water, one-eighth pound Aqua Ammonnia, one-half ounce Glycerine, one-half ounces Ether, one-half ounce Alcohol.

When cool add two quarts rain water and bottle. This is suitable for coats, pants, skirts and vests.

MRS. JOHN W. GREEN, Knoxville, Tenn.

CLEANING MIXTURE.

Dissolve four ounces of white Castile soap in four quarts boiling water, when cool add five ounces Aqua Ammonia, two and one-half ounces glycerine, two and one-half ounces alcohol, two ounces ether, cork tightly.

To clean a carpet, use about one tablespoon to a pail of water; to clean a soiled coat or black garment, use two tablespoons to a pint of strong black coffee; to clean grease spots use without diluting, clean with a brush.

CONTRIBUTED.

CLEANING MIXTURE.

Two ounces of ammonia, two ounces of alcohol, same strength as for spirits of camphor, one ounce of ether, one ounce of gum camphor, one ounce of transparent soap, add one quart of soft water Use with a sponge and keep well corked.

MRS. T.S. WEBB, Knoxville. Tenn.

COUGH REMEDY.

One ounce of Irish moss, soaked as for blanc-mange, and boiled ten minutes in two quarts of water and the juice of six lemons, sweeten to taste and str in. Drink freely, it will nourish the system and relieve the cough.

MRS. H.H. TAYLOR, Knoxville, Tenn.

TO PUT UP TOMATOES FOR SOUP.

Wash, cut out specks, put on with very little or no water, when soft, strain through a colander and return to stove to cook till thick, add a little salt. Seal while hot. You have tomatoes without seeds, or skins, and have put up nothing that has to be thrown away.

CURE FOR HOARSENESS.

Take the whites of two eggs and beat them, add two spoonsful of white sugar, grate in a little nutmeg, then add a pint of lukewarm water. Stir well and drink often. Repeat the preparation, if necessary, and it will cure the most obstinate case of hoarseness in a short time.

MRS. JOE JOUROLMON, Knoxville, Tenn.

TO EXTRACT INK FROM COTTON, SILK OR WOOLEN GOODS.

Dip the spots in spirits of turpentine and let remain several hours, then rub thoroughly between the hands and it will all dis.appear without changing either the color or texture of the fabric.

MRS. WILL INGLES, Knoxville, Tenn.

NEW TOUCHES TO OLD DISHES.

New and improving touches may be given to old and familiar dishes. Ordinary bread pudding, for example may come to the table with a coating of whipped cream sprinkled with walnut meats. Vanilla corn starch, I have discovered is doubly tempting when served with a covering layer of cut fruit. In winter, bananas, oranges or pineapples may be used with it.

M.D.

SALVE FOR POISON.

A handful of the inner bark of Alder, one of Hyssop, and one of the roots of parsley and plantain each, stew slowly in a pint of lard, strain, and it is fit for use. "The best salve for poison known, once kept as a great secret."

MRS. NELSON, Knoxville, Tenn.

SMALLPOX REMEDY.

Sulphate of zinc, one grain; fox glove (digitalis), one grain; half a teaspoon of sugar, mix with two tablespoons of water. When thoroughly mixed, add four ounces of water. Take a spoonful every hour. Disease will disappear in twelve hours. For a child, smaller doses, according to age.

MRS. B.J. STEPHENSON, Knoxville, Tenn.

SODA ASH SOAP.

Ten pounds soda ash, five pounds new lime, sifted, boil in ten gallons of rain water, ten minutes, add twenty-five pounds clean grease and boil two hours, let stand until cold, then cut out.

MRS. B.J. STEPHENSON, Knoxville, Tenn.

SEASONINGS.

When boiling chicken for salad or pressed loaf, put in a quarter of a pound of good salt pork as a seasoning. Let the chicken cool in the water.

Put sugar in the water used for basting meats of all kinds, it gives a good flavor; to veal more especially.

To give a good flavor to corn beef hash, use a good stock for moistening, with a pinch of salt, sugar and cayenne.

Three tablespoons of freshly-made Japan tea, with a bit of nutmeg, give an indescribable flavor to an apple pie.

Boston baked beans can be greatly improved by adding a cup of sweet cream the last hour of baking.

When making tomato soup, add a raw cucumber sliced fine, boil soft and strain with tomato. It gives a seasoning quite taking.

Add a cup of good cider vinegar to the water in which you boil fish, especially salt water fish.

Make snow cake with arrowroot flour; the flavor is delicious.

When boiling ham, put in a cup of black molasses, one onion, a few cloves and pepper-corns, adding a bunch of hay; the latter seasons finely. Let the ham cool in the water in which it has boiled, skin, rub with brown sugar and brown in a slow oven for an hour, basting every fifteen minutes with some of the stock in which it was cooked.

A few pieces of orange or lemon placed in an earthen jar gives cookies a delicious flavor when eaten.

CENTRAL PRESBYTERIAN.

CURE FOR TOOTHACHE.

Tablespoon of any kind of spirits, tablespoon of vinegar, teaspoon of common salt, mix and put in mouth, it gives great relief.

FROM *KNOXVILLE REGISTER*, 1820.

HINTS.

A pinch of salt in a glass of lemonade will improve the taste.

A Pretty Ornament—A turnip or carrot suspended by a cord which is kept wet will put out shoots and make a pretty ornament.

All vegetables with the exception of potatoes should be cooked in uncovered vessels.

To boil a cracked egg add a teaspoon of salt to the water, and it will cook without having any of the white come out.

Whipped Cream—The cream must be of good consistency, from thirty to thirty-six hours old, and very cold to whip well.

Wrap flour or soda on a burn.

Fainting—Place flat on back; allow fresh air, and sprinkle with water. Place head lower than rest of body.

To keep finger nails clean when polishing the stove, put a little lard under and around the finger nails and it will protect them from blacking.

Fire in One's Clothing—Do not run, especially downstairs, or out-of-doors. Roll on carpet, or wrap in woolen rug or blanket. Keep the head down, so as not to inhale the flame.

Fire from Kerosene—Do not use water. It will spread the flames. Dirt, sand or flour is the best extinguisher, or smother with woolen rug, tablecloth or carpet.

To Clean Gold or Silver—Rub well with wet prepared chalk, when dry rub well with a flannel cloth.

Hoarseness—Boil a lemon till soft, squeeze over enough sugar to make a thick jelly, use often.

If the top of a cake is sifted with flour before icing, there is less danger of its running over the sides.

Mayonnaise dressing separates when too much salt has been added to the yelks of the eggs, or when the oil is added too fast at first, or when the ingredients are warm.

Omelettes are tough when milk is added to the eggs instead of water, or when the eggs have been beaten until very light. Salt should be sprinkled over the omelette after it is partly done.

If the knife and fingers are slightly buttered when seeding raisins, the work will be robbed of its discomfort and stickiness.

To remove grass stains, soak in alcohol or molasses.

Fruit, Coffee, Cocoa, Chocolate or Tea Stains—Spread the stain over a bowl and pour boiling water through until the stain disappears.

Scorch Stains—Wet the stain with soapsuds, then spread in the sun; cover the wet stains with starch made into past with soapsuds.

To Remove Ink Stains from Cloth—Soak the article in sweet milk until the stains disappear, do it though while the ink is fresh, if the milk sours, no matter.

That salt should be eaten with nuts to aid digestion.

That a hot, strong lemonade taken at bedtime, will break up a hard cold.

That whole cloves are now used to exterminate the merciless and industrious moth. It is said they are more effective as a destroying agent than either tobacco, camphor or cedar shavings.

That a cup of strong coffee will remove the odor of onions from the breath.

That well ventilated bedrooms will prevent morning headache and lassitude.

ICE CREAM

ICE CREAM.

One-half gallon of cream or rich milk, three-fourths of a pound of sugar, three tablespoons of arrowroot, the whites of eight eggs. Let the milk and sugar come to boiling point, dissolve arrowroot in half-pint of milk and stir in boiling milk until it thickens, then beat in briskly the well beaten whites, flavor to taste and freeze.

MRS. AKIN.

ANGEL PARFAIT.

One cup sugar, three-fourths cup water, whites three eggs, one pint heavy cream, one tablespoon vanilla. Boil sugar and water till syrup threads, pour slowly on beaten whites and continue beating till smooth. Add cream beaten stiff and then freeze.

MRS. JOHN COX, Knoxville, Tenn.

APPLE CREAM.

Prepare apples as for float, then to one quart of apples put one quart of rich cream, sweeten apples before adding cream. Freeze.

MRS. E.S. McCLUNG, Knoxville, Tenn.

BISQUE ICE CREAM.

One cup of sugar to each quart of cream, vanilla to suit taste, one-half dozen stale macaroons to each quart, ground fine, freeze as other creams. This is fine.

MRS. W.K. VANCE, Bristol, Tenn.

CAFE PARFAIT OR COFFEE ICE CREAM.

One cup milk, one-fourth cup strong coffee, one-eighth teaspoon salt, one cup sugar, three cups thin cream, yelks of three eggs. Scald milk with coffee and add one-half sugar. Without straining, use this mixture for making custards, using eggs, sugar and salt. Add one cup cream and let stand thirty minutes. When cool, strain through cheese cloth and add remaining cream. Freeze.

MRS. JOHN COX, Knoxville, Tenn.

CHOCOLATE MARSHMALLOW ICE CREAM.

Three ounces chocolate, Baker's, one-half pound marshmallows, cut in small pieces, one pint sugar, one teaspoon vanilla, one-half gallon of cream. Melt the chocolate, add to it half the sugar. Put half the cream in a double boiler on the stove, when the cream reaches the boiling point add the rest of the sugar and the chocolate slowly, stirring all the time. When mixed allow to stay on stove about a minute, take off, add remainder of cream, and just before freezing, put in the cut up marshmallows.

MRS. JOHN PEYTON MOFFETT, Knoxville, Tenn.

CHOCOLATE PUDDING. (FROZEN.)

Beat the yelks of three eggs, half a cup of sugar and a level spoonful of cinnamon together until very light; add slowly a cup of milk, heated to boiling, beating well; then pour gradually over an ounce and a half of unsweetened chocolate, melted by standing over hot water. Place this mixture in a double boiler and stir constantly until it thickens. When cold, add a cup of rich cream, vanilla to flavor, and freeze. Prepare and have ready a cup of candied fruits, figs and seeded raisins. Cut the candied fruit and figs in thin slices, the raisins in halves. Make a syrup of a quarter of a cup of each of sugar and water, add the fruit, boil until it is tender and plump, then drain. Add the drained fruit to the frozen mixture when it is almost done, and finish freezing.

MRS. C.R. McILWAINE, Knoxville, Tenn.

COLUMBIA PUDDING. (FINE.)

One cup sugar, four eggs, one quart each of milk and cream, one-fourth pound each candied cherries and candied pineapple, one-half glass sherry wine. Make a custard as thick as mush of the four eggs, cup of sugar and quart of milk, when cold add the quart of cream whipped stiff. Begin to freeze, add the cherries and pineapple, chopped fine. When frozen hard, pour in the sherry wine. This makes three quarts.

MRS. B.B. BURNS, Bristol, Va.

FROZEN PUDDING.

One pint milk, two cups granulated sugar, a scant half cup flour, two eggs, two tablespoons of gelatine, one quart of cream, one-half pound of candied fruits, one tablespoon extract vanilla. Let the milk come to a boil, beat the flour, one cup sugar and eggs together, stir in the boiling milk; then add the gelatine which has been soaking one or two hours in water enough to cover it, set away to cool; when cool add vanilla, sugar and cream, freeze ten minutes, then add the candied fruit and finish freezing, take out the beater, pack smoothly and set away for an hour. To serve, dip the tin in warm water and turn out. Serve with whipped cream.

MRS. LUCY J. BROWNLEE, Knoxville, Tenn.

FROZEN PUDDING.

Beat the yelks of six eggs until very light. Boil together a pint of water and a pound of sugar for five minutes; add the yelks of the eggs. beat over the fire for just a moment; take from the fire, and beat continuously until the mixture is cold. It should be thick like sponge cake batter. Acid a quart of cream and a teaspoon of vanilla. Turn into a freezer, freeze until it is the consistency of snow. Have ready half a pint of chopped fruit, which has been soaking for an hour or two in orange juice, add this fruit and turn until the mixture is well frozen.

MRS. C.R. McILWAINE. Knoxville, Tenn.

MAPLE PARFAIT.

Five eggs, leaving out the whites of three, one and one-half cups of hot maple syrup, pour over the beaten eggs and put on the fire, and cook till it coats the spoon, cool, beat the three whites and whip one pint of cream, a pint before whipping, add to the eggs and syrup which are now cold and freeze. In the first instance the eggs are beaten separately.

MRS. ARTHUR E. DAVENPORT, Chattanooga, Tenn.

MARSHMALLOW ICE CREAM.

One-half gallon cream, one pound marshmallows, one pint sugar, one-fourth pound chocolate, vanilla. Heat the cream and sugar till sugar melts, cut marshmallows in pieces and shave or grate chocolate, add to hot cream and suger and stir all well together, add vanilla, and when cold freeze.

CONTRIBUTED.

MOCK ICE CREAM.

One gallon of milk, one pound sugar in the milk, when slightly warm put in eight tablespoons of corn starch, lightly filled. Break into the starch six eggs, mix the eggs and starch with a little cold milk, stir into the milk when slightly warm. Mix the eggs, starch and cold milk in a bowl, and then put into the warm sugar and milk; a very small pinch of salt will improve it. Cook until it is thick as good cream and tastes smooth. Stir all the time. Be sure and strain through a coarse towel. Let it be perfectly cold before flavoring.

MRS. S.B. BOYD, Knoxville, Tenn.

MOUSSE.

A plain mousse, which is a foundation for all other varieties, is made as follows: Whip cream, if not solid, drain carefully. Sweeten and flavor with wine or any preferred flavoring. Put in cans, carefully covered, and pack in ice and salt for three hours.

MRS. A.P. WHITE, Knoxville, Tenn.

ORANGE ICE CREAM.

One-half gallon of cream, six small or four large oranges, half the number of lemons, one cup of sugar to each quart of cream. Put the grated rind of one orange and one lemon and only the juice of the rest. Freeze as other fruit creams.

MRS. W.K. VANCE, Bristol, Tenn.

ORANGE SNOW.

One quart new milk, two cups sugar, one-half teaspoon vanilla. Add half of the sugar to the juice of four oranges and three lemons, and let stand two hours, stirring frequently, add rest of sugar to the milk and vanilla, and when half frozen add the lemon and orange syrup and turn rapidly.

MRS. D.F. McCARTY, Bristol, Va.

PEACH CREAM.

Mash soft peaches through colander, and to one quart of juice put one cup sugar, add one quart good cream, add more sugar, if necessary.

MRS. E.S. McCLUNG, Knoxvile, Tenn.

PEACH CREAM.

One quart rich cream, one pint peaches, mashed and strained, sweeten the peaches to taste, also the cream. Mix just as you go to freeze, as the peaches get dark by standing.

MISS ANN BELL, Knoxville, Tenn.

VANILLA ICE CREAM.

Soak one-half box of gelatine in one pint of new milk, one hour, then stir and melt over the fire till creamy, cool and pour in freezer. Add two and one-half cups sugar, three teaspoons vanilla and fill balance of gallon freezer with pure cream, freeze and pack.

MRS. THOMAS CURTIN, Bristol, Tenn.

PEACH CREAM.

Mash soft peaches through colander, and to one quart of juice put one cup sugar, add one quart good cream, add more sugar, if necessary.

MRS. E.S. McCLUNG, Knoxvile, Tenn.

PEACH CREAM.

One quart rich cream, one pint peaches, mashed and strained, sweeten the peaches to taste, also the cream. Mix just as you go to freeze, as the peaches get dark by standing.

MISS ANN BELL, Knoxville, Tenn.

VANILLA ICE CREAM.

Soak one-half box of gelatine in one pint of new milk, one hour, then stir and melt over the fire till creamy, cool and pour in freezer. Add two and one-half cups sugar, three teaspoons vanilla and fill balance of gallon freezer with pure cream, freeze and pack.

MRS. THOMAS CURTIN, Bristol, Tenn.

JELLIES, MARMALADES, & PRESERVES

GENERAL DIRECTIONS FOR PICKLES AND PRESERVES.

Wash jars and tops. Set them on a rack or dish towel in a vessel of cold water. Cover and bring to boiling point. When ready to use, remove one jar at a time, set it on a dish towel in a shallow pan of hot water, and fill to overflowing with scalding fruit and syrup. Remove all air bubbles by inserting a silver spoon around the sides of the jar. Wipe the mouth of the jar with a cloth that has been dipped in boiling water. Put on a new rubber and screw on the top. Turn the jar upside down till cold. Wipe off, label and put away in an even temperature.

Use fruit under ripe, rather than over ripe. For fruit lacking in flavor, as pears, add one slice of lemon or a stick of cinnamon to each pound of fruit.

Large fruit is cut in pieces before preserving.

Hard fruits, as quinces or pears are cooked tender in clear water and this water is used to make the syrup.

Put only a few jarfuls of fruit into the syrup at a time. Drain out all scraps of fruit from the syrup before putting in a fresh supply of fruit.

Keep fruit in cold water until ready to cook.

CONTRIBUTED.

GERMAN METHOD OF PRESERVING SMALL FRUITS.

Weigh, pound for pound, cover fruit with sugar and stand over night or several hours. Drain off syrup, boil and skim, add fruit a little at a time. As soon as thoroughly hot lift with skimmer, put on plates, cover with a glass and dry in the hot sun. Bring them in as the sun goes down and put out next day. Now roll in granulated sugar and pack in boxes.

MRS. J.H. McCUE, Bristol, Tenn.

JELLY.

Wash the fruit, if it is large, cut into pieces, leaving the skin on. Put it into a granite or porcelain kettle. With watery fruit, such as grapes, or berries, add only enough water to cover the bottom of the kettle. With fruit like apples or quinces, fill the vessel almost up to the level of the fruit. Cook till the fruit is tender, drain (without squeezing) through a flannel bag, and allow a pound of sugar to every pint of juice. Bring juice to boiling point and boil twenty minutes, removing scum as it rises. Add sugar that has been warmed in the oven, and boil till a spoonful will jell when cold. Cool the jelly slightly and put into tumblers. When cold cover with melted paraffine and put on the tin tops.

APPLE BUTTER.

Six gallons of cider, one bushel of apples, peeled and sliced, boil the cider half an hour and skim well, then add apples and cook up well before adding the sugar, flavor with cinnamon oil, and cook the butter till very thick, stirring to prevent burning. If you prefer, you can flavor with allspice.

MRS. JANE KENNEDY, Knoxville, Tenn.

APPLE BUTTER.

To three gallons of apples stewed and run through a colander, add two quarts white sugar, two quarts of brown sugar, cook down to one-half the quantity, flavor with a few drops of oil of cinnamon. "Sour Johns" make the best apple butter.

MRS. JOHN RICHARDS, Knoxville, Tenn.

TO CAN GREEN BEANS.

Gather, wash and snap the beans. Put in jar and fill to overflowing with cold water, then put on rubber and screw on top. Put hay, or excelsior in bottom of can or boiler, and put the filled jars in and cover with cold water. Let come to a boil and boil four or five hours, let cool, and then, if necessary, screw the tops again. Put in a dark place.

MRS. SLATEBLY, Bristol, Va.

TO CAN PEACHES.

Select nice yellow or white cling stone peaches, peel and quarter, or halve, or leave whole, if preferred. To every pound of peaches use one-fourth pound of granulated sugar. Put peaches and sugar with very little water into a preserving kettle and boil ten or fifteen minutes.

Use glass cans with glass tops. Place a very wet cloth in the bottom of your dish pan, which is set where the air will not strike the jars, set the jars on this. Having previously rinsed them in hot water. Have a tin funnel that will just fit into the mouth of the cans, pour in a cup of syrup first, and then fill with fruit and syrup to the top and seal tight. Turn the jar upside down and leave a few minutes, if any juice comes out tighten the top, it may be you will have to use another top, sometimes another jar, for to keep, the jar must be air-tight. When cold try the top again, sometimes you can tighten it a little more. then set away in a cool, dark place. When peeling your peaches, drop into cold water to prevent their becoming dark. Pears and quinces may be canned the same way.

MRS. S.B. BOYD, Knoxville, Tenn.

CANNED TOMATOES AND CORN.

Put corn and tomatoes, just one-third corn in a kettle and cook till tender add a little salt, pepper and sugar if you like. Can as you do fruit.

TO CANDY CITRON.

Select tender melons. Pare and halve them and remove all seeds. Make a very rich syrup with water and granulated sugar, allowing a pound of sugar to every gill of water, and placing both in a pan, set over boiling water until all the sugar is dissolved.

Place a single layer of citron in the syrup in a shallow vessel, cook very slowly until clear, remove from the syrup with a perforated skimmer, and place on a wire sieve to dry. The citron may be used as soon as dry, or rolled in sugar and packed in boxes.

MRS. WILL BELWAY DUENNER, Bristol, Va.

QUNICE CHEESE.

Cook quinces in just enough water to make tender, then run through a colander, and place on stove, in a granite pan or kettle and cook till thick. Put one-half pound sugar to a pound of fruit and cook till stiff, and when taken out in a spoon and cool, has a nice glaze. The fruit is weighed before cooking.

MISS SALLIE FAW, Johnson City, Tenn.

PEAR CHIPS.

Seven pounds fruit. three and one-half pounds sugar, one pound preserved ginger, three lemons. Peel and cut fruit in small pieces, add sugar and slice ginger, and add to fruit, boil lemons, and when done enough to pierce with a straw, remove seed and chop, then add to the other ingredients and place on stove to boil. Boil three hours, stirring occasionally to keep from burning. You can season with race ginger instead of preserved ginger.

MRS. BARNETT, Atlanta. Ga.

NUT CONSERVE

Thinly slice twelve large oranges, add the juice and grated rind of four lemons, six pounds of raisins, seeded and chopped, three pounds of English Walnuts, chopped, and one and one-half pounds of blanched almonds, chopped. Dissolve seven pounds of sugar in two pints of grape juice, add the above mentioned ingredients and simmer very slowly until reduced to a thick marmalade. Put in glasses and seal. Serve with game or roast.

This is a novel and delicious conserve, and should be in every store-room.

MISS BESSIE LIN ROBERSON, Bristol, Tenn.

VIOLET AND ROSE CONSERVE.

Pick apart half a pound of violets, put over the fire one pound of granulated sugar; add half a cup of water and half a salt spoon of cream of tartar. Stir until the sugar is dissolved and wipe down the sides of the pan; boil to the "soft ball". Add the violets to this and stir until the sugar grains and is rather brittle. While hot, break apart the leaves and throw-them on a screen to dry. Rose leaves may be conserved the same way.

MRS. WILL BEWLAY DUENNER, Bristol, Va.

CONSERVED CHERRIES.

To conserve cherries, select fine, large red cherries; stone, drain and weigh. Take an equal weight of sugar; put the sugar over the fire in a preserving-kettle and add sufficient water to melt the sugar, boil and skim. Add the cherries; push the kettle on the back of the stove where they will cook slowly until they are transparent. Throw on a sieve to dry. After they are dry, roll in granulated sugar and keep between layers of waxed paper.

MRS. WILL BEWLAY DUENNER, Bristol, Va.

SULPHURED FRUIT.

Get a sugar barrel; peel and quarter the apples. Put in the barrel about one-half bushel of the fruit, then fill a teacup half full of sulphur and put it down in the fruit, and set the sulphur on fire.

Put a heavy cloth over the barrel to keep in the fumes, and burn from two to four cups of sulphur, after each half bushel of fruit. Cannot burn too much sulphur. Have the barrel open below, so the juice will get out, as it is better. Keep filling with fruit, and burning sulphur until you have as much fruit as you want. Keep the barrel well covered all the time so gnats cannot get in.

MRS. J.L. DAVIS, Weir's Cove, Tenn.

QUINCE HONEY.

Four pints sugar, one pint water, boil until a thick syrup, add four large quinces, grated fine and cook until tender.

MRS. W.A. GREER, Knoxville, Tenn.

CHOPPED MARMALADE.

Chop sweet apples coarsely, make a thick syrup, allowing one pound of sugar to each pound of fruit. Cook the syrup until very thick, then put apples in the boiling syrup and cook until transparent, season with ginger or lemon, according to taste.

If apples are very juicy, take them out when clear and boil syrup till thick.

MRS. W.K. VANCE, Bristol, Tenn.

GRAPE FRUIT MARMALADE.

One grape fruit, one lemon. Remove the inside sections, the white skin and seeds. Use the juice, the pulp and rinds, chipped or ground very fine. To one pint add one and one-half pints of water, boil half an hour, or longer, counting from beginning to boil. Let it stand twenty-four hours in a bowl, then to one pint add one and one-half pounds granulated sugar, boil again one-half hour or longer, counting from beginning to boil. This will make nine glasses. Fresh grape fruit and fresh lemon insure best results. Orange marmalade may be made the same way, only take one lemon and two oranges.

MRS. J.F.J. LEWIS, Knoxville, Tenn.

MARMALADE JELLY.

Twelve Seville oranges, one pint of water, two lemons, and three-quarters of a pound of lump sugar to each pint of juice; wipe the oranges, then cut them in halves; put them in the saucepan with the water and let them boil about three-quarters of an hour. The juice should be strained off. Bring it to boiling point and let it boil for a few minutes. Now measure it and allow the sugar in the proportions given, put it and the juice into the preserving pan and let it boil till some of it jellies when it has become cold. If it does not do this it will require boiling longer. Pour the jelly into small pots and cover when cold. Sometimes Seville oranges are dry and hard, and if this should happen a little strained apple juice should be added, else the syrup becomes sticky instead of setting in a jelly.

MISS MARJORIE GOULD, Georgian Court.

ORANGE MARMALADE.

Six sweet oranges and three lemons, shred these and let stand in five quarts of water for twenty-four hours, then boil two hours, add six pounds of sugar and boil until it jellies.

MRS. BENJAMIN D. BRABSON, Knoxville, Tenn.

ORANGE MARMALADE.

Twelve oranges, six lemons, one gallon of-water, ten pounds of sugar. Wash the fruit, cut it and take out the seeds and grind it, soak thirty-six hours in the gallon of water, then boil tender and add sugar and cook until it jellies.

MRS. EDWIN FRAZER, Nova Scotia, Canada.

ORANGE MARMALADE.

The oranges must first be slightly grated and cut in half, then squeeze the juice from them and soak them in salt and water, two days, and in fresh water two days, (change the water each day) on the fifth day they must be put in a kettle of fresh water and boiled about fifteen minutes, then taken out and laid on a cloth that the water may drain from them, they are then to be boiled in the syrup, which should be previously clarified, one pound and a half of sugar to a pound of oranges.

MRS. WILLIAM HOUSE, Knoxville, Tenn.

ORANGE PEEL MARMALADE.

Soak peel in plain water several days, changing water every day, then boil in plain water till you can stick a straw through, drain off all the water, beat up the peel as you would fruit, till free from lumps add sugar, and cook till thick. Lemon peel will do too.

SCOTCH ORANGE MARMALADE.

Two dozen Seville oranges, or if sweet oranges are used put one-fourth lemons. Cut the oranges in halves, squeeze out the juice and set it aside. Cut up the fruit, rind and all, together, chop fine, leaving out only the seeds. Put the chopped fruit in a large bowl and add to it one gallon of water and let it stand for twenty-four hours. Then boil until tender, adding more water should it get too thick, and set aside until next day. Then weigh and add the juice which was set aside. To every pound of fruit, boiled, add one and one-half pounds of white sugar. Boil until the chips are transparent and the syrup jellies, this may be an hour or more.

MRS. BRUCE, Scotland.

BRANDIED PEACHES.

Choose firm white freestone peaches. Peel and weigh fruit; to every twelve pounds of peaches add nine pounds sugar, one pint water, put sugar and water in preserving kettle, and when it begins to boil drop in the peaches, but do not pile up. Let boil for twenty minutes, or until you can stick a fork through them. Remove with a perforated spoon and put in glass jars. Let syrup cook fifteen minutes longer and when cool add peach brandy, two-thirds syrup and one-third peach brandy, when thoroughly mixed cover the peaches with the liquid. It is best to put peaches up in small jars.

MISS VIRGINIA GREEVER, Chilhowie, Va.

APPLE PRESERVES.

Pare and core the apples. To one pound of fruit take one pound of sugar. Make a lime water by putting into as much water as a common painter's bucket will hold, a lump of lime the size of a walnut, put into this the apples and let them remain all night, pour off the water and pour on fresh water, letting them stand six hours. Make a strong ginger tea, in which boil the fruit till tender. Make a syrup of the sugar and ginger tea and boil the fruit in it till done.

MRS. A.M. FRENCH, Knoxville, Tenn.

CITRON PRESERVES.

Cut citron in thin slices, pare off outside, put in kettle with water enough to cover, boil until it can be pierced easily with a fork, skim the citron out and strain the water, put it back and allow three-quarters of a pound of sugar to a pound of citron, in this, slice two or three lemons and let boil till the syrup is quite thick, then put in the citron and boil. When transparent it is done, if boiled too long the citron will be tough.

MRS. JACOB THOMAS, Bristol, Tenn.

CITRON PRESERVES.

Pare the dark rind from the outside and scrape the soft pulp from the inside of the melon, cut in forms to suit the fancy. Soak in salt water three days, soak out the san, then boil in alum water till you can pierce the rind with a pin or straw. Put into clear water till the alum is soaked out, say two or three hours, it is well to change the water. To one pound of fruit take two of loaf sugar, make a syrup of half the sugar. Boil the citron till it becomes transparent. In two or three days take the syrup from the fruit and the other half of the sugar, boil and pour both over the citron. If any small white spots appear give the whole a few minutes boil. Drop in a few pieces of white race ginger.

MRS. JOE JOUROLMON, Knoxville, Tenn.

PEACH PRESERVES.

Weigh peaches, and to each pound allow one-fourth pound of sugar. Allow sufficient water to cover the peaches and add the sugar and boil as a simple syrup, skim and pour over the fruit and let stand over night. Next morning drain and make up as preserves with three-fourths pound sugar to each pound of fruit. Save the first syrup for flavoring, etc.

MRS. H.E. GRAVES, Bristol, Va.

STRAWBERRY PRESERVES.

Cover with a pound of sugar one quart of berries, stemmed, let stand till dissolved, or dissolve slowly on back of stove. Let come to a boil and boil furiously for fifteen minutes, let stand in the same vessel till next day, then put up in jars or tumblers and cover with paraffine, before putting on the tops of the jars.

MRS. B.J. STEPHENSON, Knoxville, Tenn.

STRAWBERRY PRESERVES.

One quart of sugar to one pint of berries, boil sugar till it becomes stringy in water, then put in berries and boil a few minutes till it jellies. Put only enough water on sugar to dissolve it.

MRS. EDWARD COYKENDAL, Knoxville, Tenn.

STRAWBERRY PRESERVES.

After the berries are washed and capped, weigh them, and allow one pound of sugar for each pound of berries. Sprinkle the sugar over the berries, in layers, and allow them to boil briskly for twenty minutes, using no water. Take them off the stove and allow them to become thoroughly cold before canning. If the preserves are made in the afternoon it is better to wait until the next morning before putting into the cans.

Have the cans sterilized as usual by boiling them, but let them be perfectly cold also when the preserves are put in, and fill them level full and seal as usual.

If these directions are carried out the berries will be plump and red and will retain their natural flavor much better than by the old method of putting into the cans hot, and the syrup will be thick and rich.

MRS. J.S. McDONOUGH, Knoxville. Tenn.

SUNSHINE STRAWBERRIES.

Take equal quantities of berries and sugar and let them heat to the boiling point. Then put in jelly glasses and place in the sunshine for about one week.

MISS GERTRUDE VANHAUSEN, Bristol, Tenn.

WATERMELON PRESERVES.

Peel and cut eight pounds of rinds, soak twenty-four hours in salt water (three tablespoons salt), and water enough to cover, soak again in alum water, three tablespoons as above, then soak twenty-four hours in fresh water.

Take one ounce white ginger root to one and one-half gallons of water, boil until tender enough to pierce with a straw, or cooked nice and tender, then to eight pounds fruit make a syrup of seven pounds sugar, put in fruit and boil till transparent. Season with cinnamon. This will keep, even if not sealed.

MRS. JACOB THOMAS, Bristol, Tenn.

SPICED APPLES.

Eight pounds sweet apples, pared and quartered, four pounds sugar, one quart apple vinegar, one ounce each of stick cinnamon and cloves.

Boil vinegar, sugar and spices together, put in apples while boiling and let them boil until tender (about thirty minutes), then put apples in jar, boil down syrup until thick, pour over apples and seal.

MRS. JACOB THOMAS, Bristol, Tenn.

SPICED CURRANTS.

Five pounds stemmed currants, four pounds brown. sugar, one pint vinegar, whole cloves, allspice and cinnamon, of each one tablespoon. Boil an hour and a half. Tie the spice in a muslin bag, which can be taken out when done. You can as well use ground spice without the bag.

C. C.

MEAT

A GOOD SUPPER DISH. (ORIGINAL.)

Chop any left overs of meat you may have, mix with enough chopped onion to season. Put a layer of bread crumbs in a greased baking dish, then a layer of meat, pepper and a very little salt, another layer of crumbs, then meat, finishing with a layer of buttered crumbs. Moisten with any kind of meat stock or gravy, or if you have neither add bits of butter to the layers of meat and moisten with water, bake about half an hour and serve hot.

MRS. E.M. BROWN, Knoxville, Tenn.

A LUNCHEON NOVELTY.

I take this porterhouse steak, which I have had trimmed of bone and fat and cut two inches thick, and put it on the broiler and broil quickly over a hot fire. I place it on a hot platter and spread both sides with this mixture I have in a cup: A tablespoon of melted butter, a half tablespoon each of salt and white pepper. On top I lay three plaintains which I have just fried in butter, the plaintains are red bananas. Over this pour half a pint of bechamel sauce, and over the whole sprinkle a tablespoon of grated horseradish. You will find this a delicious dish for a luncheon party.

LECTURE BY MRS. LEMKE.

APPETIZING FOR BREAKFAST.

Prepare a light batter in the following way: To four well-beaten eggs and half a cup of milk, add one tablespoon of flour and a little pepper. Fry till slightly brown on one side, eight or nine delicate rashers of bacon. Turn them over and then pour the batter over them. Brown the batter on both sides and serve on a hot dish.

CONTRIBUTED.

BEEF A LA MODE.

Take a round of beef, weighing five or six pounds, take out the bone and fill the space with rich forcemeat, after having made incisions all over the meat, fill with the stuffing. Draw the flap around, insert a wooden pin or two to keep it a nice shape, place it in a pan without cramping, adding about a pint of water. Bake slowly, baste frequently. Prepare your forcemeat as follows: One pint bread crumbs, two onions, two tablespoons allspice, one tablespoon cloves, red and black pepper and a little salt.

Chop the marrow you take out of the bone with a little fat of bacon or pork, if you have it, if not a spoonful of lard, rubbed into the bread crumbs, when the gravy boils away, sprinkle a couple of spoons of flour in one end of the pan to brown, then add a cup or two of rice gruel, that you pour off the dinner rice. When you take out the beef, if there is not enough gravy, rub a spoonful of flour into a smooth paste, add a little cold water, stir briskly and pour into the gravy boat. If the gravy is oily pour some off or add more flour and water. Season with pepper and salt.

MRS. C.S. KINGSBURY, Atlanta, Ga.

CORN BEEF.

One pound and a half salt to a gallon of water, one-half pound sugar, one-half ounce each of saltpetre and potash, let them come to a boil, skim and cool, pour over the beef which must be covered.

MRS. B.J. STEPHENSON, Knoxville, Tenn.

DRIED BEEF.

Two tablespoons of melted butter, add one-half pound of chipped beef. Fry until brown, add one and one-half pints of milk and one tablespoon of flour, creaming the flour with a little cold milk. Serve on toast.

CONTRIBUTED.

CREAMED DRIED BEEF.

One-half pound dried beef, one tablespoon each of butter and flour, one-half pint milk, two eggs, pepper to taste.

Place the butter in a small frying or stew pan, add the milk, and when hot, the beef, minced finely. Cook three minutes, rub the flour smooth in a little cold milk, add a dash of pepper and stir into the beef. As soon as it thickens draw the pan back, add the well-beaten eggs and serve at once. The hot gravy will cook the eggs sufficiently.

MRS. WILL BEWLAY DUENNER, Bristol, Va.-Tenn.

STUFFED BEEF HEART.

Soak the heart three hours in cold water, remove the muscles from the inside and take out every bit of blood. Open the large end enough to put in the following dressing; one-half pint bread crumbs, a little suet, chopped, a heaped teaspoonful, season highly with salt and pepper, add a tablespoon of milk and a beaten egg, stuff and roast till tender. If it seems tough, parboil the heart first and then stuff and roast.

MRS. W.K. VANCE, Bristol, Tenn.

BEEF LOAF.

Two pounds of hamburg steak (a little fat with it), one cup of bread crumbs, a small onion, salt and pepper to taste, two eggs, tablespoon of butter or beef drippings. Mix all well and shape into oblong mound. Place in pan in oven, with water as for roast chicken, baste frequently. When done, about forty-five minutes, place meat on dish and make a thickened gravy with the juices in the pan, pour over the loaf and serve. This is nice served cold.

MRS. H.N. SAXTON, JR., Knoxville, Tenn.

NICE DISH OF BEEF.

Mince cold roast beef, both fat and lean; add chopped onion, pepper, salt, and either butter or beef gravy. Put in a baking dish and fill up with mashed Irish potatoes. In mashing the potatoes add rich milk or cream. Put a piece of butter on top and brown nicely.

MISS MARY PLEAS McCLUNG, Knoxville, Tenn.

ROAST BEEF WITH RED SAUCE.

Take a four or five pound standing rib roast, have the butcher to take out the bones or break them. Put in a pan and set in the oven. Let brown and then baste every few minutes with hot water.

When it has been cooking half an hour, baste with a cup of homemade catsup or strained tomatoes, sprinkle well with flour, salt and pepper and continue to baste with the sauce in the pan, adding hot water, when necessary.

The oven should not be so hot, after the first fifteen minutes, and the roast will be done in two hours. Good hot; better cold; best broiled in butter for lunch.

MRS. W.N. PATTON, Bristol, Tenn.

SPICED BEEF.

Take a round of fresh beef, rub well with saltpetre, pour brine over to cover it and let stand for three or four weeks.

To Cook—Pare off fat and gristle and remove the bone, mix grated bread and butter, season with pepper, cloves, a little mace and celery seed, fill up the bone cavity, make a deep cut and fill with the dressing, bind tightly with muslin, stick cloves into the meat, boil in water steadily for eight or nine hours. Take off binding when meat is perfectly cold.

MRS. W.K. VANCE, Bristol, Tenn.

BEEFSTEAK.

Take choice steak, three-quarters of an inch thick, roll it slightly, but do not pound it, have your skillet quite hot, barely greasing it to prevent the steak from sticking, watch it constantly, turning it whenever it gets a little brown. When done it should be pink in the centre, though not raw. When cooked enough put it on a hot platter, sprinkle with plenty of pepper and salt, then add melted butter. Some think a tablespoon of coffee poured over it before serving an improvement.

MRS. H.H. TAYLOR, Knoxville, Tenn.

BROILED STEAK.

Wipe steak with a cloth wrung out of cold water and trim off superfluous fat. With some of the fat grease the broiler, place meat in broiler and broil over a clear fire, turn every ten seconds for the first two minutes, that surface may be well seared, thus preventing escape of juices. After the first minute turn occasionally until well cooked on both sides. Steak cut one inch thick will take eight to ten minutes, if liked rare; twelve minutes, if well done. Remove to hot platter, serve with butter and sprinkle with salt and pepper.

MRS. ELIZABETH O. HILLER, Chicago, Ill.

PAN BROILED FLANK STEAK.

Select a flank steak from prime beef if possible. Trim into shape and score with a sharp knife diagonally across both sides; gashes should be one inch apart. Sprinkle with salt, pepper and dredge with flour; placing in hissing hot, well greased iron skillet, sear quickly on one side, turn and sear on the other, continue turning until steak is richly browned. Add small pieces of beef fat to skillet when necessary to prevent steak from scorching. Reduce heat, cover skillet and let steak simmer until tender, turning occasionally. Spread with butter and serve with brown sauce.

MRS. ELIZABETH O. HILLER, Chicago, Ill.

BIRDS.

One can mushrooms, one tablespoon butter for each bird, one-half tablespoon Worcestershire sauce for each bird, salt to taste, very small piece of red pepper pod, one tablespoon port wine for each fowl.

Let all come to a boil, add birds flat down, and if the above is not enough liquor to cover birds, add enough boiling water to cover them. Move to back of stove, so that they will only simmer, and let simmer for three hours. Just before serving add one-half cup of cream with tablespoon of flour dissolved in the cream. Let all boil up once and serve on toast.

E.B.

CASSEROLE OF RICE AND CHICKEN.

Butter a mould, line it with hot steamed rice, about three-fourths of an inch deep. Fill the cavity with a mixture, two cups finely chopped chicken, seasoned to your taste, to which add one-fourth cup of cracker or bread crumbs, one egg slightly beaten and enough hot stock to make it stick together. It must not be too moist or too dry. Having filled the centre, put about one inch of rice on top, put on the buttered lid and let steam for forty-five minutes. Put or turn on a platter, garnish with parsley and serve with tomato sauce. Milk may be used in place of stock and any kind of meat.

MRS. JOHN M. ALLEN, Knoxville, Tenn.

CHICKEN COQUILLE.

Boil two tender chickens or a small turkey in as little water as will cook them tender, chop the meat very fine, make a dressing of the liquor, four well beaten eggs, four tablespoons of cracker dust, one tablespoon of butter, white or red pepper and salt to taste. Mix well together, put in a baking pan, sprinkle with cracker dust and brown in a quick oven.

MRS. BARNETT, Atlanta, Ga.

CREOLE CHICKEN.

One big fat hen cut up as for fried chicken, a tiny onion, parsley, celery, salt and pepper to season, one big generous lump of butter, two tablespoons flour.

Fry the chicken in the butter, take out, stir in flour and bit of onion, let brown nicely and pour over boiling water, stirring until smooth. Put back chicken and add boiling water to cover, pepper, herbs and salt, let simmer gently until tender, which should be in about two hours.

Always be sure to have a large enough vessel and do not let boil after the chicken is put back. Fine.

MRS. W.N. PATTON, Bristol, Tenn.

CHICKEN CROQUETTES.

Boil one chicken till tender, when cold run through a chopper, first removing bones and skin. Put a teacup of sweet milk to boil, have ready a dessertspoon of flour stirred in a little milk, stir this in boiling milk till thick as custard, add several pieces of butter and the jellied water in which the chicken has been boiled, pour on ground chicken, season with salt and pepper. When cold roll in oblong shape. dip in cracker crumbs and fry in deep fat.

MRS. EMMA BELL.

CHICKEN CROQUETTES.

Boil one chicken till tender, chop and cool, then add a boiled onion and a sweetbread, boiled and chopped very fine. Take one cup of sweet milk and boil with bread crumbs till thick, add a tablespoon of butter, mix all together well, season with salt and pepper, mix with the chicken, etc., and make out in small rolls. Dip first in a beaten egg, then in rolled crackers. Fry a light brown.

MRS. MARY CARTER, Knoxville, Tenn.

FRIED CHICKEN.

After the chicken is carefully dressed and salted, put into your pan a large spoonful of lard, flour your chicken, and when your lard is hot place the chicken in, cook slowly until ready to turn. Turn it carefully, put in a piece of butter, then pour a cup of water over it, cover closely and let cook slowly until all the water has boiled out, then fry slowly until a crisp brown. Remove chicken, which will be crisp and brown, yet soft and tender.

MRS. HOWARD ANDERSON, Beverly, Tenn.

JELLIED CHICKEN.

Boil the chicken till tender, using as little water as possible, remove meat from bones, chop very fine and season with pepper and salt and a pinch of celery seed. Put in a mould with layers of hard boiled eggs, sliced. Boil the water in which chicken led in which the was cooked till it is half boiled away, add a tablespoon of gelatine and when it is dissolved, and still warm, pour over the meat. Put in a cool place and when you are ready to use it turn out on a platter and garnish.

MRS. S.B. BOYD, Knoxville, Tenn.

CHICKEN PIE.

Cook one fat hen until the meat falls from the bones, six hard boiled eggs, cut in slices, this makes two pies, cooked in medium sized baking dishes. Cover the bottom of baking dish with strip of cooked pastry, add layer of chicken that has been pulled to small pieces, mixing white and dark meat, layer of hard boiled eggs with bits of butter, parsley, pepper and salt. Another layer of pastry, chicken and eggs; fill the baking dish with the stock that has been seasoned with one cup of milk, pepper and salt. Cover the pie with the uncooked pastry and bake in hot oven until brown. Never use the chicken bones in the pie.

FANNY M. PARK, Knoxville, Tenn.

ROAST CHICKEN.

Prepare a stuffing of fine bread crumbs, and season with salt and pepper, a little chopped thyme and parsley. Rub in one tablespoon of butter and the beaten yelk of an egg, but no other moistening. Sprinkle the chicken lightly with salt and pepper, then rub all over thickly with lard, and put in a baking pan with two cups of water.

Allow from ten to fifteen minutes cooking to a pound according to the size of the chicken. Baste frequently, and dredge well with flour from time to time after it begins to brown. For the gravy, boil the giblets in one cupful of water until done, then chop fine. Skim the gravy in the pan, stir in one tablespoon of browned flour rubbed smooth in cold water, add the giblets and serve very hot.

MRS. WILL BEWLAY DUENNER, Bristol, Va.

RAMEKINS OF CHICKEN.

Cut into cubes sufficient cooked chicken to make one and one-half cups. Have ready a cup of cooked and drained peas, fresh or canned, and a fourth of a cup of sliced mushrooms.

Melt one-fourth of a cup of butter; when hot and bubbling, add a fourth of a cup of flour and gradually half a cup each of chicken stock, cream and the liquor from the canned mushrooms. Season to taste with salt and paprika, add the chicken, peas and mushrooms and when all are mixed thoroughly, place in ramekins. Cover with browned crumbs and serve.

MRS. WILL BEWLAY DUENNER, Bristol, Va.

SMOTHERED CHICKEN.

Young tender chickens, about two pounds in weight are best.

Dress as for broiling, wash and drain well, salt lightly, dust with black pepper, and dredge well with flour.

Dredge the bottom of a baking pan thickly with flour, lay the chickens on its breast down, then cover the upper side with thin slices of streaked bacon, and lay over the bacon generous lumps of good butter. There should be chickens enough to cover the pan bottom, a single one is best cooked in a skillet. Dredge flour lightly over all, after the butter is put in, add cold water till it stands half an inch deep in the pan, cover with another pan, exactly fitting, and set in a hot oven.

Let it cook half an hour, covered, adding more water, if the first supply cooks away. Take off the upper pan, and brown until the overlay of bacon is crisp and the flour well browned on the pan.

MRS. WILL BEWLAY DUENNER, Bristol, Va.

STEWED CHICKEN.

Cut the chicken at the joints, making two pieces of each leg; cut the breast in halves and also the back; making eleven pieces in all. Put the dark meat in the stewing pan first and the white meat on top, just cover with boiling water, bring quickly to boiling point; boil five minutes, then push on the back part of the stove, where it cannot again boil, and keep it there until the meat is tender. A chicken a year old will require one hour to cook; two years old, two hours. If it boils hard it will be tough. When the meat is half done, add a teaspoon of salt. When ready to serve place in a hot dish. Put two tablespoons of butter and two of flour into a saucepan, mix. Add one pint of the water in which the chicken was stewed, you will only have about this much at the end of the cooking. Stir until boiling; add a dash of pepper; take from the fire, and add one yelk of an egg, slightly beaten, and strain it over the chicken, garnish the dish with small baked dumplings.

MRS. WILL BEWLAY DUENNER, Bristol, Va.

CHICKEN TIMBALES, COLD. (FINE.)

Heat one-half cup each of chicken stock and milk; add slowly to the yelks of two eggs slightly beaten; cook in a double boiler until thickened. Add one teaspoon gelatine softened in a tablespoon of cold water, and when slightly cooled, one-half cup of minced chicken, stirred in and the mixture poured into dainty timbale moulds and set on ice to harden. It is attractive turned out on crisp, green lettuce leaves.

KNOXVILLE COOK BOOK.

CHILLI CON CARNE.

Cut or chop two pounds of beef in small pieces, add a little suet or tallow chopped and salt to taste. Place the above in a covered pot in which you have previously heated two large tablespoons of lard. Steam till half done, now add two quarts of hot water and one or two tablespoons of Gebhardt's Eagle Chilli Powder, according to strength desired. Stir well and boil till meat is tender.

MRS. FRANK MAXWELL, Austin, Texas.

CURED HAMS.

Salt and smoke the hams in the old-fashioned way, and then pack them down in nice, sweet hay. Do not let the hams touch each other, and take them out as needed to eat.

MRS. J.L. DAVIS, Weir's Cove, Tenn.

HAM TIMBALES.

Allow one cup milk to one cup stale bread crumbs and cook, stirring almost constantly until a smooth paste is formed, add one cup cold boiled ham, finely chopped, season with four teaspoons butter, add salt and pepper to taste, then add the whites of two eggs, beaten stiff; Fill individual moulds two-thirds full of the mixture, put in a pan half full of hot water, cover with buttered paper, bake in moderate oven twenty minutes, or until firm. Remove from the moulds to a hot serving dish and garnish with sliced, hard boiled eggs and parsley.

MRS. CHARLES LEONHARDT, Knoxville Tenn.

HAM TRIANGLES.

Roll biscuit crust rather thin and cut into rounds or squares. Place on each piece a spoonful of minced ham, or other meat as convenient, moistened slightly with stock or warm water. Wet the edges of crust, fold and press closely together. Brush over with milk or yelk of egg and water, bake in a rather hot oven. Serve with a brown cream or tomato sauce.

MRS. HELEN ARMSTRONG.

BAKED HASH.

Cut some cold beef in small pieces (if underdone it will be better), add some boiled, sliced potatoes, a little minced onion, pepper and salt. Moisten with a little hot water, set it on the stove and stir until it is heated through. Then put in a deep buttered dish, mould into a nice shape, making the top smooth. Put in the oven and bake till it is quite brown, and has a thin crust. Corned beef is nice for this dish.

MRS. W.K. YANCE, Bristol, Tenn.

BEEF HASH.

Take enough scraps of meat to make about one pint and cut fine, one large Irish potato and a small onion, cut fine, pepper and salt, save as much stock from meat as possible, and if not rich enough add a piece of butter, thicken with a little flour.

Put all on together to boil and when done, serve in a hot dish.

MRS. D.Y. HENRY, Windstone, Va.

POTATO HASH.

Chop beef very fine. Boil about two dozen medium sized potatoes, take a piece of very fat middling or pork, chop it as fine as the beef, put it into a large skillet an.d after all the grease is fried out, put in the beef, and when it is browned a little, mash the potatoes and stir them in with the beef, seasoning highly with black pepper and salt. A piece of butter is an improvement. When a nice brown, it is ready for the table.

MRS. A.M. FRENCH, Knoxville, Tenn.

HASH SOUFFLE.

First make a cream sauce like the following: One teacup milk, one heaping teaspoon Kingford's corn starch, piece butter size of egg, cayenne pepper, dash of salt and some grated nutmeg. Let all come to a boil. Turn in one cup finely minced meat of any kind and let get heated through. Add two finely cut hard-boiled eggs before serving.

EMMA CHURCHMAN HEWITT.

MIXTURE FOR MEAT.

One pound saltpetre, one pound black pepper, three pounds brown sugar, eight quarts salt.

Dissolve saltpetre in one quart rain water, then add salt and dissolve it, then add pepper and sugar and mix together, rub the meat over with the mixture, fill all crevices with it and put extra thick coat on the flesh side, about like spreading butter on bread, then lay on rack to drain ten or fifteen days, skin side down, then hang up and smoke. This is sufficient for five hundred pounds.

Dissolve saltpetre the day before you wish to use it and make your mixture then so it will have time to thoroughly dissolve.

MRS. JOS. S. DONNELLY, Shaun's, Tenn.

DELICIOUS MEAT CAKES.

One egg, one pint milk and a little salt. Add enough Kingford's corn starch and flour in proportion of one teaspoon of corn starch to two teaspoons flour to make a nice batter, when griddle is ready pour on it a spoonful of batter; lay on this a spoonful of chopped meat; on this again a spoonful of batter. When first batter is browned turn with cake turner and brown other side. Fine for breakfast.

CONTIBUTED.

SAUSAGE MEAT.

Six pounds of lean, fresh pork, three pounds fat, twelve teaspoons of powdered sage, six teaspoons each of black pepper and salt, grind fat and lean, and season, and pack in a jar to use where wanted.

MRS. ANN BELL, Knoxville, Tenn.

BARBECUED RABBIT.

Boil the rabbit till tender and let the water get low in the vessel, put it in a pan with this water, a tablespoon each of Worcestershire sauce and tomato catsup, two tablespoons of vinegar, salt, pepper and butter to taste, baste frequently and serve on a hot dish.

MRS. THOMAS BERNARD, Chattanooga, Tenn.

PORK SAUSAGE.

Three pounds pork, fat and lean, half and half, ground twice, one scant tablespoon salt, one tablespoon powdered sage, one scant teaspoon black pepper, one good pinch red pepper, two small red peppers, chopped fine, mix thoroughly.

MRS. A.S. BIRDSONG, Knoxville, Tenn.

HOME MADE HOG SAUSAGE.

To ten pounds of ground pork put five tablespoons of sage, four tablespoons of salt, two tablespoons of pepper, one teaspoon mustard, mix well.

MRS. JOHN M. PRESTON, Seven Mile Ford, Va.

A SAVORY STEW.

Two pounds of fresh beef, some sliced turnips, potatoes, a carrot or two, and an onion. Put these into a sauce pan, cover with water, cook slowly for two or three hours, as the vegetables must be thoroughly done. Potatoes need not be put in at first as they require less time to cook. When the vegetables are dished, pour over them a gravy made of some of the juice, thickened with browned flour.

Dumplings served with the stew will be fund an improvement; they may be made of flour and a small piece of butter and mixed with water; boil them in a separate vessel and then put in the stew.

MRS. W.K. VANCE, Bristol, Tenn.

BRUNSWICK STEW.

A small soup bone, piece of boiling bacon, about one-fourth of a pound, if you have a chicken, use the small pieces, wings, back, neck, etc. Put in a soup kettle, let come to a boil, then let boil slowly for two hours. Then add one quart tomatoes, mashed fine, one-half dozen ears of corn, about one pint cabbage, chopped fine, four medium sized Irish potatoes, cut in small pieces, one large onion, sliced thin, one pint butter beans, a little okra, celery, macaroni, one turnip, season to taste with red and black pepper and salt.

Put in tomatoes first and other vegetables as the time of cooking requires. The stew will be ready to serve for a midday dinner. Take out bone and serve hot.

This may be made in winter by using canned vegetables, though it is better with fresh vegetables. If you like, you can add a pod of red pepper to the stew.

MRS. D.Y. HENRY, Windstone, Va.

GIPSY STEW. (CHAFING DISH.)

Put butter into pan, two cups of cold meat, chopped with a little gravy, add two chafing spoons of walnuts and cheese, add one-half stir thoroughly and put on cover, cook ten. Serve on toast.

MRS. H.P. WYMAN, Bristol, Tenn.

SCOTCH STEW.

Five pounds of the very best round steak, after cutting all the fat, bones, gristle and stringy pieces away, then pass it through a meat chopper and put in a pot; covering with water and let it stew, stirring occasionally to prevent its lumping. After it has stewed all the water up and is thoroughly done and dry, season with butter, pepper and salt to taste; this quantity takes a pound of the best rich, sweet butter.

It usually takes seven or eight hours to stew, when you first put it on drop a pod of red pepper in the pot. This is a nice dish for any meal.

MRS. J.W.S. FRIERSON, Knoxville, Tenn.

SQUIRREL OR CHICKEN STEW.

Boil squirrel or chicken quite tender, add Irish potatoes, green corn, tomatoes, okra, and let them all boil till very tender and the meat leaves the bones. Thicken as for soup and season with pepper, salt and butter.

MRS. JAMES S. BOYD, Knoxville, Tenn.

BREAD STUFFING.

Break stale bread into very fine bits and season with salt and pepper, add bits of butter and fill the body and breast of the fowl, putting in sufficient to give the fowl a plump appearance. For duck, add a little onion, an apple and pieces of celery.

MRS. CYNTHIA BROOKS BOYD, Knoxville, Tenn.

CHESTNUT STUFFING.

Shell and blanch six cups French chestnuts, cook in boiling salted water until tender. Drain and force through a potato ricer, season with one-half cup butter, one and one-half teaspoons salt, one-fourth teaspoon pepper, add one-half cup cream. Melt one-half cup butter and mix with two cups cracker crumbs. Combine mixture and fill body and breast of turkey. Half this mixture is sufficient for an eight pound turkey.

ELIZABETH O. HILLER, Chicago, Ill.

SWEETBREADS A LA BECHAMEL.

One pair of sweetbreads, one tablespoon flour, one gill of cream, one-half teaspoon of salt, one tablespoon of butter, one gill of white stock, six mushrooms or more, if you have them, chopped fine, two dashes of white pepper, yelks of two eggs. Wash and parboil the sweetbreads, remove the fibrous skin and fat and pick into small pieces. Put the butter in a saucepan to melt and add the flour, mix till smooth, add stock and cream, stir continually until it boils, then add the mushrooms and sweetbreads. When ready to serve add yelks, well beaten, salt and pepper, and if you use it, one tablespoon of sherry, and serve in a heated dish or individual paper cases.

MRS. W.K. VANCE, Bristol, Tenn.

SWEETBREADS WITH PEAS.

Put in the dish a teaspoon of butter, add three small sweetbreads prepared as follows: Stand the sweetbreads in cold water for an hour or two, then parboil and remove rough edges, membranes, sinews, etc. Then put in cold water and keep on ice till wanted.

When the sweetbreads have butter and are in danger of burning, add one-half pint of strong beef or veal broth, a celery leaf chopped fine, salt and white pepper, and one-half teaspoon of flour, browned. Turn the sweetbreads. When the sauce is reduced one-half, it is ready. When cooling, open a can of the best green peas obtainable, small French preferable, rinse by putting in a colander and pouring cold water over them. Warm thoroughly, put in salt, pepper and a tablespoon of butter. Serve peas and sweetbreads together.

CONTRIBUTED.

ROAST TURKEY.

Select a plump young ten-pound turkey, dress clean, stuff and truss. In trussing, use No. Eight cotton, because it will pull out easy, double it. Place the turkey on a rack in a dripping pan, rub entire surface with salt and spread with a butter paste, made by creaming together one-third cup butter and adding slowly one-fourth cup of flour. This is spread over breast, wings and legs. Place in a very hot oven and brown delicately, turning turkey often. Reduce heat when evenly browned, add two cups water to fat in the pan and baste every fifteen minutes until turkey is cooked. This will require from three to three and one-half hours, depending somewhat on the age of the bird. For first basting after turkey is delicately browned, use one-half cup butter melted in one cup of boiling water. If turkey is browning too rapidly, cover with a piece of heavy paper well buttered, placing over turkey, buttered side down. Remove the skewers and strings used in trussing before serving.

ELIZABETH O. HILLER, Chicago, Ill.

VEAL LOAF.

Three pounds raw veal, a piece of butter size of an egg, one heaping teaspoon of salt, one-half teaspoon pepper and two eggs, also season with onion, parsley, thyme, and a tablespoon of Worcestershire sauce.

Chop the veal fine, or use a meat grinder and mix all together and put in about two tablespoons of water. Mould in loaf, then roll it in eight tablespoons of rolled crackers and pour over it three tablespoons of melted butter.

Place in a pan and bake about two hours.

MRS. OLIVE MOODY, New Orleans, La.

VEAL LOAF.

One pound chopped veal, three eggs, one cup sweet milk, three onions, chopped fine, pepper, salt and celery seed.

Mix all well together and add enough bread crumbs to make single croquette. Have some browned bread crumbs, put them through the sifter, put what is to be your croquette in the bread crumbs and shape it as you like. The crumbs seem to sink just under the surface and become a part of the croquette, not an excessive amount of crumbs.

When all are shaped, take the yellows of four eggs, beat them, add one-half tea-cup of sweet milk, a little salt and pepper, put each croquette in this liquid, then roll in the sifted crumbs and put in a cool place until you are ready to fry.

Have a deep fat boiling, put croquettes in, turn till brown on all sides. Take out, put on brown paper to absorb grease then serve. You can re-heat these in the stove next day. Put a sprig of parsley in the top of each when you serve. Makes about forty.

MRS. JOHN M. ALLEN, Knoxville. Tenn.

VEAL RAGOUT.

Cold boiled veal cut fine, dredge with flour season with pepper, salt, and a little minced onion. Put into a saucepan with a cup of cream or milk, let come to a boil and add two hard boiled eggs.

OYSTERS

OYSTER PIE.

Prepare the crust and line a pie dish. Put a layer of oysters in the bottom of the dish, dust lightly with spiced pepper and salt, and continue thus until the dish is filled with a quart of oysters, a blade of mace and a cup of mushrooms peeled and sauted in two tablespoons of butter.

Heat to the boiling point, skim, strain and season with one-eighth of a teaspoon of salt and two shakes of pepper. Pour in the pie, cover with the crust and bake about half an hour. Before serving add a cup of stock to the pie.

MRS. WILL BELWAY DUENNER, Bristol. Va.

A FINE OYSTER PIE.

Make a rich puff paste and after greasing the baking dish, line with paste. Then season one quart of oysters with pepper and salt, one-half pound butter and half teacup of bread crumbs.

Put this in with the oysters, without the liquor and cover with paste, in strips. This pie will bake in one-half hour. If in baking, the crust browns too fast, put over it a paper doubled; if it looks dry, pour in some of the liquor, which must be boiled. Serve immediately, as paste is better just from the oven.

MRS. C.H. ALLEN, Knoxville, Tenn.

OYSTER LOAVES.

Allow one stale roll and five or six oysters for each person. Cut off the tops of the rolls, scoop out the crumbs and brush inside and out with melted butter, then put into a hot oven until slightly colored. Pick over and drain the oysters and plump them in their own liquor; season with half a teaspoon of salt, a good dusting of pepper and a few drops each of lemon juice and anchovy sauce. Add one tablespoon of cream for each roll. Fill the hot cases and serve at once.

MRS. WILL BEWLAY DUENNER, Bristol, Va.

OYSTERS.

One-half gallon of oysters, one-half pound of butter. Put the oysters after they have been drained in a biscuit pan, place the butter sliced over them, put a little salt and pepper, sprinkle with tomato catsup, according to taste. When the frill begins to show, take off. Stir all the time after they begin to cook, cook on top of the stove. Turn into a tureen.

DR. JAMES PARK, Knoxville, Tenn.

CREAMED OYSTERS AND MUSHROOMS.

Drain one quart of oysters. put three tablespoons butter in pan with four large tablespoons of flour, stir and mash lumps until perfectly smooth, and until it bubbles, then put in the oysters.

When these are heated through, add the juice that was drained from oysters, and a cup of milk or cream in which a piece of soda, about the size of a pea, has been dissolved. When this has cooked a few minutes add the mushrooms (one can thirty-five cent size), from which juice has been drained, cook until it bubbles. Then add two eggs, well beaten, very slowly, and immediately the last drop is added, take off the fire. Add one and one-half teaspoons of salt and serve on crackers or toast. This serves nine or ten persons. Stir constantly the entire time this is cooking.

MRS. C.S. NEWMAN, Knoxville, Tenn.

CREAMED OYSTERS IN PEPPERS.

Heat one quart of oysters to the boiling point. Drain and make a sauce with oyster liquor, cream, flour, butter, salt and pepper; add the oysters. Cut around stems of red or green peppers and remove stems and seeds. Turn the oysters into these cases, sprinkle with buttered cracker crumbs and brown.

MRS. H.N. SAXTON, JR., Knoxville, Tenn.

FRIED OYSTERS.

Take large-sized oysters, drain, sprinkle with salt and pepper and let stand ten minutes, then roll each one separately in bread or cracker crumbs, put into boiling hot lard, serve as soon as brown, season with butter, salt, pepper and acid sauce, or mustard and pickle.

MRS. R.S. HAZEN, Knoxville, Tenn.

TO FRY OYSTERS.

Drain the oysters well in a colander and season with salt and pepper. Have ready a pint and a half of dried bread crumbs; season slightly salt and pepper. This quantity of crumbs will "bread" fifty oysters, an ample supply for six persons. Thoroughly beat three eggs. Place a small quantity of crumbs on a plate and roll the oysters in it, adding crumbs as needed, until all the oysters have been breaded. Lay the oysters as they are thus prepared on a baking-board, sprinkled with the crumbs. Dip the oysters into the beaten egg, one at a time, and roll each in the bread crumbs again. Let them stand at least an hour if you would have them in perfection. Place a layer of oysters in a frying basket and plunge it into boiling fat, so hot that the smoke arises from the centre. Cook about a minute and a half, and drain on soft brown paper. Oysters fried in this way are brown, crisp, tender and plump.

"BLAIR"

MINCED OYSTERS.

One pint oysters, one cup toasted bread crumbs, one cup sweet milk, one egg, beat together and put in a lump of butter, size of an egg, melted, small teaspoon of chopped onion, two or three tablespoons of chopped celery, juice of half a lemon, salt, and red and black pepper to taste.

Drain and chop the oysters, add the melted butter last, put all in a vessel and cook ten or fifteen minutes, cook in shells fifteen or twenty minutes.

MISS ANN BELL, Knoxville. Tenn.

MINCED OYSTERS.

Mince two quarts of oysters fine, add one-half loaf sliced baker's bread, after it has been toasted and rolled into fine crumbs, add four eggs, beaten, one-half cup butter, teaspoon chopped onion, pepper and salt to taste.

Put on stove and stir until eggs are thoroughly cooked. When ready to serve, put in baking dish, or shells, cover with melted butter and brown.

MRS. ROBERT D. BROOKS, Knoxville, Tenn.

MINCED OYSTERS.

One quart oysters, one tablespoon onion, two tablespoons of celery, run all through meat chopper, put oysters, celery and onion in pan on stove, cook until tender, then add pepper, salt, butter to taste, also cracker crumbs, to make as thick as you wish. Transfer to a baking dish or shells. sprinkle cracker crumbs over the top, place in oven and when a delicate brown it is ready to serve.

MRS. RUSSELL, Knoxville, Tenn.

POACHED OYSTERS ON HALF SHELL.

Butter as many scallop shells as there are individuals to serve, put into each shell about six oysters with a little of the liquor, sprinkle with salt and pepper, putting bits of butter here and there over them. Set shells in a dripping pan, then in a hot oven. When done, serve on plates garnished with celery plumes, parsley or whatever is most convenient, and with toast points or fingers.

MRS. OTEY.

SCALLOPED OYSTERS.

Take the oysters from the liquor; place some in a baking dish or pan; grate bread crumbs and season highly with pepper and salt; a few celery seed over them and small bits of butter; add another layer of oysters and the seasoning; then pour over a glass of wine and oyster liquor, after grating bread over the whole. Bake till hot through.

MRS. C.H. ALLEN, Knoxville, Tenn.

SCALLOPED OYSTERS.

One can oysters, one cup cream, one-half cup butter, rolled cracker crumbs, pepper and salt. Place in the bottom of your dish a layer of powdered cracker, then a layer of oysters. Season with butter, pepper and salt, alternate the layers of crackers and oysters until your dish is filled, cover with the powdered crackers and pour over all the liquor of the oysters and one cup of cream. Place in the oven and bake thirty minutes.

MRS. H.H. TAYLOR, Knoxville, Tenn.

STUFFED OYSTERS.

Chop one quart raw oysters, put in a pan with one quart browned bread crumbs, one small onion, minced, one tablespoon butter, yelks of two raw eggs, yelks of two hard boiled eggs, a little lemon juice, salt, nutmeg, black and cayenne pepper to suit the taste. Set on stove, heat thoroughly, then fill your shells, sprinkling dry bread crumbs on the tops. Bake fifteen or twenty minutes just before serving.

MRS. E.S. McCLUNG, Knoxville, Tenn.

STUFFED OYSTERS.

Chop oysters fine, about three dozen will fill one dozen shells, mince one small onion very fine, add to the oysters with about as much bread crumbs as oysters, add nutmeg, cayenne pepper, salt, a little lemon juice, with the raw yelks of two eggs, and the hard boiled yelks of two more, a large tablespoon butter, fill the shells and sprinkle with bread crumbs. Bake about half an hour.

MRS. E.S. McCLUNG, Knoxville, Tenn.

OYSTERS ON TOAST.

Allow six oysters for each person, mince fine, beat together salt, pepper and a tablespoon of butter, and heat, when hot add the oysters, the beaten yelk of an egg and two tablespoons of cream. Stir and when the egg is set, pour over buttered toast and serve hot. This is enough for a small family, but if there are many persons you will have to make a greater quantity of dressing.

MISS RAGSDALE, Chattanooga, Tenn.

OMELETTES

OMELET.

Six eggs, beaten separately and very light, one pint of milk, a pinch of pepper, level, teaspoon salt, bake in a pan or cook in a skillet on top of stove.

ELIZABETH WILKERSON, Knoxville, Tenn.

OMELETTE.

Beat four eggs separately, two tablespoons sweet milk, one tablespoon flour and a pinch of salt. Grease the griddle with butter, pour on and when it begins to brown on one side, roll from one end.

MRS. WM. J. BROWN, Bristol, Va.

BAKED OMELET.

Three eggs, beaten separately, two-thirds cup sweet milk, couple of spoonsful of rice or grits, cold, or one tablespoonful flour, salt to taste. Butter a baking dish and beat in the whites as you put it in the pan. Bake in a moderate oven and eat at once for it will fall if allowed to stand. Do not put in the oven till you take the biscuit out to put on the table.

MRS. A.E. DAVENPORT, Chattanooga, Tenn.

CHEESE OMELET.

Make the same as a plain omelet, and as soon as it begins to thicken, sprinkle in three tablespoons of grated cheese.

CONTRIBUTED.

CREAM EGG OMELET.

Crumble two slices of bread in a cup of rich sweet milk, let the bread soak while in a separate pan, then add a heaping teaspoon of butter, pour the milk into the eggs, mix well, season with salt, pepper and onion.

Put into a well greased, then into a hot oven. When done take out and roll the same as you would a jelly roll.

Bake quickly.

MRS. SANDY McNUTT, Knoxville, Tenn.

FRUIT OMELET.

Chop raisins, currants, candied peels, oranges and lemons, figs, French prunes, or any similar fruits until you have a scant half cupful when mixed. They can be put through the meat cutter, using a coarse knife and having about equal parts of the different fruits. When the fruits are mixed add just a dash of powdered cinnamon. Put the mixture in a double boiler with the juice of an orange and allow it to cook thirty minutes. To make the omelet itself, break four eggs into a dish and beat them lightly and quickly, but merely enough to mix the yelks and whites together. Add a tablespoon of powdered sugar and a teaspoon of butter.

Melt a second teaspoon of butter in the chafing dish. Get it hot, but without allowing it to brown; then turn in the eggs. Shake the pan so they will not set. Let them brown until the egg is well cooked, lifting the set part as this is formed to allow the raw to run upon the hot pan. The moment the omelet is well set pour in the hot fruit, folding over quickly and turn on a plate. Sprinkle it with powdered sugar and serve immediately.

FRUIT OMELET.

Drop the yelks of four eggs into the mixing bowl, beat till thick and light colored, then and four tablespoons hot water, half a teaspoon of salt and a dash of pepper, then fold in the well stiffened whites. Remove the skin from three oranges, cut in long slices, reject seeds, fiber and white part, reserve a third of these slices for decoration, then fold in the remainder, first sprinkling with powdered sugar, at the same time add three tablespoons of orange juice and a teaspoon lemon juice. Heat this juice in a porcelain vessel and use in place of water. Heat and butter sides of omelet pan, pour in mixture, put over a moderate fire, shake the pan occasionally, very gently, and run a pointed knife to the centre to prevent burning. When it is puffed and it is found by raising the edges that the bottom is lightly browned, brown the top delicately on top shelf of oven or with red hot shovel. Fold once when turning out, but rather than allow overcooking which causes toughness, it is better that the omelet should show its tenderness by a slight falling apart or absence of folding, as both top and bottom being brown it is sure to look well in any event.

CONTRIBUTED.

PLAIN OMELET.

Break four fresh eggs into a bowl with four tablespoons of sweet milk, whip very thoroughly. Put a walnut of butter in the chafing dish, when very hot, run the eggs into it. Use a thin bladed knife until the bottom is loosened, but do not stir. When done, carefully roll the edge over until all rolled up. Serve on a hot plate.

OMELETTE SOUFFLE.

Break seven eggs, separate the whites from the yelks and strain them, put the whites in one pan and the yelks into another and beat both until the yelks are very thick and smooth, and the whites a stiff froth, that will stand alone. Add gradually to the yelks three quarters of a pound of powdered sugar and lemon juice to taste, next stir the whites lightly into the yelks. Butter a deep dish or a pan that has been previously heated, and pour the mixture rapidly into it, set the quick oven with coals under and on top of it and bake five minutes. If properly beaten and mixed and carefully baked, it will rise very high. Send immediately to the table or it will fall and flatten. Do not begin to make an omelette souffle till the company at the table have commenced dinner, that it may be ready to serve immediately on the removal of the meats The whole must be accomplished as quickly as possible. If well made you can turn it out on a dish. Send around with a spoon.

MRS. R.S. HAZEN, Knoxville, Tenn.

PIES

PASTRY.
To make two pies take two pints of flour, mix one with water and the other with lard, take the one mixed with water and roll it out first, then take the other and pull it out in a long roll, like a peach roll, and place it in the centre of the other. Roll both ways until it is even with the other, then take the whole of it and roll it up, cut into four parts and roll each one on the cut side.

MISS SUE DEADERICK, Knoxville, Tenn.

PASTRY.
One cup flour, three tablespoons shortening, two to three tablespoons ice water. Mix with knives, toss together and roll out. Put the water in last. Pat the dough with the pin and fold from opposite sides.

CONTRIBUTED.

PASTRY.
One pound of flour, four ounces of lard, divide the flour into two equal parts, work all the lard into one-half of the flour, work until it is a smooth dough. Take the other flour and make it into a dough as for biscuit, except do not work it quite so much. Roll it very thin, sift a little flour over it, and place the dough made of lard on it, roll until it covers the other dough, sift a little flour on it and roll as for "Peach Rolls" and it is done, cut off and roll out the size of your pan.

MRS. J.T. McTEEB, Knoxville, Tenn.

PASTRY.
One pound flour, three-fourths pound of butter, or one-half pound butter and lard mixed.

Wash salt out of butter, and beat the water out. Take half of flour and half of butter, work together and mix with cold water sufficient to make a soft dough; roll thin, pinch in some of the remaining butter, sift over this some of the flour, fold and roll out again. Continue this till all the flour and butter have been used. When rolled for baking, the pastry ought to be about one-fourth of an inch thick.

MRS. H.R. LENOIR, Knoxville, Tenn.

PASTRY.

One-half pint sifted flour, lump of lard the size of a walnut, a little salt, water enough to make rather a soft dough, work until smooth. Have ready a paste made of a generous tablespoon of lard, well creamed, into which stir flour to make paste stiff enough not to stick to the fingers. Roll dough thin on the biscuit block, which must be well floured to prevent sticking, sprinkle dough with flour and put the paste over it in bits, again sprinkle with flour and with the rolling pin cover the surface of the dough with the paste.

Now roll up as you would a jelly roll and cut into as many pieces as you want crusts. Roll these pieces out rather thin and bake in a moderate oven. This makes delicious puff pastry.

MRS. A.P. WHITE, Knoxville, Tenn.

LADYLOCK PASTRY.

Sift one pound of flour with one-half teaspoon of salt, add half a pound of butter chilled, with a fork break it and work it through the flour until it is in pea-sized pieces well coated with the flour, add one cup of ice water and mix well, using the fork; turn out on a thickly floured pastry board, dredge with flour and roll out thin; dust with flour, fold in thirds and roll out the opposite way. Do this three times, rolling alternate ways each time. For ladylocks roll out about one-quarter of an inch thick. Cut in inch-wide strips, beginning at the small end, wind the tube with the pastry ribbon, allowing the edges to overlap slightly. Bake in a very hot oven, and fill them while warm, if they are to be used as an entree, or main dish at the family luncheon. With a sweet filling they make a nice dessert, if desired for an entree, the filling may consist of green peas, asparagus tips, cauliflower, mushrooms, sweetbreads, game or fowl, cut small and made moist with a rich cream, Hollandaise or Bechamel sauce. The molds cannot always be found in the shops; but any tinner can make them; they should be five inches in length, one and three-eighths in diameter at the large end and one-half inch at the small end.

FRANCES PECK.

PIE CRUST.

One cup of flour, a pinch of soda about the size of a pea, two tablespoons of lard and enough water to make a stiff dough, this makes one pie.

BLANCHE MARSHALL, Bristol, Tenn.

APPLE PIE WITH CARAMEL SAUCE.

Line pie pans with carefully made pastry. Fill with crisp, acid apples, thinly sliced and moistened with a little water. Season with butter, sugar and nutmeg. Cover with pastry and bake until crisp, but not brown. They must cook slowly enough to make the apples quite tender.

Make a caramel sauce of two cups of light brown sugar, moistened with maple syrup, add a lump of butter the size of a walnut and cook a few minutes until it begins to thicken. Beat a moment and spread over each pie. Do not cook the caramel too hard. This is a nice sauce for cherry pie.

MRS. DANIEL BRISCOE, SR. Knoxville, Tenn.

BROWN SUGAR PIE.

One egg, one cup brown sugar, one tablespoon butter, a dash of nutmeg, mix well and turn into a pan lined with pastry made as follows: one cup of flour, a pinch of salt, one rounding tablespoon lard, rub flour and lard together and mix well with a very little ice water.

MRS. DAVID DUNN, Bristol, Tenn.

CARAMEL PIE.

One heaping cup brown sugar, yelks of two eggs, scant cup of sweet milk, big lump of butter, two level tablespoons of flour, one teaspoon vanilla.

Mix all together and cook until stiff. Put in cooked crust and cook several minutes.

MRS. S.R. McCHESNEY, Bristol, Tenn.

CARAMEL PIE.

Place three-quarters of a cup of sugar in a frying pan and stir until it turns a light brown, then add two tablespoons of hot water, when this has become thoroughly mingled with the sugar, pour in a pint of hot milk and remove at once from the fire. After the hot sugar has become fully blended with the milk, pour the whole over three beaten eggs, add a little salt, pour the custard into a crust and bake until a knife dipped into it will come out free from egg.

MRS. ED. M. BROWN, Knoxville, Tenn.

CARAMEL PIE.

Five eggs, one cup butter, two cups sugar, one heaping preserves, sour ones are best, one teaspoon vanilla, bake in crust.

This makes three pies.

MRS. ELLEN WRIGHT, Damascus, Va

DAMSON CARAMEL PIE.

One cup of butter, one cup of damson preserves, mashed, four yelks one-half cup of sugar. Beat very light and bake in pastry. Serve hot or cold.

MRS. HATTIE KING TAYLOR, Bristol, Tenn.

CHESS PIE.

Four eggs, one tablespoon flour, two cups sugar, three-fourths cup butter, one cup cream. Bake in a good pastry.

MRS. B.J. STEPHENSON, Knoxville, Tenn.

COCOANUT PIE.

One-half pound grated cocoanut, three-fourths pound powdered sugar, three ounces butter, whites of five eggs, wine glass white wine, one light tablespoon rose water, one-half nutmeg, grated, add eggs last and bake in pastry. Good.

MRS. OTEY, Bristol, Va.-Tenn.

CHOCOLATE PIE.

Four tablespoons grated chocolate, one pint cold water, yelks of two eggs, two tablespoons corn starch, six tablespoons sugar.

Cook until thick, bake rich pastry shells first, then pour filling in and whip the whites of the eggs to a stiff froth and put on top. Return to the oven long enough to set well.

MRS. ELLA P. ANDERSON, Knoxville, Tenn.

CHOCOLATE PIE.

Four eggs, beaten separately, two scant cups sugar, beat sugar and yelk together, four tablespoons of corn starch, six tablespoons of grated chocolate and two and one-half cups of boiling water, cooked together, till chocolate is dissolved.

Cool this mixture and stir into the eggs and sugar and cook until thick and smooth. Cook crust first, fill with mixture and put meringue, made of the four whites on top of the two pies.

MRS. KATE WALKER, Ebeneezer, Tenn.

CRANBERRY AND RAISIN PIE.

Two cups of cranberries and one of raisins, chopped fine, sweeten with two cups sugar, add a cup of water and a little flour sprinkled over the berries. Bake in two crusts.

MRS. SAMUEL HOSS, Bristol, Va.-Tenn.

CREAM PIES.

Yellows of five eggs, one one pint granulated sugar, one tablespoon flour, one pint rich cream.

This quantity will make two puddings. Bake in a paste. Make a meringue of the five whites.

MRS. C.S. NEWMAN, Knoxville, Tenn.

APPLE DUMPLINGS.

Peel and core the apples and fill the holes with butter, sugar and nutmeg, if you like. Inclose each apple in a nice pastry; place in a deep pan or dish, over which pour a little warm water, sweetened, melted butter and a little nutmeg. Bake till a light brown.

If the water should cook out before the dumplings are done, add a little more. Serve with sauce. One cup sugar, one-half butter, beat well and grate a little nutmeg lightly on the top.

CONTRIBUTED.

CONFEDERATE BOILED CUSTARD.

Twelve eggs, one-half gallon sweet milk. Beat the yellows with one teacup of molasses and just before stirring it in the milk add one teaspoon of soda.

REBECCA E. DAVIS, Virginia

LEMON PIE.

Three-fourths cup sugar, three-fourths cup boiling water, three tablespoons flour, one egg, yelk, juice and a portion of grated rind of one lemon, one teaspoon butter.

Mix flour and sugar, and the boiling water, stirring constantly. Cook two minutes, add the butter, egg yelk, and the juice and rind of the lemon. Line a pan with pastry and pour in the mixture, which has been cooled and baked until pastry is done. Cool slightly and cover with meringue, then return to the oven and brown meringue.

Meringue—Beat whites of two eggs until stiff, add gradually two tablespoons of sugar and continue beating, then add one-fourth teaspoon vanilla.

MISS ELIZABETH McCHESNEY, Bristol, Tenn.

LEMON PIE.

Four eggs, yelks only, two cups of sugar, juice and grated rind of two lemons, one pint of water, two tablespoonsful of corn starch. Let the water boil, dissolve corn starch in a little cold water and stir in boiling water, beat yelks and sugar together and add boiling water and corn starch. Make a meringue of the whites with four tablespoonsful of sugar and flavor with a little lemon juice. This makes the filling and meringue for two pies.

CONTRIBUTED.

LEMON PIE

Line the plate with plain crust, also put a rim around the edge. Prick the crust so it will not rise in the center, and put in oven and bake quickly. For the filling, cook in a double boiler until it thickens, one cupful of sugar, one tablespoonful of corn starch, one salt spoonful of salt, one lemon (the juice and grated rind), one beaten egg, and one cupful of hot water. When the crust is done, turn the cooked mixture into it; then beat the whites of three eggs very stiff and add gradually three tablespoonfuls of powdered sugar, pile it lightly over the pie and color in the oven a delicate brown.

LEMON PIE.

Three lemons, juice and grate, two cups sugar, one cup milk, six eggs, yelks only, two tablespoon corn starch, one and one-half tablespoons butter.

Bake in rich puff paste. Beat up whites with eight tablespoons sugar, spread over pies when done, and return to the stove until brown.

MISS NELLA C. MOSS, Knoxville, Tenn.

MINCE MEAT.

One pound tenderloin beef, chopped fine, three pounds suet, chopped fine, one pound brown sugar, three pounds each of raisins and currants, three-fourths of a pound of citron, chopped, one ounce of nutmeg, mace and cloves.

Pack in a stone jar and pour over it one quart of brandy, to every pie allow a tumbler of wine. The beef should be cooked.

MRS. G.M. BURNS, Knoxville, Tenn.

MINCE MEAT.

Two pounds beef, lean, two pounds raisins, four pounds suet, six pounds apples, six pounds sugar, one-half pint whiskey, half-gallon blackberry wine, one-half teaspoon cloves, four teaspoons cinnamon, one teaspoon each of pepper and salt.

Cook the beef till tender, cool and chop, peel and chop apples, also chop suet and raisins. Mix suet and sugar, raisins, apples, the beef which must be cold, spices, wine and whiskey and stir all well together, seal in jars.

MRS. S.B. BOYD, Knoxville, Tenn.

MOCK MINCE MEAT.

Bread crumbs, currants, raisins, sugar, molasses, vinegar, water, one teacup of each, mixed thoroughly, one tablespoon of cinnamon, one teaspoon salt, one teaspoon cloves and one teaspoon of nutmeg, a little ginger. Put in a good pastry and serve hot.

MRS. W.K. VANCE, Bristol, Tenn.

MOCK MINCE MEAT.

One cup raisins, two cups sugar, one egg, lump of butter, one cup bread crumbs, one cup vinegar. Bake in pastry crust. This is sufficient for two pies.

MRS. SANDY McNUIT.

MINCE PIE.

Pare and core two pounds apples, one pound suet, two pounds raisins, stoned, chop these separately, very fine, add two pounds currants, one ounce cinnamon, one pound sugar, the peel of one lemon grated, juice of a sweet orange, a beef tongue boiled and chopped fine, a little mace, rose water, cloves, one pint of Madeira, one pint brandy, mix well together, put in a stone jar and keep from the air. Whenever it is used, season more highly the quantity you wish with wine, brandy, rose water, orange juice, sugar, and some citron.

MRS. WILLIAM HOUSE, Knoxville. Tenn.

MOLASSES PIE.

One cup molasses, one tablespoon each sugar and butter, three eggs. Bake in crust, makes one pie.

CONTRIBUTED.

PUMPKIN PIE.

Three eggs, three cups pumpkin, two cups cream. one and one-half cups sugar, cinnamon to taste. Beat the eggs together, add pumpkin and sugar and stir, then beat in the cream. This makes two pies.

MRS. JOHN RICHARDS, Knoxville. Tenn.

PUMPKIN PIE.

Get a good, sound, yellow pumpkin, not too large. Put very little water on it and stew it. When soft drain all the water off, strain through a sieve while hot.

For a quart of stewed pumpkin take six or more eggs, a pinch of salt, a heaping teaspoon of ginger, about a pint of milk, two good tablespoons of sugar, put milk in gradually, the last thing. The main thing is to get in eggs enough, and if the batter does not look good and yellow add two or three more. A pint of milk may not be needed, or more may, judgment must be used. Bake in puff paste.

C. C.

RAISIN PIE.

Boil one pound of raisins, one quart of water and one cup molasses together for an hour, then add one tablespoon of flour, small piece of butter, spices to taste. Bake in two crusts. Makes three pies.

MRS. BRANCH KEEBLER, Bristol, Va.

SILVER PIE.

Peel and grate one large Irish potato; add the grated rind and juice of a lemon, also add beaten white of an egg, one teacup of white sugar, one of cold water. Bake in pie tins lined with good paste; spread the top with a meringue, set in oven and brown, then before serving, dot with bits of jelly.

MRS. RUSSELL, Knoxville, Tenn.

TRANSPARENT PIE.

Two-thirds of a cup of butter, one cup of sugar, yelks of two eggs, cream until very light, then add three big spoonsful of cream, bake in a crust and stir while baking.

Use whites of eggs for the meringue. The best pie I ever ate.

MRS. HARRY ANTRIM, "Eastview",
Buckingham Co., Va.

PICKLES

ARTICHOKE PICKLE.

Wash thoroughly and pour over them a strong, hot brine, let stand twelve hours or longer, if not convenient to make, soak for a few hours in water to draw out some of the salt, then scald for a few minutes in vinegar.

Throw away the vinegar and pour over the artichokes some fresh vinegar in which you have scalded allspice, cloves, mace, cinnamon and whole black pepper, some brown sugar, about two pounds to a gallon of vinegar. After pouring the hot vinegar over, add a few cloves of garlic, or a few onions. When cold cover closely and keep in a cool place.

MISS ANN BELL, Knoxville, Tenn.

CABBAGE PICKLE.

For a two gallon jar, take cabbage enough quartered to fill it, then pour on it hot brine; let the brine remain on it four days. Squeeze them out of the brine and pour weak vinegar over them, letting it remain several days, then take strong vinegar and put into it two ounces of cinnamon bark, cloves to suit the taste, and two ounces of turmeric, put this over the cabbage and tie closely. Add a good teacup of brown sugar and a few cloves of garlic or an onion or two.

MRS. M. McCLUNG, Knoxville, Tenn.

YELLOW CABBAGE PICKLE.

Select cabbage not too large, quarter and sprinkle with salt, let it stand over night; wash out salt and cook until tender in weak vinegar, into which turmeric enough to color a pretty yellow has been mixed. Throw this vinegar away, and to one-half gallon of good vinegar, put a scant quart of brown sugar, one tablespoon of ground mustard, mixed smooth, one small teaspoon each of whole cloves, whole allspice, whole black pepper, a few sticks of cinnamon, a little mace, a little root ginger. Boil for five minutes, place cabbage in a jar, sprinkle celery seed and white mustard seed between layers, pour the hot vinegar over; add a few cloves of garlic or one or two medium sized onions. When cold, tie up and keep in a cool, dry place.

MRS. A.P. WHITE, Knoxville, Tenn.

YELLOW PICKLE.

Take nice hard heads of cabbage, quarter them and tie up with thread; place in a jar and pour over them strong salt and water as warm as the jar will bear; let it stand two weeks; then take the cabbage out, place on a table, with a cloth on it, in the sun for several hours, then put back in the jar in plain cold vinegar, let it stand three to four weeks.

Pour off the vinegar, mix through the cabbage; small onions, celery seed, mustard seed, sliced horseradish and a pod or two of green or red pepper. Take cloves, nutmeg, cinnamon, mace, scald a few minutes in a quart of vinegar and pour over the cabbage; then fill up with cold vinegar. Mix the plain vinegar with sufficient turmeric to give the cabbage a good color, then add the spiced vinegar. The spices and the turmeric can be placed in little bags if desired.

MRS. S.B. BOYD, Knoxville, Tenn.

YELLOW CABBAGE PICKLE.

Cut and quarter the cabbage and put a layer in the kettle, sprinkle with salt, turmeric, mustard seed, grated horseradish, black and red pepper, celery seed, ginger, then another layer of cabbage and then spices until the kettle is full, cover with vinegar and cook slowly. When done, spread on dishes to cool and afterwards put away in a jar of fresh, cold vinegar, seasoned with mustard seed, made mustard, pepper, horseradish, celery seed, turmeric and other spices and a little brown sugar. It is better to put the spices in thin muslin bags.

MRS. HENRY A. CHAMBERS, Chattanooga, Tenn.

CANTALOUPE SWEET PICKLE.

Take ripe cantaloupes, pare and cut into moderately small pieces, cover with vinegar and let them stand twenty-four hours. Measure off the vinegar and throw away one quart, then to each remaining quart add three pounds brown sugar, one ounce stick cinnamon, one-fourth ounce cloves and a few blades of mace. Place the mixture on the fire, and boil hard for twenty minutes, skimming well, then add the melon and boil all together for fifteen minutes. Do this for three successive days, skimming well each time, then put into jars for use. When done, it is better to take out the spices, as they make the pickle dark, after remaining in it a long time.

MRS. HENRY A. CHAMBERS, Chattanooga, Tenn.

CANTALOUPE SWEET PICKLE.

Seven pounds fruit, three pounds sugar, one quart vinegar, stick cinnamon, cloves, allspice to taste. Put vinegar, spices and sugar on stove to make syrup, then put in cantaloupe and cook till clear.

CONTRIBUTED.

CHERRY PICKLE.

Seed cherries and weigh, cover with apple vinegar for twenty-four hours, then pour vinegar off and throw away. Put cherries in earthen bowl and cover with sugar, pound for pound and let stand, stirring from two to three times a day (getting sugar well up from bottom), for three or four days, or until sugar is all dissolved, then seal in jars. Do not use for two months after making.

MRS. ROGERS VANGILDER, Knoxville, Tenn.

CHERRY PICKLE.

Stone cherries and weigh them. Put in an earthenware bowl and cover well with apple vinegar. Let stand for twenty-four hours. Pour off the vinegar and put the cherries back in the bowl. Take the same number of pounds of sugar that you have fruit and pour on top of the fruit without stirring.

Let this stand for twenty-four hours again. Then stir up twice a day until all the sugar is entirely dissolved. Put in glass jars and do not use for three months.

MISS SANNA M. WEBB, Knoxville, Tenn.

CHOW CHOW.

Take one peck green tomatoes, five onions, three heads of solid cabbage, one dozen green peppers. Chop separately, then mix, salt well and drain over night.

Put in a porcelain kettle one pound brown sugar, half a cup grated horseradish, a teaspoon of ground black pepper, a teaspoon of ground mustard, a tablespoon each of whole white mustard and celery seed. Cover with vinegar, boil and pour on the pickles in a jar. Do this several successive days, then put away in glass jars.

MRS. J.N. MOORE, Knoxville, Tenn.

CHOW CHOW.

One peck of green tomatoes, sliced thin, throw over them one teacup of salt, let stand over night and then drain off. Chop very fine the tomatoes, take six large onions, seven pounds of cabbage, three pods of red and three pods of green peppers, chop them all separate. Take three quarts of vinegar, two quarts of brown sugar, let come to a boiling heat, stir in the above ingredients; let all come to the boiling point and add the spices; allspice, cinnamon, cloves white mustard seed, celery seed, two heaping teaspoons each, one tablespoon of yellow turmeric powder to give the whole a rich color.

MRS. T.A. GHORMLEY, Knoxville, Tenn.

CHOW CHOW.

One peck green tomatoes, chopped fine, sprinkle with salt and let stand over night, then drain and press out all the water. Add two medium sized heads of cabbage, one-half dozen pickle, one dozen onions, one dozen red peppers, all chopped fine, four pounds brown sugar, three ounces white mustard seed, four ounces ground mustard, one ounce celery seed, one ounce turmeric.

Put in a kettle and cover with good apple vinegar and boil thirty minutes.

MRS. S.R. McCHESNEY, Bristol, Va.-Tenn.

CHOW CHOW.

First prepare vegetables of all kinds as for table use and then cut up into moderately small pieces and put in a jar.

Take half a pint of good strong mustard that has been made up several days, half a pint of flour, one pint sugar and one gallon vinegar. Take sugar, flour, mustard, red and black pepper, celery seed, mustard seed, ginger and turmeric and mix with a little vinegar to a smooth thick paste. Place the vinegar on the fire and when it boils, pour the paste into it, stirring all the time, until it is as thick as boiled custard, then, while hot pour into the jar over the vegetables and let stand ten days, or two weeks before using. Cucumber pickles from the grocery with onions are very nicely prepared in this way.

MRS. HENRY A. CHAMBERS, Chattanooga, Tenn.

CHOW CHOW.

Chop fine one head of cabbage, salt to taste and set away in cool place till next day, then drain off all the water and put on a slow fire with one quart of vinegar, one tablespoon of celery seed, one-half cup of white mustard seed, one-half cup of green nasturtium seed, one-half teaspoon of black pepper. Stir all together until boiling hot, then seal.

ALBERTINE LUTTRELL VANCE, Knoxville, Tenn.

CABBAGE CHOW CHOW.

Four large heads of crisp cabbage, one quart of finely chopped onions, two quarts of vinegar, or enough to cover, two pounds brown sugar, two tablespoons each of ground mustard, black pepper, cinnamon, turmeric, celery seed, one tablespoon each of allspice, mace, powdered alum. Pack the cabbage and onion in alternate layers with a little salt between and let stand until next day. Then scald vinegar, sugar and spices together and pour over the cabbage and onion after you have carefully drained off the salt water. Do this for three mornings in succession, on the fourth morning boil for fifteen minutes all together. When cold pack in small jars. Keeps well. Ready for use as soon as cold.

CONTRIBUTED.

CUCUMBER PICKLE.

Soak your cucumbers in cold water until the salt is thoroughly extracted and then put in vinegar and let it simmer over the fire until they assume a pretty green color; then spread on a dish and let stand to cool, and when convenient put in clear vinegar for several days, then put in your vinegar, which should be previously spiced as follows: To one gallon of good cider vinegar, add one ounce each of mace, cloves, long peppers, black pepper, two ounces each of cinnamon, celery seed, white mustard seed, allspice, one ounce of black mustard seed, one-half pound grated horseradish, a handful of garlic, a handful of nice large raisins.

If you want it sweet add three pounds good brown sugar to every gallon of vinegar. Make a syrup of the sugar and the spiced vinegar and add it.

MRS. J.S.W. FRIERSON, Knoxville, Tenn.

CUCUMBER SWEET PICKLE.

Slice cucumbers that have lain in salt and water, about one-fourth inch thick. Soak the salt out and boil in alum water half an hour. Wash through several waters to get the alum taste out, then boil in ginger tea half an hour.

Make a syrup of one quart of vinegar, one pint of water and three pounds granulated sugar to four pounds of cucumbers, season with cinnamon, cloves and mace and boil till the syrup is thick enough.

MRS. SUSAN H. BOYD, Knoxville, Tenn.

CUCUMBER SWEET PICKLE.

Take cucumbers that have lain in brine, cut in slices about one-fourth of an inch thick and soak in fresh water until all the salt is extracted.

Cover eight pounds of cucumbers with water and add two ounces of powdered alum and boil half an hour; soak alum out in cold water and cover with fresh water and add enough root ginger to make a strong tea and boil half an hour.

Make a syrup of three and one-half pounds of brown or white sugar to four pounds of fruit, three pints of water and five pints of vinegar; add three small red peppers, one-half ounce of whole cloves, one-third ounce whole mace, one ounce stick cinnamon, one-fourth pound raisins, two lemons sliced, and seeds taken out, two tablespoons (level) celery seed, a few grains of black pepper, and boil until the syrup is thick enough.

CONTRIBUTED.

SLICED CUCUMBER PICKLE.

Two dozen large cucumbers, sliced and boiled for an hour in vinegar enough to cover them; set aside in the hot vinegar. Next day drain off this vinegar and throw away. To the cucumbers add one gallon of vinegar, one pound sugar, one tablespoon each of ginger, garlic, black pepper, celery seed, turmeric, scraped horseradish, one teaspoon each of mace, allspice, cloves, one-half teaspoon of cayenne pepper. Boil two hours, when cold it is ready for use.

ENGLISH PICKLE.

One dozen green peppers, one dozen cucumbers, one-half peck of green tomatoes, one head cauliflower, one quart small onions, one-fourth pound each of mustard seed, ground mustard, celery seed, ten cents worth of turmeric. Soak the cucumbers in salt water eight days, then soak in clear water until the salt is extracted, mix all the ingredients together (except the white mustard seed) in a gallon of good vinegar and boil half an hour. When cold, add the mustard seed.

MRS. H.H. TAYLOR, Knoxville, Tenn.

GERMAN PICKLE.

To one quart of vinegar put one and one-half pounds of sugar, one teaspoon each of white mustard seed, mace, cloves, race ginger, cinnamon, two and one-half pounds of peaches, pared and cut into quarters. Put all into the vinegar and boil until the fruit is soft, boil and skim the syrup every other day until there is no danger of fermentation.

This keeps nicely, only gets a little darker.

HODGE PODGE,

One gallon cabbage shredded, one gallon sliced round cucumbers, four onions sliced, four bell peppers sliced round, one ounce of white mustard seed, one ounce black mustard seed, one cup ground mustard, one ounce celery seed, two heaping tablespoons salt, two coffee cups brown sugar.

Put cucumbers and cabbage in granite kettle, stir in salt, add onions and peppers, also sugar. Pour over this mixture enough cider vinegar to wet thoroughly. Put on stove, when hot add mustard wet in vinegar and seeds. Boil for ten minutes, more sugar may be added, if not sweet enough.

MRS. R.M. HOSKINS, Knoxville, Tenn.

HOTCH POTCH PICKLE.

All kinds of vegetable for pickles, cabbage, cucumbers, young cantaloupe, muskmelon, green tomatoes, young corn, beans, onions, few green peppers and horseradish. You can use more or less, as you please; also green peaches if you like. Cut up small and sprinkle with salt and let remain a few hours. To each gallon thus cut up, put one-fourth pound of good mustard, rubbed to a paste with pure sweet oil, one tablespoonful each of powdered mace, cinnamon, allspice, cloves, celery seed, red and black pepper, two teacups of brown sugar, one ounce of turmeric, half a pound of white mustard seed. Squeeze the vegetables from the salt and water, put them in a stone jar, adding the spices and vinegar sufficient to cover, put the jar in a kettle of cold water and let it boil an hour. The largest portion of cabbage is used, the turmeric and mustard seed are put in after it boils, and more vinegar, if necessary.

MRS. MARY ANN BAKER.

MANGOES.

Take three gallons of good vinegar, put in two pounds of sugar, two small teacups of ground cinnamon, one box ground mustard, one handful of black pepper, the same of white ginger cracked, two pods of red pepper and some mustard seed.

Soak the mangoes, (small green cantaloupes are the best,) put them in a kettle with some alum and grape or cabbage leaves, and let them simmer till they are green and seem tender. Take out a piece large enough to clean them nicely, rinse well and fill with mustard seed, celery seed, a few cloves, a good deal of cinnamon, and some horseradish, scraped. Slice four onions and salt them, let them stand a few hours, rinse and put them in. One-half a tea-spoon of celery seed will be sufficient for the largest mango. Spread a cloth with beeswax, tie them up and let them stand a few days in the sun, then put away in jars.

MISS SUE DEADERICK, Knoxville, Tenn.

DELICIOUS PEACH MANGOES.

One peck of soft peaches, put in salt and water for twenty-four hours. Then take out the stones, return to the salt water for six hours. Make a stuffing of one-half pint of small onions, a little green ginger, one ounce of celery seed, one ounce of black mustard seed, one-third ounce of turmeric, a pound of sugar, or more, if preferred sweet. Mix this stuffing with enough sweet oil to make a stiff paste, stuff and tie up each peach and put in the jar, cover with cold vinegar.

MRS. MARY ANN MATTHEWS, Washington, D. C.

GREEN PEPPER MANGOES.

First, after gathering the peppers, slit between the veins and take out the seed, leaving stems on.

Second, prepare a brine of cold salt water, strong enough to bear up a fresh egg, which pour over. the seeded peppers, fresh brine must be poured over them for three successive days and the old brine poured off, care being taken to have the old water poured from the peppers inside.

Preparations for stuffing; one-half bushel of peppers, eight pounds chopped cabbage, one pound grated horseradish, one-half pound each white mustard seed and celery seed, two tablespoons of ground black pepper, some add chopped onions, two tablespoons salt, two pints brown sugar, place in jars and over each layer sprinkle a little brown sugar, crushed race ginger, cloves, mace, cut up onions, horseradish and a little cinnamon. Fill the jars with vinegar, then cover the jars as tightly as possible.

Stuff the mangoes and sew up the slit with a double flax thread, use a large needle and small wrapping twine.

MRS. H.H. TAYLOR, Knoxville, Tenn.

MELON RIND SWEET PICKLE.

Pare and cut the rind in any shape wanted, put it in brine for two or three days, then wash the salt out, put it in alum water, one teaspoon of alum to one quart of water, leave it in one day and night, then wash out the alum. Make a syrup of sugar and vinegar, three pounds of sugar to four of fruit, when boiling put in the melon, tie different spices in a cloth and boil with it. Boil till the syrup thickens. If after a few days the syrup becomes thin, boil again, repeating it till it is thick.

MRS. E. BOLLI, Knoxville, Tenn.

MIXED PICKLES.

One gallon of cabbage, one-half gallon of green tomatoes, one quart of onions. Chop all very fine and mix well, adding two tablespoons of salt. Let stand until next day, then press well.

One-half gallon pure cider vinegar, two tablespoons each ground ginger, cloves, mustard, three tablespoons cinnamon, a tablespoon each black pepper and allspice, two tablespoons celery seed, one and one-half pounds sugar; add sugar and spices to vinegar and boil half an hour, mix peppers and mustard with cabbage.

It is ready for use at once.

MRS. SAMUEL HOSS, Bristol, Va.

MUSTARD PICKLE.

One gallon cabbage, cut coarse, one-half gallon silver skin onions, two red peppers. Salt each separately twenty-four hours before using them. Then scald in vinegar separately, in which a little turmeric has been dissolved. Throw the vinegar away, and to two quarts of fresh vinegar, add three tablespoons of mustard, make smooth with a little vinegar. Bring the vinegar to a boil and pour over the scalded cabbage. Put in jars and fasten tight.

MRS. MOODY CHURCHWELL, Knoxville, Tenn.

MUSTARD PICKLE.

One quart small cucumbers, one quart large cucumbers, sliced, one quart small onions, one head cauliflower, four green peppers, one quart green tomatoes, cover with one cup of salt and two quarts water, and let stand twenty-four hours, then let them come to scalding heat and drain through colander.

Paste—Six tablespoons mustard, one cup sugar, one cup flour, two quarts vinegar, one tablespoon turmeric. Smooth together in a small quantity of the vinegar and stir constantly until it thickens. Stir pickles into paste. It is then ready to can.

I make my paste in a double boiler, then turn it over my pickle. It is very good.

MRS. E. V. FISH, Central Falls, R.I.

MUSTARD PICKLE.

Two quarts cucumbers, two quarts onions, one quart green tomatoes, two small tomatoes, six large peppers, two quarts cabbage.

Boil in cold water until tender; then drain over night. Make a dressing of three quarts of vinegar, put in a porcelain kettle. One more quart vinegar, one ounce turmeric, one ounce ground mustard, four cups sugar, two cups flour. Add these to the three quarts vinegar and boil until it thickens, then pour over pickle and stir all together.

MRS. C.T. LEONHARDT, Knoxville, Tenn.

PICKLE.

Two quarts cucumbers, cut up, four heads cauliflower or two heads cabbage, two quarts little onions, six green peppers, two coffee cups sugar, two coffee cups flour and two of olive oil, one gallon vinegar, one ounce turmeric, one ounce celery seed, one pound mustard.

Cut vegetables, soak over night in weak brine, in morning put on stove and let come to a boil with a small lump of alum. Mix condiments and let come to a boil. After vegetables have boiled up once, take out and squeeze, then put in condiments, putting back on stove to boil up once more. Seal in jars.

Cucumbers bought in bulk, put up in brine, can be used just as well, so pickle can be made any time the other things can be secured.

MRS. PATTON, Chattanooga, Tenn,

PEACH PICKLE.

Eight pounds of cling peaches after they have been peeled, three and one-fourth pounds of brown sugar. three and one-fourth pints of vinegar.

Put peaches in a stone jar, boil sugar and vinegar together and pour while hot over the peaches, do this every other day for a week. If at the end of the week the peaches do not seem tender, put them with the syrup in a kettle, and bring all to a boil, putting in at same time one teaspoon of whole cloves, a half teaspoon of whole spice, a small piece of cinnamon bark and a root of race ginger.

MRS. H.R. LENOIR, Knoxville, Tenn.

PEACH PICKLE.

Peel your peaches, pack in salt, let stand four days and nights, then take out, brush off the salt and dry in dishes three days, then put in water twelve hours and then add your spices. Put first a layer of peaches, then sprinkle spices, etc. To one gallon of vinegar add one-fourth pound black mustard seed, one-fourth pound white mustard seed, one tablespoon box mustard, one teaspoon cayenne pepper, one-half ounce mace, two ounces cinnamon, one ounce each of ginger, horseradish, garlic, four large onions cut fine, one tablespoon black pepper, one ounce turmeric, mixed with vinegar. The same mixture of spices makes delightful cucumber and cabbage pickle.

MRS. HOWARD, Tuskeegee, Ala.

PEPPER PICKLE.

One-half bushel of peppers, cut around the stem and remove all seeds, replace the stem. Make a brine that will float an egg, boil it and pour over the peppers; repeat this every other morning for three times.

Then prepare the stuffing as follows: Eight pounds of chopped cabbage, one and one-half pounds white mustard seed, one pound black mustard seed, one pound of grated horseradish, one-half pound celery seed, two pints brown sugar, one-half dozen onions, chopped fine, two tablespoons of salt, two tablespoons black pepper. Mix thoroughly and stuff the peppers; then sew the little caps on with coarse thread.

Put a layer of peppers in a jar, then sprinkle over them a large handful of brown sugar, some sliced onions, broken up horseradish, a sprinkle of white mustard seed, black mustard seed, celery seed, broken up ginger, cinnamon, mace, cloves, allspice a little broken up red pepper. Put another layer of peppers, then another, sprinkling of all these ingredients, and so on, until the jar is full. Mix up some ground mustard and pour half a teacupful over the top.

Fill the jar with the best vinegar. One or two cloves of garlic imparts a delightful flavor to any sour pickle.

MRS. E.S. McCLUNG, Knoxville, Tenn.

SPANISH PICKLE.

Three dozen cucumbers, cut lengthwise and crosswise, two heads of cabbage chopped, one-half gallon of onions cut and put in salt. One hour after salting squeeze all separately and add one ounce of celery seed, one ounce turmeric, one-half pound white mustard seed, three pounds brown sugar, one tablespoon ground mustard, vinegar enough to cover the mass thoroughly, then put it on the fire and bring it to a boil, add cloves, spice and cinnamon to taste. Put up in jars.

CONTRIBUTED.

SPANISH PICKLE.

One peck of cucumbers, cut in one inch pieces, two dozen small onions, sliced, one dozen green peppers, sprinkle a cup of salt over this and let stand twenty-four hours, put in a bag and drain over night.

The next morning cover with one gallon of vinegar, heated with one ounce turmeric powder and one ounce each of mustard and ginger.

MRS. SAMUEL HOSS, Bristol, Va.-Tenn.

SOUR PICKLE.

One gallon vinegar, one small box mustard, two ounces allspice, one ounce cloves, one-half ounce mace, one-fourth pound mustard seed, one ounce ginger root, two ounces turmeric, two or three pods red pepper or a teaspoon of powdered red pepper, two lemons. Pound half the spices. Put the vegetables in strong salt water and let stand three days, then take them out and wash in fresh water and put into the vinegar. If cabbage is used it must not be washed, but dried in the sun. The jar must be kept in hot sun and stirred every day. Any vegetables used for pickles can be used and may be added from time to time until the jar is full.

MRS. EDWIN H. FAY, Knoxville, Tenn.

SOUR PICKLE.

After the salt has been soaked out of the cucumbers, place them in a kettle and cover with vinegar and water, half and half, add a pod of red pepper and a lump of alum about the size of a hickory nut, pound the alum. Let them simmer till a good green, say half an hour. Take them out and drain, then place in jars. Boil a pint or more of vinegar with a pinch each of cinnamon, cloves, mace, black pepper, celery seed and ginger and a tablespoon of sugar. Pour over the pickles and fill up with cold vinegar. You may add a little onion, horseradish and white mustard seed, but do not cook them. If one does not like pickle so highly spiced, just use cinnamon, cloves and red pepper and put in without boiling.

MRS. S.B. BOYD, Knoxville, Tenn.

SWEET PICKLE.

Wash the peaches and put them in a jar; to every gallon of vinegar put three pounds of sugar, put mace, cinnamon and cloves in the vinegar, pour it boiling hot over the peaches, repeat pouring over the hot vinegar three or four times. You can suit your own taste as to the spices to stick the cloves in the peaches looks very pretty.

CONTRIBUTED.

SWEET PICKLE.

Boil together one gallon of good vinegar, seven and one-half pounds brown sugar, two ounces each of ginger, cloves and cinnamon. After these have boiled well, put in fifteen pounds of peeled clingstone peaches and boil slowly together two or three hours.

MRS. LUCY J. BROWNLEE, Knoxville, Tenn.

DAMSON SWEET PICKLE.

Take as much vinegar as will cover the fruit. To every pint add one pound sugar, cloves, spice and cinnamon to your taste. Boil the vinegar every day for five days and pour over the fruit, the sixth day boil all together.

MRS. SOPHIE K. HUNTER, Knoxville, Tenn.

SWEET PEACH PICKLE.

To seven pounds of fruit, put three pounds of sugar, one pint of vinegar, mace, cloves, cinnamon and mustard seed. Put the sugar on the fruit, let it stand till it makes a syrup, then add the vinegar and spices and let it boil until the fruit is cooked.

MISS BETTIE ALEXANDER, Lexington, Va.

SWEET PEACH PICKLE.

To three pounds of fruit take one and one-half pounds of brown sugar, one pint vinegar, with spices to suit the taste, boil the vinegar and sugar together and pour it your the fruit, let it stand all night, then boil the syrup and fruit together till the syrup is thick enough.

MRS. B.J. STEPHENSON, Knoxville, Tenn.

SWEET PEACH PICKLE.

To three pounds fruit take one and one-half pounds sugar, one pint vinegar, with spices to taste. Boil sugar, vinegar, and spices together and pour over fruit, let stand all night, then boil syrup and fruit together. So soon as cold, it is fit for use.

MISS SUE DEADERICK, Knoxville, Tenn.

SWEET PEACH PICKLE.

Pare the peaches and to every pound of peaches, put half a pound of sugar. Dissolve the sugar in vinegar, allowing three pints to every seven pounds of fruit. Put the peaches in a stone jar with cinnamon, boil the sugar and vinegar and pour over the peaches. The next morning set the jar in a vessel of cold water, put on the stove and boil until the peaches are done.

MRS. E.S. McCLUNG, Knoxville, Tenn.

SWEET PICKLED PEACHES.

Seven pounds of fruit, one pint vinegar, three and one-half pounds sugar, if vinegar is very strong weaken with a little water. Make syrup and drop peaches in and let remain till they prick easily with a fork, stick about three cloves in each peach. If you use ground cinnamon tie up in a cloth and drop in syrup, if stick cinnamon, put a piece in your can. This recipe is nice for pears also.

MRS. H.P. WYMAN, Bristol, Tenn.

SPICED PEACHES.

Five pounds peaches, not too ripe, two pounds brown sugar, one quart vinegar, one-half ounce each of mace and cinnamon bark, a few cloves and one tablespoon of white mustard seed. Bruise spices slightly and put in a thin muslin bag, boil vinegar and sugar, skim it and put in the fruit, let cook till tender. Pour off syrup, scald and pour over the fruit again for two or three mornings. Free stone peaches are best, cut in halves.

MRS. W.K. VANCE, Bristol, Tenn.

SPICED PEACHES.

To seven pounds of peaches make a syrup of one pint of cider vinegar, and three and one-half pounds of sugar, brown or white (I prefer granulated). After it has boiled put in enough peaches to cover the bottom of the kettle. When they boil take them out to cool, then heat again before putting in the cans. Boil a small bag of cinnamon and cloves in the vinegar and sugar.

MRS. MARY ANN MATTHEWS, Washington, D. C.

SWEET PEAR PICKLE.

Peel the pears, leaving on the stems and boil until tender in enough water to cover them. Then to seven pounds fruit add three pounds of sugar, one quart best vinegar with mace, cloves, allspice and cinnamon to taste. Boil all together until the syrup thickens.

MRS. JOHN M. BROOKS, Knoxville, Tenn.

SPICED PLUMS, DAMSONS.

Six pounds plums, three pounds sugar, three teaspoons cinnamon, one and one-half teaspoons cloves, two teaspoons mace, three teaspoons allspice and a pint of vinegar. Boil slowly until thick, say about three hours, stirring frequently. This is fine.

MRS. ELLA WICKS, Knoxville, Tenn.

GREEN TOMATO PICKLE.

Slice one peck of green tomatoes and one dozen large onions, sprinkle each layer with a little salt and set away for twenty-four hours. Drain through a sieve and put into a kettle with pepper pods, one-fourth of a pound of mustard seed, one ounce each of allspice, mace, black pepper, one-half ounce cloves, two pounds brown sugar, cover the whole with strong vinegar and allow it to simmer until the tomatoes look clear. When done add one box mustard.

MRS. HENRY A. CHAMBERS, Chattanooga, Tenn.

GREEN TOMATO SWEET PICKLE.

Slice and boil in ginger water, green tomatoes, until the wild taste is removed, then to two pounds tomatoes add one and one-fourth pound sugar and one pint vinegar, spice highly with cinnamon, mace and cloves and boil for a few minutes.

MRS. HENRY A. CHAMBERS, Chattanooga, Tenn.

RIPE TOMATO PICKLE.

Take small ripe pear shaped tomatoes, prick each with a fork, pack in salt, alternate layers and let stand eight days, then for one night let them stand in vinegar. To one peck tomatoes add one box good mustard, one-half ounce each of cloves and pepper and one dozen large onions; slice onions and let them stand in salt one night. Fill a jar with alternate layers and cover with good vinegar.

MRS. SOPHIE K. HUNTER, Knoxville, Tenn.

SWEET TOMATO PICKLE.

Slice green tomatoes about one-fourth of an inch thick, boil in ginger water until the wild taste is removed. To two pounds of tomatoes add one and one-half pounds sugar, one pint good vinegar and spice with cloves, cinnamon and a little mace. Boil until syrup seems rich and thick.

MRS. A.P. WHITE, Knoxville, Tenn.

UNIVERSAL PICKLE.

One gallon best vinegar, one-half pint salt, one pound brown sugar, two ounces each of cloves, allspice, mace, ground ginger, white mustard seed, black pepper, and turmeric; if desired, one box mustard, three dozen sliced onions, a little horseradish. Mix all well together and drop in your vegetables as you gather them, having them perfectly dry; can use any kind. Set jar in the sun a few days and stir up frequently.

MRS. W.K. VANCE, Bristol, Tenn.

VIRGINIA MIXED.

One-half peck green tomatoes, twenty-five medium sized cucumbers, fifteen large onions, one-half peck small onions, four heads cabbage, one pint horseradish, one-half pound white mustard seed, one-fourth pound ground mustard, one-half cup ground black pepper, one-half pint salad oil, one ounce celery seed, one-half ounce ground cinnamon, two ounces turmeric.

Cut up vegetables coarsely, mix with salt thoroughly, let stand twenty-four hours, drain and put vinegar and water over it, let stand a day or two, drain and mix thoroughly. Boil one and one-half gallons cider vinegar and pour over three mornings, the last time add one pound sugar, mix oil and ground mustard in a little of the vinegar and pour over the pickles when they are cold.

MRS. W.K. VANCE, Bristol, Tenn.

PUDDINGS

ALL THE YEAR ROUND PUDDING.
Line a pie dish with paste, spread on this three ounces of any kind of jam, raspberry is the best, then beat well in a basin the following: three ounces bread crumbs, the same of sugar and of butter, the rind and juice of half a large lemon; add this to the pastry and jam and bake half an hour.

MRS. JOHN M. ALLEN, Knoxville, Tenn.

APPLE PUDDING.
One teacup stewed apples, one teacup of sugar, four eggs, butter the size of an egg, one-half teaspoon of lemon.

"MIMIE", Knoxville, Tenn.

GREAT GRANDMA'S APPLE PUDDING.
One pound of sugar, one pound of butter, one pound of stewed apples, twelve eggs, beaten light, flavor to the taste. Bake in puff paste. You can use sweet or Irish potatoes or mush instead of apples.

MRS. ISABELLA STEPHENSON BOYD, Knoxville, Tenn.

"THAT LITTLE APPLE PUDDING."
Two cups fine apple sauce, two yelks, sugar, nutmeg. Beat well. Meringue.

MRS. HATTIE KING TAYLOR, Bristol, Tenn.

TWO APPLE PUDDINGS.
Beat one-half pound butter and one-half pound sugar to a cream, add six eggs, leaving out the whites of three, a glass of wine, brandy, rose water each, a little cinnamon and nutmeg. Stew the apples and mash through a colander, throw in the peel of an orange while stewing, when cool put half a pound of apples into the other ingredients, should it not be sufficiently acid, add the juice of an orange, bake in puff taste.

MRS. WILLIAM HOUSE, Knoxville, Tenn.

APPLE CUSTARD.

Two teacups of apples, stewed and strained, two teacups sugar, one teacup butter, seven yelks, the juice of one lemon. Take the whites of five eggs and half a cupful of sugar, beat very light and spread over the pudding, brown slightly.

MRS. C.S. NEWMAN, Knoxville, Tenn.

BAKED BLACKBERRY PUDDING.

One quart flour, one pint molasses, teaspoon soda in molasses, three pints berries, a little salt. Bake about an hour and a half in covered dish in moderate oven. Serve with flavored hard sauce.

MRS. W.U. GREENE, Brooklyn, N. Y.

BAKED INDIAN PUDDING.

Scald three pints new milk, stir in it one pint of fine Indian meal. When cool add salt, seven eggs, one-half pound raisins, one-fourth pound butter, sugar and spice to the taste. Bake in a tin pan an hour and a half.

MRS. WILLIAM HOUSE, Knoxville, Tenn.

BAKEWELL PUDDING.

Line a baking dish with pastry. Put in a layer of acid preserves, then beat four eggs with one teacup of sugar and one of melted butter, pour this over the preserves and bake without a top crust.

MRS. MARY McCLUNG, Knoxville, Tenn.

BISHOP DUDLEY PUDDING.

Five eggs, beaten separately and beaten very light, three teacups of flour, one of granulated sugar, one of butter, one of cream or rich milk, one-half pound of raisins, after they are stoned, two ounces candied orange peel, steam or boil three or four hours. The mould should be too close for water to get in, or better not to submerge it. Eat with Fairy sauce.

LUCY ASHMORE, Sanibel, Fla.

BOILED PUDDING.

Two teacups chopped suet, one cup each of molasses and sweet milk, two cups raisins, one teaspoon each of cream of tartar and soda, and salt, three and one-half cups flour. Mix all carefully, give a good beat up. Tie in a square of cloth which has been wet in boiling water and well floured, put in boiling water and let boil hard for three hours, turning several times. I put half a cup of sugar in molasses to make it sweet, but the receipt does not call for it.

MRS. McCRUM, Lexington, Va.

BOILED PUDDING.

One pint of milk, six tablespoons of flour, two eggs, pinch of salt. Boil one hour and eat with sauce.

C. C.

BREAD PUDDING.

One pint grated bread, one quart milk, tablespoon of butter, one cup sugar, four eggs, season with some essence. Whites of eggs may be made into a meringue for the top. The above is particularly nice when seasoned with a lemon. Grate the rind in the pudding and put the juice in the meringue.

MRS. W. E. BELCHER, Knoxville, Tenn.

BREAD PUDDING.

Slice bread, not too thick, spread each piece with butter and acid jelly, cherry or strawberry preserves. Pack into baking dish, pour over this one quart sweet milk with one cup sugar and the yelks of four eggs, stirred well into it. Bake until brown on top, eat with hot sauce in winter, in summer use plain cream.

MRS. WILL HAZEN, Knoxville, Tenn.

BROWN BETTY.

Grease a pudding dish with butter, put into this a layer of nice cooking apples, chopped fine, then a layer of bread crumbs, with sugar sprinkled over and bits of butter. Repeat layer of apples and of bread crumbs until dish is nearly full, having crumbs, butter and sugar on top. Pour one cup of boiling water on and cover until done, then remove lid and let the top brown. Eat with cream and sugar, or clear sauce.

MRS. ALLEN S. MEBANE, Knoxville, Tenn.

CARAMEL CUSTARD.

One quart milk, five eggs, one and one-half cups sugar, teaspoon vanilla, one-half teaspoon salt. Scald the milk, add to the sugar, after stirring constantly until melted and light brown. Beat the eggs slightly, add salt and pour in the hot milk. Add vanilla, strain into a buttered mould, set in a pan of hot water and bake about thirty minutes.

MRS. MARY JONES.

CARAMEL PUDDING.

One quart milk, yelks four eggs, one large cup of brown sugar (browned until melted), three large table-spoons corn starch dissolved in a little milk. Let milk come to a boil and pour into the beaten eggs. Add brown sugar, then corn starch. Let this boil until thick. Pour into pudding pan, flavor with vanilla. Make a meringue of whites and set in oven to brown slightly. Serve cold with whipped cream. (Use double boiler for boiling custard.)

CARAMEL PUDDING.

One cup brown sugar, one quart sweet milk, four eggs, four tablespoons corn starch, one tablespoon of butter. Place sugar in pan, put in the oven to brown, watch carefully, as sugar burns quickly, after it is browned put in milk and let it dissolve, cook in a double boiler. After the sugar has melted add the beaten yelks and corn starch and let all cook until thick (this should be smooth and velvety), remove from the fire, beat and add butter, flavor with vanilla and put in a baking dish. Beat the four whites with four tablespoons of white sugar, spread on pudding and bake till light brown, serve cold. It is delicious with cream, plain or whipped.

MRS. H. SPENCER, New York City.

CHESS CAKE.

Yelks of twelve eggs, one pound white sugar, one pound butter, flavor to taste. Beat all together and cook in double boiler until the consistency of thick cream, then bake in pie tins lined with tea cake dough, made by the following receipt: Four eggs, three cups sugar, one cup of butter, one-half cup of buttermilk, with one scant teaspoon of soda dissolved in it. Enough flour to make a dough stiff enough to roll, flavor with lemon. Bake in oven and when cool stack together with boiled icing.

MRS. ARCHER A. PHLEGAR, Bristol, Va.-Tenn.

CHOCOLATE PUDDING.

One pint of sweet milk, one-half cup of sugar, one tablespoon of corn starch, one and one-half tablespoons of grated chocolate, vanilla to taste. Put corn starch, sugar and chocolate in the cold milk, put on the stove and stir all the time, by the time the chocolate is melted the pudding is done. Put in a mould and serve with whipped cream.

MRS. A.S. BIRDSONG, Knoxville, Tenn.

CITRON CUSTARD. (PREACHER PIE.)

Eight eggs, one and one-half cups sugar, three-fourths cup butter. Beat yelks well with the sugar, add butter creamed. Put pastry on pans and line with bits of citron and whole seeded raisins, over this pour above mixture and bake one hour. With whites and eight tablespoons sugar make meringue and spread on pies and put in oven until brown. This makes two pies.

MRS. JAMES A. HENSLEY, Knoxville, Tenn.

COCOANUT PUDDING.

Yelks of four eggs, one pint of grated cocoanut, one pint of sugar, one-half cup of butter, three-fourths cup of sweet milk. Bake in crust.

COCOANUT PUDDING.

Whites of six eggs, three-fourths pound sugar, one-half pound cocoanut, one teaspoon corn starch, one pint sweet milk. Add more milk if you wish to make more than three puddings. Bake in rich pastry.

MRS. J.W.S. FRIERSON, Knoxville, Tenn

COCOANUT PUDDING.

The whites of six or eight eggs well-beaten, a tablespoon of sugar to each egg, one tablespoon of butter, grated cocoanut to make it pretty stiff. Grate the cocoanut, cream the butter, put sugar and cocoanut into the butter, and lastly, the eggs, bake in pastry, bake a light brown.

COCOANUT PUDDING.

One cocoanut, grated, one and three-fourth pounds sugar, one half-pound butter, eight eggs. Cream butter, add sugar and eggs well beaten, two wine glasses wine, and cocoanut. Bake in pastry when done, cover with the whites of the eggs, heaten stiff with a little sugar, brown nicely.

MRS. SOPHIE K. HUNTER, Knoxville, Tenn.

COCOANUT PUDDING.

One can condensed milk, one-half loaf bread, stale, one large tablespoon of butter, one-half pound of cocoanut, nine eggs, sweeten to taste. Soak bread in enough milk to moisten, put all together and stir. Bake about one hour, the slower the better.

"UNCLE JOHN," Cook on the "Emson", Caloosahatchie River, Fla.

CORN STARCH PUDDING.

Two eggs, three tablespoons corn starch, a good teacup of sugar, three pints milk, one teaspoon of lemon. Flavor with lemon and serve with whipped cream.

MRS. A.P. WHITE, Knoxville, Tenn.

COTTAGE PUDDING.

One pint flour, one-half pint of sugar, one-eighth pound of butter, two eggs, one-half pint of sweet milk, two teaspoons of baking powder. Bake one-half hour. To be eaten with sauce.

MRS. JOHN T. BRUCE, New York City.

COTTAGE PUDDING.

One cup sugar, one egg, one cup milk, one large cup flour, three tablespoons melted butter, two teaspoons cream of tartar, one teaspoon soda. Bake half an hour.

MRS. J.A. RAYL, Knoxville, Tenn.

DATE PUDDING.

Whites of eleven eggs, one pound sugar, one-third pound pecan meats (broken), one pound dates (seeded), flavor with vanilla. Beat eggs until stiff, add fruit, nuts, sugar and vanilla. Bake slowly until brown. Serve with whipped cream. If entire amount is made it is better to use two baking pans. It should be eaten the day it is made and it is served without sauce.

DATE PUDDING.

One cup each of dates, English walnuts, ann sugar, two eggs, two heaping tablespoons flour, one teaspoon baking powder, and vanilla to flavor. Bake forty minutes in well buttered pans, serve hot, with whipped cream.

MRS. H.M. SIMMONDS, Knoxville, Tenn.

DELMONICO PUDDING.

One quart sweet milk, four eggs, four tablespoons corn starch, four tablespoons sugar, mix yelks and corn starch well together, pour the boiling milk into this, add a spoonful of butter, flavor to taste. Pour into a deep dish and bake. When ready to serve beat to a stiff froth the whites of two eggs with two tablespoons of sugar, spread on top.

MRS. A.M. FRENCH, Knoxville, Tenn.

FIG PUDDING.

Six ounces each of sugar, suet and bread crumbs, three eggs, teacup milk, one and one-half pounds figs, cut fine, two teaspoons baking powder, one wine glass of brandy, one grated nutmeg, steam three hours in a mould. Grate the bread, chop the suet, removing all strings, rub suet and bread crumbs together, to this add the baking powder and figs, beat the yelks and sugar together and add the milk, put all together, adding the whites last. Serve with liquid sauce, flavored with brandy and nutmeg. If you cannot get suet, good rich butter will do.

MRS. J.W.S. FRIERSON, Knoxville, Tenn.

FRUIT PUDDING.

Three eggs, one cup sugar, one-half cup butter, one cup jam or preserves, one-half cup flour, one teaspoon soda in two spoons sour milk or cream, spice to taste. Steam or bake and serve with sauce or whipped cream.

MRS. HOWARD ANDERSON, Beverly, Tenn.

GINGER PUDDING.

One pint molasses, half a pint of butter, four pints flour, one tablespoon each of ginger, cinnamon and spice, one teaspoon soda, in a cup of buttermilk, four eggs beaten separately. Mix the molasses with the yelks, spices, also the butter, flour and whites of eggs, and lastly, the soda and milk. Bake.

MRS. B.J. STEPHENSON, Knoxville, Tenn.

GINGER PUDDING.

Three eggs, three cups flour, one cup butter, one cup each of sugar and molasses, one heaping teaspoon of yeast powder and a tablespoon of ground ginger.

MRS. A.P. WHITE, Knoxville, Tenn.

GRAHAM PUDDING.

One and one-half cups of graham flour, one cup of sweet milk, one-half cup of molasses, one cup of raisins, or one cup of raisins and figs mixed, one teaspoon of soda. Steam three or four hours and eat with a hard or liquid sauce.

MISS BRANCH KEEBLER, Bristol, Va-Tenn.

GRAHAM PUDDING.

One cup each of molasses, sweet milk, seeded and chopped raisins, one-half cup washed currants, one egg, two cups graham flour, sifted, one teaspoon of cinnamon and one of soda, dissolve the soda in the milk. Steam three hours. Serve with a sauce, flavored with vanilla.

MRS. BARNETT, Atlanta, Ga.

GREEN PUDDING.

Put into a pan four eggs, one cup of butter, two cups of sugar. Season to taste, set on the stove, stir until warm through, but must not boil, then bake in pans lined with pastry. This is enough for two puddings.

CONTRIBUTED.

HASTY PUDDING.

Four eggs, beaten separately, four tablespoons of flour, one pint of sweet milk, bake thirty minutes. Eat with a sweet sauce.

MRS. RACHEL M. ROGERS, Knoxville, Tenn.

HERODOTUS PUDDING.

Half-pound of bread crumbs, fine, half-pound of chopped figs, (you can use the cooking fig), six ounces of beef suet, chopped, six ounces brown sugar, two eggs. Mix all together and put in a mould, or a little bucket and steam or boil three hours (water must not get in it). Eat with any kind of sauce you prefer. In making the butter and sugar sauce it is much improved by breaking an egg in it just before it is done.

MRS. T.C. CHALMERS, New York City.

JAM CUSTARD.

Three eggs, one-half cup rich milk, nearly one-half cup butter, jam enough to make moderately stiff. This will make two custards. Bake in crust.

MISS BRANCH KEEBLER, Bristol, Va.

JELLY CUSTARD.

Two-thirds of a cup of butter, one cup sugar, one cup acid jelly, six eggs. Cream butter and sugar and beat jelly in well. Beat eggs, omitting three whites for meringue, and add, mixing thoroughly. Bake in crusts until set and add meringue, set back in stove until a light brown.

MRS. H.M. SIMMONDS, Knoxville, Tenn.

JEFF DAVIS PUDDING.

Three cups flour, one cup each raisins, sugar, butter, buttermilk or sour cream, four eggs, heaping teaspoon baking powder mixed in the flour. Boil in a bag, or steam in a mould, boil two hours, flour the bag well, after dipping it in boiling water. After it is done take out and dip it into cold water so it will turn out easy. Serve with a nice, rich sauce, flavored with vanilla.

MRS. J.W.S. FRIERSON, Knoxville, Tenn.

KENTUCKY PUDDING.

Three-fourths of a cup of butter, two and one-half cups of sugar, three eggs, one cup of cream, three tablespoonsful flour, season with lemon and bake in paste.

MRS. ARCHER A. PHLEGAR, Bristol, Va.-Tenn.

LEMON PUDDING.

Six eggs, beaten separately, one teacup butter, four cups sugar, one cup sweet milk, two tablespoons corn starch, juice of four lemons. Bake in crust. This will make six puddings.

MRS. MARY CARTER.

LEMON PUDDING.

Peel one lemon and boil the peel until tender, changing the water three times, takes one and one-half hours, then cut it up fine with the pulp of the lemon, rejecting the thick under skin and seeds. Add one teacup of water, three cups white sugar, three eggs and butter the size of a hen's egg, also a few spoonsful of grated crackers or bread. Beat all together until light and bake in rich pastry. If desired a meringue can be made. A lemon pudding is really not complete without a meringue.

MISS SUE DEADERICK, MRS. J.T. McTEER,
Knoxville, Tenn.

LEMON PUDDING.

One cup sugar, four eggs, two tablespoons of corn starch, three lemons, juice of both and rind of one, one pint milk, one tablespoon butter. Heat the milk to boiling and stir in the corn starch, which has been wet with a few spoonsful of cold water. Boil five minutes, stirring constantly, while hot add butter and set away to cool. Beat the yelks of the eggs light and add sugar, mixing thoroughly; then add lemon juice and grated rind. Beat this to a stiff cream, and add gradually to the corn starch, milk, when the latter is cold. Stir all smooth, put in a buttered baking dish and bake. When done, cover with meringue and brown.

MRS. W.W. CARSON, Knoxville, Tenn.

LEMON PUDDING.

Twelve eggs, leaving out the whites of seven, beat yelks and whites with the sugar, having a large tablespoon of sugar to each egg, if it does not appear very stiff put in more sugar, and to this pour in one-half pound of drawn butter, not melted to oil. Flavor with essence of lemon to taste.

MRS. B.J. STEPHENSON, Knoxville, Tenn.

LEMON PUDDING

Six eggs, two cups sugar, three lemons, one cup butter, one goblet water, three tablespoons corn starch, beat yellows of eggs and sugar to a cream, add the water, with corn starch dissolved in it, grate the peel of lemon and add it and the juice and then the butter, bake in a crust till well done. Beat the whites with one teacup sugar, put on top, place in oven and bake a light brown. The above makes two puddings.

MISS ANN BELL, Knoxville, Tenn.

LEMON PUDDING.

Six eggs, one-fourth pound of butter, two and three-fourth pounds of sugar and a few drops of oil of lemon, not extract. Beat the eggs well but not separately, add the sugar and beat till they are light, then the melted butter and lastly the oil of lemon. Bake in pastry in a slow oven.

MRS. HENRY A. CHAMBERS, Chattanooga, Tenn.

LEMON PUDDING.

One-fourth pound butter, two and three-fourth pounds sugar, six eggs, four drops oil of lemon, beat well together and bake in paste. This makes three puddings.

MISS HARRIET PARK, Knoxville, Tenn.

LEMON PUDDING.

Bake the crust before the filling is put in, pricking in several places to prevent blistering. One cup of sugar, one tablespoon of butter, yelks of two eggs, one cup of boiling water, juice and grated rind of one lemon, one tablespoon of corn starch, dissolved in cold water. Stir it in the hot water and cook till clear, then add butter and sugar, when creamy push aside till nearly cool, then add the lemon and beaten eggs, fill the crust and bake about twenty minutes. Make a meringue of the two whites and put on top and bake.

MRS. J.H. McCUE, Bristol, Tenn.

LEMON PUDDING.

Three pints sweet milk, six eggs, four butter crackers rolled, the juice of two lemons, the rind of one, grated, sugar and salt to suit the taste. It must be made the day previous to eating.

MR. McMULLEN's NEW YORK RECIPE.

LEMON PUDDING.

Yelks of eight eggs, eight tablespoons of sugar, the same of melted butter, lemon to taste. Stir eggs, sugar, butter and lemon together and bake in puff paste. Stir, do not beat.

MRS. CYNTHIA K. BOYD, Knoxville, Tenn.

LEMON PUDDING.

Six eggs, leaving out four whites for meringue, twelve tablespoons of sugar, one-half teacup melted butter, two teaspoons extract of lemon. Have pastry ready baked, not too done, pour in mixture and bake slowly until set. Make a meringue of the whites, sugar and a little lemon, place over the top of pudding and brown slightly.

MRS. A.P. WHITE, Knoxville, Tenn.

LEMON OR MOCK COCOANUT PUDDING.

One pound white sugar, three-fourths pound butter, which must be creamed, the whites of twelve eggs well beaten, and two tablespoons of corn meal. Flavor with lemon and add a meringue if desired.

MISS SUE DEADERICK, Knoxville, Tenn.

MAURICE PUDDING.

Whites of eight eggs, beaten to a stiff froth, four ounces flour, half-pound sugar, pint rich milk. After the eggs are well-beaten add the sugar by teaspoonsful, flavor cream with rose water or lemon, then add the eggs and flour alternately, beat well, butter a baking dish and bake quickly, but have the heat regular, as it falls easily. It must not stand after being mixed. Serve with butter and sugar sauce. If you like add a very little soda to the pudding. It is best eaten as soon as baked.

MRS. R.S. HAZEN, Knoxville, Tenn.

MEAL PUDDING.

Nine spoons of sugar, seven spoons of meal, eight eggs, stir the meal in last, melt the butter. Eat with a sauce.

MRS. WILL INGLES, Knoxville, Tenn.

MERINGUE PUDDING.

One quart sweet milk, one pint bread crumbs, one cup sugar, grated rind of one lemon, small pinch of salt, yelks of four eggs, well beaten, bread to be soaked in the milk for about fifteen minutes. When all is well-mixed put in a deep dish and bake until about the consistency of boiled custard. While this is baking beat the four whites to a stiff froth with a cup of sugar and the juice of one lemon, after the pudding is sufficiently baked and almost cold, put the meringue on with a large spoon and bake it a very light brown. To be eaten cold.

MRS. J.A. RAYL, Knoxville, Tenn.

MOLASSES PUDDING.

Three cups flour, one cup each of molasses and melted butter, one cup hot water, one teaspoon soda, bake in, pudding pan. Sauce for same: Butter and sugar worked to a cream, add hot water to make it the proper consistency, flavor with vanilla.

MRS. MARY A. BYARS, Bristol, Va.

MOLASSES CUSTARD.

Two cups molasses, one cup sugar, one tablespoon butter, six eggs. Set molasses and butter on the back of the stove until mixed, then cool. Beat eggs and add sugar to eggs, then stir all together. Add enough nutmeg or cinnamon to flavor. Fill crusts very full and bake by slow fire.

MRS. H.M. SIMMONDS, Knoxville, Tenn.

NONPARIEL PUDDING.

One quart sweet milk, four eggs, the whites of three for the meringue, one cup cake or bread crumbs (sponge cake is best), one tablespoon melted butter, one cup sugar, juice and a little of the peel of the lemon, grated. Soak crumbs in milk, beat eggs light, mix all well and bake.

MRS. R.S. HAZEN, Knoxville, Tenn.

ORANGE PUDDING.

Yelks of two eggs, one cup of sugar, two tablespoons of corn starch, one and one-half cups of sweet milk. Boil in double boiler till thick, cool and add three oranges, peeled and broken into bits, also more sugar, if needed.

For Meringue—Cook one-half cup of sugar till it "hairs", then add the beaten whites.

MRS. J.H. McCUE, Bristol, Tenn.

PECAN PUDDING.

This dessert is very simple, but delicious. Roll finely one dozen stale macaroons and mix lightly with a pint of cream whipped until stiff. Add one cup of pecan meats, which have first been put through a meat chopper and mix in thoroughly. Pack in a covered mold or pail and bury in ice and salt four hours. Turn out and serve with more whipped cream.

MRS. MARY JONES, Knoxville, Tenn.

PLUM PUDDING.

One-half pound butter, one-half pound suet, freed from strings and chopped fine, one-half pound sugar, one and one-fourth pounds flour, one pound raisins, seeded, chopped and dredged with flour, one pound currants, picked over carefully, after they are washed, one-eighth pound of citron, shred fine, six eggs, whites and yelks beaten separately, one-half pint milk, one-half cup brandy, one-fourth ounce each of cloves and mace, one grated nutmeg. Cream the butter and sugar, beat in the yelks, when you have whipped them smooth and light; next put in the milk; then the flour, alternately with the beaten whites, then the brandy and spice, lastly the fruit, well dredged with flour. Mix all thoroughly, pour into pudding mould or cloth and boil five hours.

MRS. W.W. CARSON, Knoxville, Tenn.

PLUM PUDDING.

One quart milk, one pound raisins, one pound currants, one pound sugar, one pound suet, one pound grated bread, ten eggs, citron, brandy, cinnamon, nutmeg and cloves to the taste. Boil it two hours. Half the quantity will make a good sized pudding for a small family.

MRS. JENNIE HOUSE, Knoxville, Tenn.

PLUM PUDDING.

One cup citron, two cups currants, two cups raisins, four cups of bread crumbs, six eggs, one cup butter, one cup sugar, one cup sweet milk, one teaspoon nutmeg, one teaspoon cinnamon, one teaspoon soda. Cream butter, add well beaten eggs and stir in sugar. Mix the dry ingredients together and dissolve the soda in the sweet milk. Combine all ingredients and boil for five hours in well buttered tins.

AN ENGLISH PLUM PUDDING.

One pound each of raisins and currants, one pound best beef suet, chopped very fine, two ounces almonds, blanched and pounded, mix in one pound of sifted flour, one pound grated bread crumbs, two ounces each of candied citron, orange and lemon peel, half a grated nutmeg, a blade of mace, one-half pound powdered sugar, and a little salt. Mix all the above, then moisten the whole with ten beaten eggs, one-half pint of cream, a glass of brandy and a glass of wine, white. It must not be thin, or the fruit will settle at the bottom. Tie it carefully in a cloth or bag, well buttered and boil it four hours. Sift white powdered sugar over it and just as you send to the table pour brandy over it and set it on fire so as to have it in a blazing condition. Serve with wine sauce.

MRS. MARY McCLUNG, Knoxville, Tenn.

ENGLISH PLUM PUDDING.

Three-fourths pound of suet, one pound of sugar, one and one-fourth pounds of bread crumbs, one and one-half pounds each of currants and raisins, one pound of citron, twelve eggs, well beaten, one pint sweet milk, juice of three lemons, one heaping teaspoonful of salt, one single handful of flour, one teaspoonful of baking powder in flour, one tablespoonful of cinnamon, one-half tablespoonful of cloves, one glass of wine, one glass of brandy. Mix suet and sugar first, then crumbs and flour and then fruit, then brandy and wine and spices, then milk, then eggs last, mix even with the hand. Grind suet in a meat chopper (a sausage chopper will not do,) you can chop it fine with a knife. Put it into greased moulds, baking powder cans will do nicely and steam eight hours. If you wish a two pound pudding put that much in the can, it does not rise very much, nor does it shrink in weight. Serve with sauce.

MRS. FLANDERS, Palace Hotel, Knoxville, Tenn.

ENGLISH PLUM PUDDING.

Two pounds seeded raisins, two pounds currants, well washed, one-half pound citron, sliced, two pounds bread crumbs, (no flour), two pounds chopped suet juice and grated rind of three lemons, six eggs, beaten, two pounds light brown sugar, four grated nutmegs, one tablespoon salt. Mix all the fruit thoroughly with the bread crumbs, etc., then add eggs and enough milk, a little at a time, to make it moist enough to stick together, not wet. Fill bowls the desired size, even full cover with cloths tied on tightly and boil steadily for eight hours, put away in the bowls and when wanted for use boil one hour, serve with ice cream and rich wine sauce. These will keep all winter. I make half the quantity and put them all in one large boiler with the boiling water coming just half way up the bowls.

MRS. GEO. A. WILLIAMSON, Brooklyn, N. Y.

ENGLISH PLUM PUDDING.

Four eggs, heaping half pint sugar, one pint suet, one pint milk, one pint bread crumbs, one pint flour, one coffee cup citron, one-half teaspoon salt, one-half teaspoon cinnamon and nutmeg, one-half box currants, one box raisins, one quart chopped apples, one-half wine glass brandy. Four currants and raisins with part of the flour, mix ingredients together thoroughly and bake in well greased pan.

MRS. C.T. LEONHARDT, Knoxville, Tenn.

PLAIN PLUM PUDDING.

One cup of raisins, or currants, one cup suet or butter, three of flour, or four of bread crumbs, one of sugar, one-half cup molasses, one of butter or sweet milk, one-half teaspoon soda, two eggs, steam three hours.

MRS. C.H. ALLEN, Knoxville, Tenn.

POOR MAN'S PUDDING.

Put in a baking dish two tablespoons of rice, three of sugar, a little cinnamon and small piece of butter and one quart of sweet milk. Have a slow fire and cover the pan. When the rice grains have bursted take the cover off and let it brown. It will cook slowly about an hour and a half or two hours. Put it in to cook early in the morning and have it cool to serve. Flavor with a teaspoon of vanilla, if preferred.

MISS CONVERSE, Burlington, Vt.

TWO POTATO PUDDINGS.

One-half pound butter, one-half pound sugar, beat to a cream, four eggs, beaten light and added by degrees, one-half pound potatoes, boiled and mashed through a colander, then put with the butter and sugar, add brandy, wine and rose water, a glass each, a little nutmeg and cinnamon and a tablespoon of cream. Bake in puff paste.

MRS. JENNIE S. HOUSE, Knoxville, Tenn.

PRUNE PUDDING.

Cook prunes very soft, use one large cup of prunes mashed fine and run through a sieve, beat whites of six eggs very stiff, mix lightly with prunes, flavor with wine, bake rather quickly and serve with cream, either plain or whipped.

MISS NELL RHEA, Shoun's, Tenn.

PUMPKIN PUDDING.

To one pint of pumpkin put through a sieve, add one pint of milk or cream, and a small piece of butter, melted, six eggs, beaten separately, six spoonsful of sugar, bake in a crust and use the whites on top as a meringue. Flavor with ginger and lemon peel or extract to taste.

MRS. TOOLE, Knoxville, Tenn.

PUMPKIN PUDDING.

One egg, one cup brown sugar, one cup pumpkin, first peeled, cubed, stewed tender and pressed through a sieve, one teaspoon cinnamon, one-half teaspoon ginger, one-half teaspoon salt, milk to thin as desired. Bake in a moderate oven in puff paste and when nearly done lift to upper shelf to receive rich brown shade.

MRS. J.H. McCUE, Bristol, Tenn.

"UNEEDA" PUMPKIN PUDDING.

Five eggs, four cups of sugar, one-half cup of flour, one teaspoon of baking powder, three-fourths of a pound of butter, one small sweet potato, and one quart of stewed pumpkin, both run through a sieve, two teaspoons of lemon extract. Beat the yelks, add part of the sugar, cream the butter and add the rest of the sugar to that, then mix together and beat well, add the potato and pumpkin and the flour, in which you have sifted the baking powder, add lemon extract, beat well and fold in the whites. Bake in puff paste. This quantity will make five large puddings.

HENRY HOWARD, Cook on the "Uneeda", Orange River, Fla.

QUEEN OF PUDDINGS.

One pint of nice bread crumbs in one quart of sweet milk, one cup sugar, yelks four eggs, well-beaten, piece of butter size of an egg, rind of one lemon, grated, the juice of the lemon and one cup white sugar. Bake in a pan. Spread a layer of acid jelly over the pudding, putting on top a meringue made with the whites, a tablespoon of sugar to each white. Brown slightly and serve with rich cream.

MRS. JAMES S. BOYD, MRS. WILL INGLIS, Knoxville, Tenn.

THE QUEEN OF PUDDINGS.
One pint of bread or cake crumbs, one quart of sweet milk, one cup of sugar, the yelks of four eggs, well beaten, the rind of a fresh lemon, grated fine (I use nutmeg or vanilla frequently), a piece of butter size of an egg, bake until well done. Beat the whites of the four eggs to a stiff froth, add in a cup of sugar and lemon to taste, or juice of a fresh lemon, spread over the pudding a layer of any kind of preserves or jelly, then pour the eggs and sugar over and place in the oven until lightly browned.

RICH PUDDING.
One cup of sugar, two cups of butter, four eggs, flavor with vanilla. Bake in pastry.
MRS. JAMES KENNEDY, Knoxville, Tenn.

RAISIN CUSTARD.
Three eggs, two cups sugar, nearly one cup butter, one-half pound raisins, juice of two lemons. This will make two nice custards.
MISS BRANCH KEEBLER, Bristol, Va.

SOUFFLE PUDDING.
Four eggs, beaten separately, four tablespoons flour, one pint sweet milk, bake in dish and eat with sauce.
CONTRIBUTED.

SPICE CAKE PUDDING.
Four eggs, two teacups sugar, one cup butter, one-half cup sweet milk, four cups flour, one teaspoon each cinnamon and nutmeg, tablespoon ginger, add raisins if desired. Bake in pan. Serve with sauce.
MRS. WILL INGLIS.

STEAM PUDDING.
Four eggs, three teacups flour, one cup each butter and sweet milk, one teaspoon baking powder, two cups sugar. Cream butter and sugar together, break eggs into this and beat thoroughly, add milk, and lastly, flour and baking powder, season with extract of lemon. Steam one hour and serve with sauce. A teacup of raisins or currants can be added if desired. They should be mixed with the flour.
MRS. A.P. WHITE, Knoxville, Tenn.

STEAM PUDDING.
Three eggs, butter the size of one egg, two tablespoons of sugar, one teaspoon of baking powder, one-half teacup of sweet milk, steam half an hour.
CONTRIBUTED.

STEAM PUDDING.
Three cups flour, one-half cup each of sugar and molasses, one-fourth cup melted butter, one cup each of cold water and raisins, one teaspoon of soda, steam three hours.

Sauce—One cup sugar, one-half cup butter, two-thirds cup cold water, yelks of two eggs, flavor to taste. Let come to a boil slowly. The whites of the two eggs are beaten to a stiff froth and stirred in just before using.
MISS ANN BELL, Knoxville, Tenn.

AUNT MARY'S STEAM PUDDING.
Two cups bread crumbs, two tablespoons flour, one egg, one cup sugar, one cup each currants and raisins, one-fourth teaspoon ginger, one-half teaspoon cinnamon, moisten with milk, steam three hours. Eat with hard sauce.
MRS. LUCY BROWNLEE, Knoxville, Tenn.

STEAMED FRUIT PUDDING.
Put in your mixing bowl one heaping cup of bread crumbs, two scant cups flour, one cup of molasses, one cup of sweet milk, one teaspoon each of salt, cloves and cinnamon. Stir one and one-half teaspoons baking powder in milk, two well-beaten eggs, one cup of chopped suet and one-half pound of figs, chopped fine, or raisins and currants rubbed thoroughly with flour. Steam in well-greased mould or cloth for two hours. This makes quite a large pudding.
MRS. NATHANIEL TAYLOR, Bristol, Tenn.

SUET PUDDING.

Four cups flour, one cup of chopped suet, one cup of raisins or cherries, one cup molasses, one cup lukewarm water, one large teaspoon baking powder. Sift the baking powder in the flour, add suet and raisins, then molasses and water. Dip the bag in cold water and flour inside. Put it in warm water and boil pudding three hours, putting a plate in the bottom of the boiler to prevent scorching. In dishing, empty the bag on one plate and transfer to another to prevent the water making the pudding sticky. Serve with a nice sauce.

MISS MARY PLEAS McCLUNG, Knoxville, Tenn.

SUET PUDDING.

One cup suet, one and one-half cups milk, one cup syrup, three and a half cups flour, one cup raisins, three eggs, two teaspoons cream of tartar, one teaspoon each of soda and salt. Chop the suet very fine, the salt, soda and cream of tartar sifted with the flour, the raisins washed and rubbed through the flour. Rinse the bag in cold water and flour the inside to prevent sticking, allow room to swell, tie it strongly. The water must boil when it is put in and be kept boiling till it is taken out. If more water is necessary use that which is boiling, cover the kettle to confine the steam, boil three hours. When done plunge in cold water and turn out immediately, eat hot, serve with wine sauce or cream and sugar.

MRS. E. BOLLI, Knoxville. Tenn.

SUET PUDDING.

One-half pound suet, one cup each of currants, raisrns, brown sugar, fruit juice, one-half cup milk, three eggs, one nutmeg, one teaspoon salt, one dessert spoon soda, flour to make thick as fruit cake. Boil in a pudding mould four hours.

Sauce—To one pint boiling water add a heaping cup sugar, one tablespoon butter, pinch of salt, one tablespoon corn starch, dissolved in cold water, season with nutmeg or vanilla, boil half an hour. If good and well cooked it will be clear. Or to a tablespoon of currant jelly add a tablespoon of hot water, beat well and add to the above just before serving, omitting other flavoring.

MRS. G.M. BURNS, Knoxville, Tenn.

SWEETMEAT PUDDING.

Lay a thin puff paste all over the dish or pie pan and take any two kinds of preserves you may fancy of a dark and light kind, alternate with a spoonful of each until the bottom of the pan is covered. Beat the yelks of eight and the whites of two eggs with a gill of cream, one-half pound each of butter and white sugar, beat all together and when the oven is ready, pour it over the preserves and bake. Make a meringue of the remaining six whites and flavor with vanilla. This quantity will make two puddings, if baked in an ordinary pie pan.

MISS SUE DEADERICK, Knoxville, Tenn.

SWEETMEAT PUDDING.

Five or six eggs, one cup sugar, one and one-half cups sweet milk. Beat the yelks and sugar together, add the milk, flavor to taste, also add one tablespoon of flour or corn starch to thicken and place on the fire, stirring all the time. When about as thick as boiled custard remove from the fire and pour into a pudding dish, having first lined it with pastry or cake and spread with preserves, then place it in the oven and let it remain till stiff enough to bear the meringue. Beat the whites, putting a tablespoon of sugar to each white, spread over the pudding, let it remain in the stove just long enough to become a light brown.

MRS. J.A. RAYL, Knoxville, Tenn.

SWEET POTATO PUDDING.

One pound of sweet potatoes, boiled in a little water; when done take them out, peel them and mash them very smooth; beat eight eggs very light; add to them half a pound of butter, creamed, half a pound of granulated sugar, half a teaspoon of powdered cinnamon, a very little nutmeg, one wine glass of rose water, one gill of sweet cream; stir all well; then add the sweet potato, a little at a time; mix all together, stirring very hard; then butter a deep dish, put in the pudding and bake three-quarters of an hour; or line a pie plate with puff paste put in the pudding and bake twelve minutes.

MRS. S.B. BOYD, Knoxville, Tenn.

SWEET POTATO PUDDING.

Boil and mash the potatoes perfectly smooth, or press through a colander. To two cups of potatoes add two cups of sugar, one cup of butter, one glass of brandy or wine, five eggs and cinnamon, and nutmeg to the taste. Beat the eggs thoroughly, but not separately, add sugar, then potatoes and mix well, then pour in the butter, melted, then the spices, brandy or wine, and also a little salt. Bake in pastry. This quantity makes three puddings.

MRS. HENRY A. CHAMBERS, Chattanooga, Tenn.

TAPIOCA PUDDING.

One cup of tapioca, soaked two hours on the back of the stove in one quart of water. Butter a pudding dish well, and place in it pared and cored apples; season the tapioca with tablespoon of sugar, very little cinnamon or nutmeg and salt. Pour it over the apples and bake until the apples are thoroughly done. Eat with sugar and cream.

MRS. ALLEN S. MEBANE, Knoxville, Tenn.

TAPIOCA PUDDING.

Wash one cup of Tapioca through three waters, then soak for two or three hours. Take four eggs, two cups sugar, half cup butter, two cups sweet milk, teaspoon of spice and a little vanilla, reserve two whites for the meringue. Beat yelks and whites separately, cream butter and sugar, mix all the ingredients well and bake in a pan slowly. When done, make a meringue with the two whites and two tablespoons of sugar, put back in the oven and brown it slightly.

MRS. ROBERT VESTAL, Knoxville, Tenn.

TRANSPARENT PUDDINGS.

Yelks of six eggs, one pint sugar, one-half pound butter. Cook butter and sugar together, add eggs to this while boiling hot, stir rapidly. When thick enough, put into pastry and bake a light brown. Meringue can be used, if preferred. This quantity makes two puddings.

MRS. WILL HAZEN, Knoxville, Tenn.

TRANSPARENT CUSTARD.

Two eggs, one cup white sugar, one heaping tablespoon of butter, one teaspoon of flour. Beat well and cook in a double boiler until sugar is dissolved, then flavor with lemon, pour into crust and bake. Does not require a meringue.

MRS. W.N. PATTON, Bristol, Tenn.

TYLER PUDDING.

Four eggs, two cups sugar, one-half cup cream, one cup melted butter, season with nutmeg and bake in shells.

CONTRIBUTED.

VEGETABLE PUDDING.

One cup each of grated carrot and Irish potato, raw, one cup each of raisins, flour, sugar, one teaspoon each soda, cinnamon, allspice, one nutmeg, grated, butter size of an egg, grate and add carrots last. Steam three hours and eat with hard or brandy sauce.

MRS. ED. DIXON, California.

VELVET PUDDING.

One quart of milk, three tablespoons corn starch, yelks of three eggs, sweeten to taste and flavor. Boil the milk with a little salt, beat eggs, sugar and starch together until light, adding a little cold milk to thin it. Add this to the boiling milk, stirring briskly until it is of the proper consistency. Beat the whites of eggs with two tablespoons of sugar, place on top of the pudding and brown.

CONTRIBUTED.

VELVET PUDDING.

Five eggs, six tablespoons of corn starch, three pints of milk, one cup sugar. Let the milk come to a boil, then add the yelks of eggs and corn starch beaten together with the sugar. When the milk boils put a little of it into the eggs and sugar, then stir all into the milk and boil until thoroughly done. Pour into a baking dish and meringue the top with the whites. Season to taste.

CONTRIBUTED.

VELVET PUDDING.

Five eggs, beaten separately, one teacup sugar, four tablespoons of corn starch, three pints sweet milk. Beat yelks of eggs and sugar together, add starch, which has been dissolved in a little milk. Boil milk and while hot pour slowly over the eggs, sugar and starch. Return to the fire and boil until very thick, stirring all the time. Flavor to taste, then pour into a baking pan. Beat the whites to a stiff froth, add half a cupful of sugar, cover the top and brown slightly. Serve with whipped cream and sugar. (Use double boiler for boiling the custard.)

CONTRIBUTED.

VIENNA PUDDING.

One cup sifted meal, made in batter, stir in a quart of boiling water. Take one quart mush, one teacup butter, one teacup sugar, four eggs, season with lemon and bake in crust.

MRS. C.H. ALLEN, Knoxville, Tenn.

SALADS

SALAD DRESSING.

One and one-half teacups vinegar, six eggs, one teaspoon mustard, two tablespoons sugar, one-half tablespoon celery seed, salt and pepper to taste. Cook till thick.

MRS. A.E. DAVENPORT, Chattanooga, Tenn.

SALAD DRESSING.

One cup vinegar, one cup sweet milk, one heaping tablespoon sugar, one heaping tablespoon butter, one-half teaspoon salt, one teaspoon mustard, celery seed to taste, red and black pepper, two teaspoons of flour, three eggs.

Mix mustard, sugar, flour, milk, and seasoning to a smooth paste. Boil vinegar with butter and mix with other ingredients. Boil all together and keep stirring constantly until done, beat whites to a froth and add last.

MISS MARY FRANCISCO, Knoxville, Tenn.

SALAD DRESSING.

One-fourth teaspoon black pepper, one-half teaspoon salt, one teaspoon sugar, yelks of two hard boiled eggs, mashed smooth in one-half tablespoon of melted butter, not hot, one tablespoon of hot vinegar, cream as you like it.

ELIZABETH FISHER, Washington, D. C.

BOILED SALAD DRESSING.

One tablespoon sugar, one-half teaspoon salt, one-half teaspoon mustard. Mix these together dry.

Boil one-half cup strong vinegar, and pour slowly, stirring hard over one egg, beaten light, add sugar, salt, and mustard, after they have been wet with a little vinegar, then set all on the stove and let it thicken, stirring constantly. When cold add two tablespoons of rich cream.

MRS. W.W. CARSON, Knoxville, Tenn.

BOILED DRESSING.

Yelks of six eggs, two tablespoons of sugar, two tablespoons of melted butter, one-half cup each of vinegar and cream, one teaspoon of mustard, two teaspoons of salt, one-fourth teaspoon of cayenne pepper. Cook in double boiler until it thickens like custard. This is nice for tomatoes or slaw.

BOILED SALAD DRESSING.

One tablespoon salt, one-half tablespoon flour, one and one-half tablespoon sugar, one and one-half tablespoon of oil or melted butter, one teaspoon mustard, a little red pepper, three-quarters of a cup of vinegar, yelks of two eggs.

Mix all the dry things together, add vinegar, stir until smooth; put in butter or oil; cook until thick; beat eggs lightly, add milk to them and pour hot mixture slowly into milk and eggs, stirring all the time; return to fire, cook until as thick as custard. This may be used for all kinds of vegetable salads and some kinds of fish.

CREAM SALAD DRESSING.

Cream salad dressing is made by mixing sour cream with enough vinegar, pepper and salt to season the salad palatably.

MRS. WILL CHAMBERLAIN, Knoxville, Tenn.

CREAM DRESSING FOR SLAW.

Two tablespoons sweet whipped cream, two tablespoons sugar and four tablespoons vinegar, beat well and pour over cabbage, salted and cut fine.

THE WHITE HOUSE COOK BOOK.

FRENCH DRESSING.

One tablespoon vinegar, three tablespoons olive oil, one-half saltspoon pepper and a few shakes cayenne, one saltspoon salt.

Put condiments in cold cup, add vinegar, mix, add gradually, stirring all the time the oil. Mix just before serving and do not let stand.

MRS. JOHN COX, Knoxville, Tenn.

LETTUCE OR SLAW DRESSING.

One-half cup milk, one-half cup vinegar, one tablespoon sugar, one teaspoon each salt, mustard, Worcestershire sauce, butter size of a walnut, yelks of two eggs.

Mix all together and cook until thick as cream, stirring to prevent burning.

MRS. A.S. BIRDSONG, Knoxville, Tenn.

MAYONNAISE DRESSING.

Yellow of one egg, teaspoon salt, teaspoon mustard, one-half teaspoon white pepper, oil and vinegar, or oil, juice of one lemon.

Beat egg well, add salt and mustard, mix well, then add oil, drop by drop until it begins to thicken, then slowly add lemon juice or vinegar, and then the oil until the dressing becomes as thick as you like.

MRS. H.N. SAXTON, JR., Knoxville, Tenn.

MAYONNAISE DRESSING.

Mix one teaspoon mustard, dry, one teaspoon sugar, one-half teaspoon salt, one-fourth saltspoon cayenne with two egg yelks, beat well, add slowly one-half pint of olive oil and one-half cup of vinegar, if curdled add another yelk.

CONTRIBUTED.

QUICK MAYONNAISE.

Beat light yelks of two eggs, put in this a small lump of butter, one-half teaspoon French mustard, a little red pepper, salt and a cup of vinegar, stir all together in a porcelain saucepan, set in boiling water and then stir till thick.

MRS. BARNETT, Atlanta, Ga.

QUICK MAYONNAISE.

Beat well yelk of one egg, add a pinch of salt, a tablespoon of vinegar, a tablespoon of olive oil, butter size of a marble. Stir briskly over slow fire until creamy.

ALBERTINE LUTTRELL VANCE, Knoxville, Tenn.

DRESSING FOR RAW TOMATOES.

One teacup brown sugar, pour into sauce bowl, then stir in one saltspoon of salt, pepper and ground mustard and enough vinegar to make a thick syrup. Serve cold.

MRS. E.S. McCLUNG, Knoxville, Tenn.

DRESSING FOR SLAW.

Cut cabbage very fine and put in a dish and sprinkle with a teaspoon each of salt and pepper. Beat the yelks of two eggs, stir in half cup of cream and half cup of vinegar, one teaspoon sugar. Place on fire and stir till thick as custard, add one teaspoon of mustard and celery seed, if you like, and when the dressing is almost cold, pour over the cabbage and serve.

H. LEIGH TAYLOR, Portsmouth, Ohio.

SLAW DRESSING.

One teacup of vinegar, one-half teacup sugar, one teaspoon salt, one-half teaspoon mustard, stir together, beat into it two eggs, then stir in vinegar and mix thoroughly. Put on fire and stir till it comes to a boil, take off, add about a tablespoon of butter, if pepper is liked add one-eighth of a teaspoon, let it get cold, then pour on cabbage, cut fine.

MRS. JNO. M. ALLEN, Knoxville, Tenn.

SLAW OR SALAD DRESSING.

One teaspoon mustard, one teaspoon salt, one tablespoon flour, one-half cup sugar, three eggs, one cup vinegar, one cup cream or milk, one tablespoon butter, pinch of celery seed.

Mix dry ingredients thoroughly, add eggs, beating well; then add vinegar slowly and then milk. Put in double boiler and stir all the time it is cooking.

MRS. RICHARD P. JOHNSON, Knoxville, Tenn.

SLAW DRESSING.

Beat yelks of three eggs with one-half cup of sugar, two tablespoons melted butter, one tablespoon salt, one cup of cream or milk, one teaspoon corn starch, dissolved in a little of the milk, one teaspoon of dry mustard, one cup of vinegar, a little cayenne pepper, and lastly, the whites of the eggs, beaten stiff.

Cook in double boiler. It will keep for days, if kept in a cool place.

MRS. B.I. HUGHES, Rome, Ga.

SALAD DRESSING WITHOUT OIL.

Beat the yelks of two eggs light, add two tablespoons of vinegar, one tablespoon of salt, one-half teaspoon of pepper.

Cook over hot fire until it thickens, then cool. Whip one-half cup of cream, add to cooked eggs, stirring all the while until well mixed.

MRS. LUCY BROWNLEE, Knoxville, Tenn.

SIMPLE, BUT FINE DRESSING.

To each yelk of an egg use one tablespoon of vinegar. Scald vinegar, pour over eggs slowly, put on stove, stir constantly until thick; season and add half the quantity of sweet cream.

MRS. HECTOR COFFIN, Knoxville, Tenn.

PREPARED SEASONING.

Four spoons of mustard, six spoonsful of salt, one spoonful of red pepper. Prepare and keep in jar to use from. Many persons prefer this to mayonnaise.

MRS. HECTOR COFFIN, Knoxville, Tenn.

VINEGAR.

Mix one quart of molasses with three gallons of rain water and one pint of good yeast, it will ferment in a few weeks.

MISS ANN BELL, Knoxville, Tenn.

SALAD IN APPLE CUPS.

Select large firm apples and cut off the top about one-fifth of the depth of the fruit. Hollow out the interior of cup and cap leaving the shell about a quarter of an inch thick. Put a pea of butter in a pan to melt. Beat an egg slightly, season and add a teaspoon of milk. Turn this in the melted butter and stir until thick and creamy. Add a mixture of chopped English walnuts, celery and pineapple, and when the entire mixture is creamy pour into the cups and place them on ice. Before serving add a little mayonnaise and salt and pepper.

CONTRIBUTED.

ASPARAGUS SALAD.

One bunch or one can of asparagus, one head of lettuce, one-fourth teaspoon white pepper, one-half teaspoon salt.

French Dressing, made as follows: One-fourth teaspoon salt, one-fourth teaspoon white pepper, three tablespoons olive oil, ten drops onion juice, one tablespoon vinegar, one-half tablespoon lemon juice. Mix the salt, pepper and onion juice and one tablespoon of the olive oil, then add alternately the remaining oil, vinegar and lemon juice. Wash and crisp the lettuce, cook and cool the asparagus or open, drain and rinse, if canned, dry on a clean towel, cut in inch pieces and arrange on the lettuce leaves, season with salt and white pepper. Turn the dressing over all and serve.

MRS. C.R. McILWAINE, Knoxville, Tenn.

BANANA SALAD.

Cut bananas into slices, lengthwise, as thick as a dollar; arrange then on a dish so that the ends of the long semi-circular slices meet and form a hollow square. Pour over them a gill of sherry made very sweet with sugar, and into which you have put one teaspoon of lemon juice; let them get ice cold, then fill the centre with whipped cream piled high.

For those who object to wine, prepare the bananas as above and pour over them a dressing made as follows.

A gill of thick white syrup (sugar dissolved in as little water as possible), the juice of half a lemon and the yellow rind of two dark skinned oranges rubbed on lumps of sugar, which must be dissolved in the syrup. Fill the hollow centre with sliced oranges.

CATHERINE OWENS.

BRAZILIAN SALAD.

Equal parts of green grapes cut lengthwise with seed removed, and a few candied cherries, to which add small quantity of chopped celery, pineapple and apple with English walnuts and raisins cut fine.

A little lemon juice added as you thoroughly mix all ingredients is desirable. Serve on lettuce with mayonnaise and whipped cream.

MRS. R.H. SANSOM, Knoxville, Tenn.

CELERY SALAD.

Chop fine, three bunches of celery with a small head of cabbage. Take a teacup of vinegar, yelks of two eggs, a tablespoon of butter, one teaspoon each of mustard and salt, one tablespoon of sugar and a pinch of cayenne pepper. Mix these ingredients together smoothly, heat till it begins to thicken, stir till partly cool, then add two tablespoons sweet cream. Pour over the salad just before taking to the table. If thicker than desired add more vinegar.

MRS. ASA HAZEN, Knoxville, Tenn.

CHERRY AND CELERY SALAD.

One head lettuce, one box cherries, one head celery. Wash and crisp the lettuce, stone the cherries, chop the celery into dice. Mix celery and cherries with enough mayonnaise to moisten thoroughly. Arrange on lettuce leaves with spoonful of mayonnaise on top of each serving.

MRS. C.R. McILWAINE, Knoxville, Tenn.

CHERRY SALAD.

Remove the stones from large white canned cherries and in their place, put the half of a pecan meat. Arrange on lettuce hearts and serve with French dressing or mayonnaise.

MRS. R.H. SANSOM, Knoxville, Tenn.

CHICKEN SALAD.

For two large chickens, the yellows of nine hard boiled eggs, one-half pint melted butter, one-half cup Durkee salad dressing, one pint best vinegar, one teaspoon black pepper, two teaspoons mixed mustard, one teaspoon salt, celery seed to suit the taste.

Cut up the chicken, mix as much chopped cabbage as necessary, this is in case you cannot get celery, add celery seed and set aside, some boiled ham is a great addition, pour the dressing over a short time before serving.

MRS. T.S. WEBB, Knoxville, Tenn.

CHICKEN SALAD.

Remove the meat from three cooked chickens, cut carefully into pieces like dice, add a little vinegar and salt and let stand for several hours. Then cut celery into dice until you have enough in bulk to be about one-third less than that of the chicken. Mix thoroughly with the chicken. Add to the mixture a cold dressing previously cooled, add the pulverized yellows of six eggs, if necessary pepper and salt can be added.

For those persons who like salad oil, a separate mayonnaise dressing can be prepared which can be used or refused according to the preference of each individual.

Recipe for Cooked Dressing—One and one-half tumblers vinegar, yellows of three raw eggs, one teaspoon raw mustard, saltspoon salt, tablespoon salad oil or melted butter, teaspoon sugar, a little lemon juice and pepper.

Scald the vinegar, beat the eggs thoroughly and stir gradually into the scalding vinegar. Add mustard, salt and pepper. The oil must be stirred in carefully from first to last, sugar and lemon juice at the last. Stir the whole carefully until it is ready to boil. Then remove from the fire and set aside to cool.

MRS. ADRIAN TERBY, Knoxville, Tenn.

CHICKEN SALAD.

One chicken, boiled until tender, twice as much chopped celery as chicken, yelks of two hard boiled eggs and a little salt.

Dressing—One cup vinegar, if too strong, dilute with one-third water, small lump butter. Place this on stove and heat thoroughly. Mix together dry, one-half teaspoon each of mustard and pepper, one teaspoon salt, two tablespoons sugar; add this mixture to two eggs, which have been beaten light. Pour this slowly into the hot vinegar, and stir until it thickens.

MRS. W.W. CARSON, Knoxville, Tenn.

CLUB SALAD.

One fat chicken cooked tender, and let stand in broth over night, two bunches celery, one-half pound English walnuts. Cut in dice and mix with double quantity of salad dressing just before serving.

MRS. SAMUEL MITCHELL, Bristol, Va.

CUCUMBER SALAD.

Three large cucumbers, three potatoes, cut dice shape, as much cabbage chopped as cucumbers, six hard-boiled eggs, salt and pepper to taste, cover with mayonnaise dressing and serve.

CUCUMBER ASPIC.

One box Minute Gelatine, made by recipe on box. Add to it, when cool, one large cucumber, grated and strained so as to have only the juice. Season with salt, pepper, onion juice and vinegar, and color deep emerald with spinach coloring.

Pour in a mould, the hollow rim or circle is attractive, and put on ice to congeal. Serve on platter of crisp, head lettuce leaves and fill in centre with a fluffy yellow dressing with whipped cream beaten in it.

MRS. R.H. SANSOM, Knoxville, Tenn.

CUCUMBER BOATS.

Take prettily shaped medium sized cucumbers; about one inch from each end and cut down half an inch, then across the cucumber, which leaves it boat shaped.

Scoop out the inside, chop and mix with French dressing, return to the cucumber boat, which put on ice until ready to serve on a crisp lettuce leaf.

MRS. J.T. McTEER, Knoxville, Tenn.

CUCUMBER AND TOMATO SALAD.

Peel and cut in blocks, tomatoes and cucumbers. Serve on lettuce leaf with French dressing.

Or remove skin from tomatoes by dipping in hot water. Take sharp knife and remove center of tomato. Prepare cucumber and cut in small dice. Sprinkle little salt over and mix with dressing. Fill the tomato with this and then put dressing on top. Serve on lettuce leaf.

MRS. JOHN COX, Knoxville, Tenn.

EGG SALAD.

Chop hard boiled eggs coarsely, with a little cold chicken, one or two sweet peppers, chopped fine, salt and pepper. Pour over this a good French salad dressing and serve on a lettuce leaf.

MRS. W.K. VANCE, Bristol, Tenn.

FRENCH FRUIT SALAD.

Two oranges, two bananas, twelve English walnuts, one head lettuce, mayonnaise. Wash and put the lettuce to crisp. Peel the oranges, cut in slices, remove the seeds, then cut the slices in small pieces. Peel the bananas, cut crosswise into thin slices, crack the nuts and break the meats into small pieces. Arrange the lettuce for individual serving. Place a layer of bananas, then oranges, then bananas in each lettuce cup and dress with the mayonnaise, garnish with the nuts. Chopped white grapes may be added.

MRS. C.R. McILWAINE, Knoxville, Tenn.

FROZEN FRUIT SALAD.

Make a salad of Malaga grapes, apples, celery and nuts, cover very thickly with mayonnaise dressing. Put in a covered can and pack in ice for about four hours. When hard cut in slices and serve on a lettuce leaf.

MRS. W.M. HOUSE, Knoxville, Tenn.

FRUIT SALAD.

One-fourth grape fruit, one-third orange, one dozen strawberries. Peel orange and grape fruit and serve on lettuce leaf with dressing.

MRS. JOHN COX, Knoxville, Tenn.

FRUIT SALAD.

Four oranges, one can pineapple, one pound grapes. Dressing: Three tablespoons of vinegar, one tablespoon sugar, one teaspoon mustard, one-half teaspoon salt, pinch red pepper, small piece butter. Cook in double boiler until thick and when ready to serve beat in one pint whipped cream. This will serve fifteen people.

CONTRIBUTED.

FRUIT SALAD.

Slice equal quantities of bananas, mellow apples and celery, mix with salad dressing and serve at once on a bed of lettuce.

MRS. SAMUEL MITCHELL, Bristol, Va.

FRUIT SALAD.

One bunch of celery, four large apples, one-half pound Malaga grapes, one-half pound of English walnuts. Mix with mayonnaise and serve on lettuce leaves. Seed grapes.

MISS PASCAL HALL, Hagerstown, Md.

HYDEN SALAD.

One gallon cabbage, cut fine, one-half gallon green tomatoes, cut fine, one quart onions chopped, (throw away the juice), one pint green peppers, seeded and chopped, four tablespoons mustard, two tablespoons ginger, one tablespoon cinnamon, one tablespoon cloves, three tablespoons celery seed, three tablespoons of salt, two pounds sugar, one and one-half gallons strong vinegar, mix together and boil thirty-five minutes.

MRS. ARCHER A. PHLEGAR, Bristol, Va.

KNOXALL SALAD-CHICKEN CREAM.

One tablespoon Knox's Gelatine, one-fourth cup cold chicken stock, three-fourth cup hot chicken stock, highly seasoned, one cup heavy cream, salt and pepper, one cup cold cooked chicken, cut in dice.

Soak gelatine in old stock, dissolve in hot stock, and strain. When mixture begins to thicken, beat, using an egg beater, until frothy. Then add cream beaten until stiff, and chicken dice. Season with salt and pepper. Turn into one-fourth pound baking powder tins and chill.

Salad Dressing—One and one-half teaspoon Knox's Gelatine, two tablespoons cold water, yelks of two eggs, one teaspoon salt, one and one-half teaspoons sugar, one-fourth teaspoon pepper, a few grains of cayenne pepper, one teaspoon mustard, one-fourth cup lemon juice, one-half cup hot cream, one and one-half table spoons butter, whites of two eggs, one-half cup heavy cream.

Soak gelatine in cold water until soft, dissolve by standing in hot water then strain. Beat yelks of eggs and add salt, sugar, pepper, cayenne, mustard, lemon juice and cream. Cook over hot water until mixture thickens, stirring constantly, then add butter and gelatine. Add mixture gradually to whites of eggs, beaten until stiff and when cold fold in cream beaten until stiff. Mold and chill. Turn chicken cream from molds, cut in one inch slices and arrange on lettuce leaves. Put a spoonful of salad dressing on each slice and garnish with one-half English walnut meat or pecan nut meat. Cut celery into small pieces, there should be three cupfuls. Break into pieces one cup pecan of English walnut meats and brown in a moderate oven. Mix celery and nut meats, sprinkle with one-half teaspoon salt and add to one-half the salad dressing. Surround each slice of chicken cream with celery and nut mixture.

MISS AMELIA SULZBACHER, Chillicothe, Ohio.

MACEDOINE SALAD.

Take cold boiled potatoes, beets, string beans, carrots, turnips, canned peas and anything else you may wish to add; provide plenty of dressing and you have a fine relish.

CONTRIBUTED.

NASTURTIUM SALAD.

A really delicious salad can be made by combining ripe tomatoes, cold boiled potatoes, and both the tender leaves and blossoms of the nasturtium. Choose a shallow glass dish, and arrange the leaves and flowers around the edge, forming a border with the stems running down toward the centre. Place the sliced tomatoes and potatoes in the dish in alternate layers with a little finely chopped onion here and there. Pour a French dressing over the whole, and let stand on ice for half an hour before serving. Toss all together, the leaves and flowers and the other ingredients, and serve as usual. The leaves will be found to have soaked up the dressing through their stems, and to have a peculiarly pungent and delicious flavor. The blossoms are greatly liked by many persons, but can always be laid aside if their unusual flavor is not found to the taste.

CONTRIBUTED.

NILE SALAD.

One-fourth pound of chicken, one pair of sweetbreads, five cups celery, one-half pint each of almonds and pecans, four tablespoons lemon juice, one quart mayonnaise. Boil chicken until tender, then boil sweetbreads with chicken thirty minutes, chop and mix all with salt, pepper, nuts, lemon juice, then add mayonnaise. Serves twenty persons.

MRS. RUSSELL, Knoxville, Tenn.

NUT SALAD.

One pound English walnuts, shelled, white meat of one chicken, one pint of mayonnaise dressing, garnish with sliced olives, serve on lettuce leaves or in fresh tomatoes.

MRS. RUSSELL, Knoxville, Tenn.

ORANGE SALAD.

For six plates pare three oranges perfectly clean and cut across the grain, separate sections and cut again. Place on lettuce. On top of orange, put one teaspoon of finely minced onion, then add two tablespoons of chopped celery to each plate. Sprinkle lightly with salt and serve very cold, with mayonnaise.

MISS MARGARET BURNS, Bristol, Va

PEPPER SALAD.

Remove the skin from six green peppers and chop them fine, peel one red pepper and chop it very fine; peel and chop a Spanish onion, weighing a quarter of a pound; peel and chop six tomatoes; mix with these ingredients two teaspoons of salt, carefully separate the leaves of two heads of lettuce, wash them in plenty of cold water and dry them by shaking them in a towel.

Arrange the lettuce and chopped salad in a salad bowl in layers, pour over it half a cupful of salad oil and three tablespoons of vinegar and serve.

MRS. WILL CHAMBERLAIN, Knoxville, Tenn.

PERFECTION SALAD.

One-half package of Knox's gelatine, one-half cup cold water, one-half cup vinegar, juice of one lemon, one pint of boiling water, one-half cup sugar, one teaspoon salt, two cups celery, cut in small pieces, one cup finely shredded cabbage, one-fourth can sweet red peppers, finely cut.

Soak gelatine in cold water two minutes, add vinegar, lemon juice, boiling water, sugar and salt. Strain and when beginning to set add remaining ingredients. Turn into a mold and chill. Serve on lettuce leaves with mayonnaise dressing, or cut in dice and serve in cases made of red or green peppers.

A delicious accompaniment to cold sliced chicken or veal.

MRS. JOHN R. COOKE, New Castle, Pa.

PINEAPPLE SALAD.

Cut off the bottom end of a ripe pineapple, leaving the green end intact.

Scoop out the inside and mix with this, English walnuts, celery, and a little each of orange and apple, cover with mayonnaise and return the mixture to the hull of the pineapple, place on a plate with some of the salad falling out of the hull. This is very attractive on a silver platter.

MRS. C.S. NEWMAN, Knoxville, Tenn.

POTATO SALAD.

Peel and cut in pieces, not too small, Irish potatoes enough for dinner, boil in salt water till nearly done, drain off the water and put with them two or three sliced onions, with salt and pepper. Take more than half pint of vinegar and a piece of butter size of an egg, put them in a separate saucepan, adding to it the yellows of two eggs, one-half cup sweet cream, teaspoon mustard, well beaten together. Pour the mixture over the potatoes and onions and simmer ten or fifteen minutes.

MRS. A.M. FRENCH, Knoxville, Tenn.

POTATO SALAD.

One pint of cold boiled potatoes cut into dice, or shaved, season with salt and pepper, put a layer of potatoes in a fancy dish, the yelk of a hard boiled egg rubbed through a sieve, one teaspoon chopped parsley, moisten with French dressing. Yelks of three eggs, beaten well, one teaspoon mustard, two of salt, one-fourth saltspoon of cayenne, two scant tablespoons sugar, two of melted butter or olive oil, one cup cream or milk, whites of the three eggs beaten stiff, put all in a double boiler and cook till slightly thickened, last after cooking it, add one-half cup of hot vinegar. When cold pour over salad.

CONTRIBUTED.

POTATO SALAD.

Be sure to cut the potatoes up while hot and add a little finely chopped onion, so that the flavor of the onion goes thoroughly through them. Pour a French dressing over all and set aside to cool. When ready to use place on lettuce and garnish with parsley. You will find by putting the dressing on while the salad is hot, that the potatoes will be saturated with the dressing and yet firm.

CONTRIBUTED.

POTATO AND CUCUMBER SALAD.

Yelks of five eggs, one-half teaspoon of salt, little red pepper, one tablespoon of sugar; beat all together, then add one-half cup of melted butter, one-half cup of vinegar; put on stove, cook until thick. Before using add one-half cup of whipped cream. Have potatoes cut up in cubes, cucumbers sliced and add dressing just before serving.

RICE SALAD.

Two cups of boiled rice, one cup of red beets, boiled and chopped, one cup of celery cut rather fine. Make the dressing as for ordinary salad, cream is better than oil.

MRS. WILL CHAMBERLAIN, Knoxville, Tenn.

RUSSIAN SALAD.

Use equal parts of cold, boiled potatoes and white beans, well salted, cut into dice. Chop fine a little onion, celery and parsley, just enough to flavor it nicely. Add hard boiled eggs, cut into small pieces, say two eggs to a medium dish of salad. Mix it all thoroughly with a plentiful supply of French dressing and serve on lettuce.

Instead of using French dressing a little tiny bit of mayonnaise, strong mustard is delicious.

CONTRIBUTED.

SLAW.

Shred a head of cabbage very fine, sprinkle with salt and black pepper. Then take one cup vinegar, one tablespoon of butter, one teaspoon of sugar, one teacup three-fourths full of cream, with an egg mixed in the cream.

Put the vinegar, butter and sugar in a porcelain stew pan, let it come to the boil, then put in the cabbage and cream, let it come to the boil again, then put it in the dish and cover. It is ready to serve.

MISS EMMA EVANS, Knoxville, Tenn.

TOMATO SALAD.

Like most other kinds of salads it should be dressed only just before serving, and for variety, Spanish onions and sweet peppers may be mixed with the tomatoes; for the dressing use either the French dressing or mayonnaise.

TOMATO SALAD.

As far as possible use tomatoes of uniform size. Put them in a pan and pour boiling water over them to remove the skins. After this has been done place them in a cool place to become firm. Select the small curled leaves of the lettuce, forming a separate bed for each tomato. Slice each tomato, replacing the slices, so that the tomato is perfect once more. Put one in each little lettuce bed, and on its top a good lump of stiff mayonnaise.

CONTRIBUTED.

TOMATO AND CUCUMBER SALAD.

Take medium size, smooth tomatoes, pare nicely, cut off tops and remove seeds without breaking cells, chop cucumbers, a little onion, also celery if you wish, marinate with French dressing, stuff tomatoes with the mixture. Place on lettuce leaves and serve with mayonnaise. A red radish placed on plate adds to appearance.

MISS MARGARET BURNS, Bristol, Va.-Tenn.

TOMATO AND CUCUMBER SALAD.

Alternate slices of dressed tomato and cucumber along the sides of a salad bowl, with a line of heart leaves of lettuce between these. Decorate the slices of a tomato with stars of mayonnaise dressing.

MRS. C.R. McILWAINE, Knoxville, Tenn.

TOMATO AND GELATINE SALAD.

Soak a half box of gelatine in a pint of boiling water. When dissolved, add the strained juice of half a can of tomatoes. About one pint of the juice would be right. Strain through a cloth to keep the seeds from going in. Season well with salt. Pour it in a mold, (a ring mold is prettiest), and set it away to get firm; then turn it out on a shallow dish, which has been dressed with lettuce leaves. Fill in the centre of the ring with celery mayonnaise. Have plenty of mayonnaise so that the gelatine may be well flavored when eaten. It is a very artistic dish and very refreshing.

CONTRIBUTED.

SALMON SALAD.

One large can of salmon, cut the salmon into small pieces and mix with the following dressing: Yellows of three hard boiled eggs, two tablespoons butter, mixed with the eggs while hot, one heaping tablespoon of sugar, one-half teaspoon salt, one dessert spoon of made mustard. Chop whites of eggs very fine, and mix with above and last, add one-half cup vinegar.

MRS. W.W. CARSON, Knoxville, Tenn.

SALMON SALAD.

One can salmon, bones picked out, one-half teaspoon salt, pinch pepper, tablespoon olive oil, one-half tumbler good vinegar, four pickles, chopped fine, four tablespoons French salad dressing. Mix all well together and garnish with parsley.

MRS. SANDY McNUTT, Knoxville, Tenn.

SPANISH SALAD.

Cut cold chicken in dice, boil large Spanish chestnuts, carefully remove all skin, cut in half, mix with chicken, and an equal quantity of celery.

Cover with mayonnaise and serve on lettuce.

MRS. C.S. NEWMAN, Knoxville, Tenn.

STRING BEAN SALAD.

Boil white wax string beans in salted water until tender, let get cold. Place on salad dish, arrange sliced tomatoes around the edge, with mayonnaise on the top and serve very cold. If you do not have the tomatoes, cold, sliced beets are very nice. This is a pretty dish and good too.

MRS. MARY ANN MATTHEWS, Washington, D. C.

SWEETBREADS AND CELERY.

Cut cold cooked sweetbreads into dice and mix with equal quantity of celery. Cover with mayonnaise and garnish with lettuce.

MISS WILL CHAMBERLAIN, Knoxville, Tenn.

VEAL SALAD.

Three pints chopped veal, cooked, one pint chopped celery or cabbage, tender part, if cabbage, use celery salt. From eight to ten eggs, boiled hard, whites chopped, yelks smoothed down while hot with butter size of an egg, small tablespoon of mustard, teaspoon sugar, vinegar to thin about like thick molasses. Cheaper than chicken and about as good.

MISS MARGARET H. BURNS, Bristol, Va.

VEGETABLE SALAD.

One small can French peas, one pint chopped tomatoes, one cup chopped celery, one cup chopped nuts. Mix and pour over it this dressing:

Dressing—Three eggs, beaten until smooth, one-half cup vinegar, one teaspoon sugar, one teaspoon mustard, one tablespoon butter, one-fourth teaspoon black pepper and one-half teaspoon of salt, cook till thick, when cold, thin with a little cold vinegar.

MRS. JOSEPH W. OWEN, Bristol, Tenn.

WHITE WAX CHERRY SALAD.

Stone one can of white wax cherries, replace seed with filberts or any nut preferred, small can of chunk pineapple, drain thoroughly of sweet syrup, let stand five minutes in juice of one lemon, tablespoon of olive oil, speck of red pepper, serve on headed lettuce, adding a few red cherries and mayonnaise made very firm.

MRS. BENJ. D. BRABSON, Knoxville, Tenn.

SANDWICHES

SANDWICH HINTS.

Fairly stale, rather close-grained bread is best; spongy new bread is never successful. A tin, or a regular sandwich loaf saves great waste and labor in cutting them neatly, and all of one size. Have a sharp knife, cut thin slices and trim off the crust.

Finely chopped chicken or tongue, or ham, covered with a crisp lettuce leaf, torn in fairly small pieces, and dipped in a mayonnaise sauce. Thin small pieces of ham or beef are excellent with a little horseradish sauce spread on top. Tomatoes, peeled, sprinkled with oil, salt, pepper, a few drops of vinegar and a dust of chopped parsley.

CONTRIBUTED.

SANDWICH SUGGESTIONS:

Cut rounds of brown or white bread, butter and place between the rounds chicken salad.

A sandwich composed of cream cheese, stuffed olives, ground, and mayonnaise dressing, either between zephyrettes or light bread is fine.

A nice sandwich is made of hard boiled eggs, put through the grinder, with English walnuts, then mix with mayonnaise and put between thin slices of bread.

Canned salmon, mixed with mayonnaise and spread on a lettuce leaf between slices of bread is another, and a peanut sandwich is very nice. If you cannot get the peanut paste, take roasted peanuts and mix to a paste with butter and salt, and put between thin slices of bread.

MRS. A.S. BIRDSONG, Knoxville, Tenn.

CHEESE AND OLIVE SANDWICHES.

Beat the cream cheese until soft, to one small roll add six olives, stoned, chopped fine and a dash of cayenne pepper. Spread on thin slices of white bread and press together, cut in any desirable shape.

MRS. WILL BEWLAY DUENNER, Bristol, Va.

CHEESE AND PIMENTO SANDWICHES.

Make any cooked dressing or mayonnaise and with it mix one-half pound of cheese, grated, not melted, a little cream added makes it delicious. When thoroughly mixed spread upon the bread and then spread the pimento and a lettuce leaf on this. I prefer the mixture spread on both pieces of bread. You can cut up stuffed olives and use just as you do the pimentoes.

MRS. FRANK DAVIS, Bristol, Tenn.

CLUB SANDWICHES.

These delectable morsels call for white bread toasted crisply. The filling may be of grilled ham or bacon, or of broiled chicken with the addition of a taste of either of the first two meats. A morsel of either broiled ham or bacon always gives an extra fillip to chicken. A leaf of delicate lettuce is put on first on a slice of the toast; then comes the meat, with a sprinkle of salt, cayenne, and a squeeze of lemon juice for the final notes. Most sandwiches are better without butter, and these call absolutely for the broiling of the meat. This cooking and the toast realize the name "club sandwich".

CONTRIBUTED.

DRESSING FOR HAM SANDWICHES.

Two and one-half cups butter, two tablespoons dry mustard and a little sugar. Pour one pint of warm vinegar on the butter and mustard, stir to a cream, then add six well beaten eggs. After all is well mixed, put the whole in a pan and cook until thick; a small quantity of celery seed is an improvement. Chop or grate the ham and mix well with the dressing when cold.

MRS. WM. J. BROWN, Bristol, Va.

FIG AND NUT SANDWICHES.

For figs and nuts use the soft figs that come in baskets or boxes. Chop the figs soft, putting a very little flour on the chopping-knife to keep them from sticking and add to them an equal amount of chopped pecans or other kind of nuts. Mix together with cream until it will spread readily. These are especially good when used with brown bread, cut thin.

MRS. WILL BEWLAY DUENNER, Bristol, Va.

FIG-PECAN SANDWICHES.

One-half pound Turkish figs, one-half pound golden dates, one-half pound pecan nuts, one-half pound shelled Jordan Almonds. Run all through a meat chopper and mix thoroughly, pack in round baking powder tins and press down firmly, let stand over night. When wanted for use, dip can into hot water, and loosen contents with knife, cut into very thin slices and place between rounds of buttered bread.

MRS. MARY JONES.

LEMON-BANANA SANDWICHES.

Lemon-banana sandwiches are a great favorite. The bananas are sliced round, thinly, and lemon juice, a few drops, squeezed on each slice, then a pinch of sugar. The slices of bread or bun for these sandwiches are spread with cream instead of butter, and the banana laid on the half slice in a single layer of the prepared fruit.

MRS. WILL BEWLAY DUENNER, Bristol, Va.

RUSSIAN SANDWICHES.

Spread thin slices of Boston brown bread stamped out in oval shape and lightly buttered with Neufchatel, or any cream cheese. Spread, also an equal number of slices stamped out and buttered with fine, chopped olives and pimentoes mixed with mayonnoise dressing. Press together in pairs with a crisp heart leaf of lettuce between each pair. Serve while the lettuce is fresh.

MRS. WILL BEWLAY DUENNER, Bristol, Va.

SWEETBREAD SANDWICHES.

Wash the sweetbreads and put them in a sauce pan with just enough boiling water to cover them. Put in a scant teaspoon of salt and two tablespoons of vinegar. Keep them simmering for twenty minutes, then drain them and let them stand for half an hour. When they are cold, break them into small pieces and work to a paste with a sliver fork, adding three tablespoons of fine bread crumbs, one tablespoon of melted butter, one tablespoon of thick, sweet cream, and salt and white pepper to season highly. Heat very slowly and let just simmer for five minutes. Let the mixture cool before putting on bread.

E. B.

TURKEY SANDWICHES, IMPERIAL.

Cut slices of whole wheat bread, one-fourth of an inch in thickness, spread lightly with butter, then with a thin layer of minced ham or tongue, seasoned with a pinch of cayenne pepper, arrange slices of cold turkey (preferably the breast meat) on top of the ham and cover with mayonnaise dressing. Place on individual plates, garnishing each sandwich with squares of aspic jelly and a tiny star of hard-boiled egg. Serve with blanched crisp celery.

MRS. WILL BEWLAY DUENNER, Bristol, Va.

SHERBETS

SHERBET.

Squeeze the juice of fourteen lemons into a bowl, throw in the half pieces also, sweeten two gallons of water with eight full teacups of loaf sugar, add the lemon juice and strain through a colander, when this begins to freeze stir in the whites of eight eggs, well beaten.

MRS. SOPHIE K. HUNTER, Knoxville, Tenn.

CAPE MAY ICE.

One-half gallon of good strong lemonade, one quart of fresh strawberries mashed through a strainer and sweetened, one can of grated pineapple. Mix well and freeze.

MRS. A.P. WHITE, Knoxville, Tenn.

FROZEN CRANBERRIES.

Boil two quarts of cranberries till soft; strain through a jelly bag; add one pint of sugar to the liquid and partly freeze; then add the stiffly beaten whites of four eggs, freeze and let stand for two hours or more. This is lovely to take the place of cranberry jelly with turkey. Serve in sherbet glasses.

MRS. M.A. DOOLEY, Washington, D. C.

THE FIVE THREES.

Three lemons, three oranges, three bananas, three big cups sugar, three cups water. Squeeze lemons, chop peeled oranges and bananas, make a syrup of water and sugar, and when cool, add the lemons and oranges and freeze, makes almost half a gallon.

MISS NELL RHEA, Shoun's, Tenn.

WELSH GRAPE SHERBET.

One and one-half pints grape juice, two pints water, one and one-fourth pounds sugar, juice of one lemon. Mix, freeze medium stiff. Take whites of two eggs and two tablespoons powdered sugar, beat thoroughly, stir into sherbet and freeze as hard as possible. Let stand for one hour or more.

MRS. C.T. LEONHARDT, Knoxville, Tenn.

GINGER SHERBET.

Boil a pound of sugar and a quart of water together for five minutes, then add the juice of three lemons. Strain and set aside to cool, when very cold, add half a cupful of syrup. Turn into a freezer and freeze as you would ordinary water ice.

MRS. C.R. McILWAINE, Knoxville, Tenn.

GRAPE SHERBET.

Make a syrup of three cups white sugar and one quart water, let cool, add the juice of two or three lemons and of two big bunches of black grapes. Concords are best, put into freezer can and add water to fill a little less than two-thirds full. Freeze until the paddle begins to be heavy, open and add the beaten whites of three eggs, put on lid and turn until stiff, take out paddle and stir down and pack. Let stand an hour or longer. This is enough for a gallon freezer.

MRS. W.N. PATTON, Bristol, Tenn.

LEMON SHERBET.

One quart of milk, four lemons, one pint sugar, shave the rind of three lemons and pour one one-fourth cup of boiling water, let stand until cool. Put milk into freezer and pack as for freezing, then pour in lemon juice and sugar; strain the water from rind and add to the lemon juice and sugar. The milk must be cold before other things are added or it will curdle.

MRS. E.V. FISH, Central Falls, R.I.

PEACH SHERBET.

One quart fresh peaches, mashed smooth, one quart water, one pund sugar or more, if peaches are acid. Mix and freeze. Stir in whites of three eggs well beaten when it begins to freeze.

MRS. A.P. WHITE, Knoxville, Tenn.

PINEAPPLE SHERBET.

One can grated pineapple, juice two large lemons, two pounds sugar, five pints water. Put in the freezer and as soon as it commences to freeze add the beaten whites of three eggs.

MRS. E.S. McCLUNG, Knoxville, Tenn.

PINEAPPLE SHERBET.

Grate one can of pineapple, add one teacup sugar, pour over it one quart boiling water, let it stand till cold, add two grated lemons, one cup sugar, one and one-half pints water. When it begins to freeze add whites of three eggs well beaten.

MRS. SOPHIE K. HUNTER, Knoxville Tenn.

PINEAPPLE SHERBET.

One can grated pineapple, one quart boiling water, two and one-half cups white sugar, two lemons, one tablespoon gelatine. Put the water, sugar, and juice of lemons on the fire, add the gelatine and let boil till sugar and gelatine is dissolved, add grated pineapple and when cold freeze. You can omit the pineapple and thus have a lemon sherbet. The gelatine will dissolve more quickly if soaked in a little water.

MISS BRANCH KEEBLER, Bristol, Tenn.

PINEAPPLE SHERBET.

Two cans pineapple, pour over it two quarts boiling water, strain into this the juice of four lemons, add five cups sugar, and just before freexing beat in the whites of six eggs, beaten to a stiff froth.

MRS. ARTHUR WALTON, Tazewell, Va.

RASPBERRY SHERBET IN JELLY CUPS.

Heat and strain one quart canned raspberries. Freeze a pint of milk five minutes; add the raspberries, strained and cooled. Freeze until stiff. Make a lemon jelly and mould in large deep muffin cups. When ready to serve the sherbet, turn out the jelly, scoop out the centres, and fill with sherbet.

MRS. C.R. McILWAINE, Knoxville, Tenn.

STRAWBERRY FRAPPE.

One quart of berries rubbed through a colander and sweetened to tast, and one quart of water. Take one tablespoon of gelatine and cover with cold water for about fifteen minutes, then add one teacup of hot water. When cool, mix all together and freeze. When half frozen add the beaten whites of two eggs. Whipped cream added with the eggs in any quantity is a great improvement.

MRS. M.A. DOOLEY, Washington, D. C.

FROZEN STRAWBERRIES.

Take two quarts of berries and mash well, to this add one cup of sugar and juice of one lemon, put in baking powder cans and pack in larger vessel with ice and salt for one hour. Take out of can and slice and serve with whipped cream. This is a good way to use small berries.

MRS. H.M. SIMMONDS, Knoxville, Tenn.

SOUPS

DIRECTIONS FOR MAKING VARIOUS KINDS OF SOUPS.

Of course there is hardly a time when one does not have ham, beef or lamb, often the bone out of steak. I seldom buy a soup bone, unless for a good lot of okra soup. I do not allow these to go back to the kitchen. but strip off meat and put in the refrigerator for soup the next day.

If I had for instance, a steak bone only, I would boil, and to that add a can of good canned soup. Then in boiling rice I would pour the water off and put in my soup, the same way with potatoes and turnips, which seasons very much better than clear hot water.

Often I put but one-half a can of soup stock, if I thought it rich enough, always add a lump of butter, about the helping of butter to a butter plate.

Now to change the soup, I often in using canned soup or in just water boiled either from soup bone or bones left of ham, lamb or beef, put in the soup one day, rice and tomatoes, another time season with green peppers, chopped fine; the same soup next day with a few slices of lemon sliced thin, tastes entirely different; the same soup another day, seasoned with celery, chopped celery and parsley, is very different, and so on.

If you take a ham bone or piece of bacon, say half a pound and boil enough turnips for dinner, after taking out your dish for dinner leave about two tablespoons of turnips, add a tablespoon of sweet milk, pepper nicely, salt and add a few sprays of parsley for looks and you have a delicious soup. When I have asparagus I take up my dish for dinner, chop about three pieces fine and put back in water, being already salt, would pepper and put butter in and with a few sprays of parsley there was my soup for dinner.

A quart of sweet milk boiled and into this, potato (white) fixed as for table with butter and creamed nicely (if left from the day before it is all right) about two cups full to a quart of milk, into this put just the least bit of grated onion, a small piece of butter and a few sprays of parsley and just before taking off the fire, stir into it quickly the yelk of an egg, previously stirred with a little milk. Do not salt until in tureen ready for table to prevent curdling.

Corn soup may be made very much the same way. Of course it is nicer in summer when you can get green corn and have it grated. A nice corn in cans makes a very nice soup. Cook the corn, add a light half teaspoon of sugar, light quart of milk, let come to a boil, add corn to this and a teaspoon of flour, creamed into a tablespoon of butter. Just before taking off the fire add yelk of an egg, previously stirred in a tablespoon of milk, add salt and pepper to taste, after being dished in the tureen.

Now in Okra soup, a roast beef bone, if you have it, with a little piece of pork, or a chicken, or part of one, a quarter or even half a peck of okra and plenty of tomatoes, or half the quantity of okra and tomatoes, a whole bell pepper, taking out the seed, one carrot, one large onion, one or two potatoes, and a liberal supply of green pepper, chopped fine and put in just as you are taking the soup off the stove. After all it is the seasoning that makes soups palatable.

A delicious oyster soup is made in this way: To one gallon of oysters, take one quart of milk and yelks of six eggs. Strain liquor from oysters and put it on to cook. If you have not as much liquor as solid oysters, make it as much by adding hot water. While the liquor boils, have the milk getting hot in another vessel and when it comes to a boil pour it on the well beaten yelks of the eggs. Take two large spoonsful of butter and cream with the same quantity of flour and put in the hot custard and stir until smooth. When the liquor boils well, add the oysters and then the custard. Season with the least bit of grated onion, a tiny bit of nutmeg and pour over toast, if you like it, right in your soup tureen.

I do not care for the toast that way, but prefer the bread cut in tiny squares and toasted very brown or fried either in lard or strip of bacon, in with lard.

I frequently take one quart of oysters, one pint of milk and yelks of two eggs and make as above.

When eggs are added to soup it is more nutritious. It is best to make soup the day before using, so that it may be allowed to get cold. and have all grease taken from it.

CONTRIBUTED.

BISQUE OF CLAMS.

Take a pint of clams and place them, with their own liquor and a pint of water, in a porcelain kettle over the fire. When they commence to simmer, take them out and mince them; replace in the kettle with a tea-spoon of chopped onion and the same amount of parsley, and a bit of mace. Simmer fifteen minutes; strain and return to the fire with a pint of stock. Thoroughly mix a teaspoon of flour with one of butter and pour the soup slowly over it. It ought to be of the consistence of cream. Finish by adding half a pint of hot cream and a little cayenne. The soup must not boil after cream is added.

MRS. S.B. BOYD, Knoxville, Tenn.

BOUILLON.

One and one-half pounds beef, one beef bone, two and one-half quarts water, one ounce salt, two carrots, two onions, about two cloves, three leeks, one-half head celery, one-half parsnip, cook thoroughly, strain and serve clear.

MRS. R.S. HAZEN, Knoxville, Tenn.

BOUILLON.

Two pounds of beef, no fat, and one chicken and boil thoroughly all day, skimming carefully all scum and grease, put in one onion, some celery and the usual pot herbs for soup, and let them boil with the meat. It is usually made the day before and thoroughly cooled so that all the grease rises to the surface and is skimmed off, when cold.

The next day put it on and boil up again, it must be strained and when cold should be about the consistency of jelly, Season to taste, salt and pepper, whole cloves and mace are tied in a little bag and boiled in it and a glass of wine is added when about to serve.

The whole secret is thorough boiling and continual skimming until perfectly clear. It must boil slowly, or rather simmer all day, at the back of the stove.

MRS. T.C. CHALMERS, New York City.

CELERY SOUP.

Make good beef broth, skim off the fat, and thicken with a little flour, mixed with water. Cut into small pieces one large bunch of celery, boiling them in the broth until very tender. When done add a cup of rich cream with pepper and salt, or in place of the cream use a tablespoon of butter.

MRS. ALLEN S. MEBANE, Knoxville, Tenn.

CHICKEN SOUP.

To one tablespoon of flour, add one teacup of milk or cream slowly, then the yellow of one or two eggs, beat them well together, then add slowly one quart or more of the boiling stock from the chicken. Let boil until thick enough to serve. Butter, salt and pepper to taste.

MRS. W.M. HOUSE, Knoxville, Tenn.

CORN SOUP.

Take the cobs, after cutting the corn from them, scrape them, put the cobs and scrapings in a kettle and boil, add a little thickening, a small piece of butter, then salt and pepper to taste. It is very delicate. A little cream or milk added is quite an improvement.

CONTRIBUTED.

CREAM OF CELERY SOUP.

One quart of finely chopped celery. Cover with one quart of water, simmer gently for twenty minutes. Press through a colander. Put one quart of milk in a double boiler. Rub together two tablespoons of butter and two of flour; add and stir until smooth and thick. Add a rounding teaspoonful of salt, a salt spoon of white pepper; add the celery mixture. Strain the whole through a fine sieve, bring to boiling, serve at once.

MRS. C.R. McILWAINE, Knoxville, Tenn.

CREAM OF PEA SOUP.

Soak three-quarters of a pint of dried peas over night in a quart of water; in the morning, add boiling water, cover closely and simmer gently four or five hours, then rub through the colander to remove skins. Just before the peas are done, prepare one and one-half pints potatoes cut in thin slices. Cook until tender, in very little water. Rub through colander. Add the potatoes to the sifted peas, and milk enough to make three and one-half pints in all. Return to the fire, add a small head of celery, cut in finger lengths, let all simmer together fifteen minutes. Remove the celery with a fork, add salt and a cup of thin cream. This should make about two quarts of soup.

MRS. C.R. McILWAINE, Knoxville, Tenn.

IRISH POTATO SOUP.

Peel and boil eight medium sized potatoes with a large onion sliced. some herbs, salt and pepper. Press through a colander. then thin it with rich milk and add a lump of butter, more seasoning, if necessary. Let it heat well and serve hot.

MRS. W.K. VANCE, Bristol, Tenn.

GUMBO (AN OLD CREOLE RECEIPT).

Fry slowly together one sliced onion and a tablespoon of drippings or a slice of salt pork. Add a pound of lean beef, cut in small pieces, stew quickly. Dredge with a heaping tablespoon of flour and, cook until brown.

Add three pints boiling water, one pint peeled and sliced tomatoes and one pint sliced okra. Cover and simmer for an hour and a half, adding salt and pepper to taste. Chicken may be used instead of beef, or crabs or shrimp. In the latter case these should be previously boiled and the meat picked out and added last. A little chopped ham is always an improvement. Serve with boiled rice. The gumbo should be very thick.

MRS. C.R. McILWAINE, Knoxville, Tenn.

GUMBO SOUP.

Fry a young chicken until brown, then put on in cold water with one onion, salt, pepper, about a quart of young tender pods of okra, cook until thoroughly done. Two or three ripe tomatoes added, twenty minutes before taking from the fire improves the soup.

This same seasoning added to any kind of soup stock is good, if you can't "catch a chicken".

MRS. W.K. VANCE, Bristol, Tenn.

GUMBO.

Fry one grown chicken and boil it two hours in a stove pot full of water. Add one quart of sliced tomatoes, one quart of sliced okra, boil three hours longer, half an hour before dinner add one small onion, chopped, salt, pepper and sugar to suit the taste. A small slice of boiled ham is thought to be an addition to the flavor. Do not add more water unless there is danger of burning. Serve with rice at table. The above may be varied by adding more okra or tomatoes, if preferred.

MRS. S.S. BOOTH, Vicksburg, Miss.

CHICKEN GUMBO.

Heat some fat in a fryer, wash, and cut up in pieces one pint of okra, put into fat and fry a light brown, add one onion, cut into small pieces, let it brown and add one tablespoon of flour, browned. Now add one quart of tomatoes cut fine, one ear of green corn, grated; let all boil together for a few minutes, add this to soup stock that has been previously strained. Season highly with cayenne and salt.

Cut up one chicken in small pieces, fry in boiling fat and add to soup. Must be very thick. Serve with or without boiled rice.

MRS. B.B. BURNS, Bristol, Va.-Tenn.

OX TAIL SOUP.

Take one or two tails, wash clean and put in a gallon of cold water, add a small handful of salt; when the meat is well cooked, take out the bones.

If this is boiled the day before needed, let it stand till cold and skim off the fat. An hour and a half before dinner, put on to cook with an onion, four or five cloves stuck in it, a carrot, cut in thin slices, or any other vegetable you prefer.

MRS. W.K VANCE, Bristol, Tenn.

OYSTER SOUP.

To one gallon oysters, two quarts milk, one quart cream, one pound of butter. Put the liquor, milk, cream, and one-half of the butter in a kettle; when it comes to a boil add the oysters, the remaining butter with one tablespoon of flour worked in it, pepper and salt to taste. Take off as soon as it comes to a boil, add crackers if desired.

MRS. JAMES KENNNEDY, Knoxville, Tenn.

OYSTER BISQUE.

Cover half a pint of finely chopped celery with a pint of water, stew slowly half an hour. Drain and wash twenty-five oysters, put in a saucepan and shake over the fire until they have boiled for five minutes. Drain, this time saving the liquor. Chop the oysters fine; add them to the liquor. Now mix the celery and oysters together, add to them a quart of milk. Rub together two tablespoons butter and two of flour; add this to the mixture and cook ten minutes longer, strain through a fine sieve. Add a rounding teaspoon of salt, saltspoon of white pepper. Serve at once in bouillon cups.

MRS. C.R. McILWAINE, Knoxville, Tenn.

QUEEN VICTORIA'S FAVORITE SOUP.

One cup chopped chicken meat, one pint chicken broth, one pint sweet cream, one-half cup cracker or bread crumbs, yelks of three eggs, teaspoon salt, one-half teaspoon pepper. Soak the cracker crumbs in a little of the cream. Drop the yelks of three eggs into hot water and boil until hard, chop the chicken until it is as fine as meal, add the soaked cracker to it, press the hard yelks through a coarse wire strainer and add all to the broth with salt and pepper, then strain the whole through, a colander, pressing through all of the meat. Heat in a double boiler for half an hour and serve.

MRS. DANIEL BRISCOE, SR., Knoxville, Tenn.

TOMATO SOUP.

Boil for ten minutes, a quart of tomatoes and a pint of water, a slice of onion, a bay leaf, and half a teaspoon of celery seed. Rub together one and one-half tablespoons of butter and three tablespoons of sifted flour; add this to the soup, stir until boiling and add salt to taste and a dash of red pepper. Strain, reheat and serve with squares of buttered toast.

MRS. ALLEN S. MEBANE, Knoxville, Tenn.

RUSSIAN SOUP. (BORSCH)

Boil four medium sized beets, or use canned beets, when cold cut in slices about one quarter of an inch thick and then in narrow strips the same width.

Heat one quart of good beef stock which has been already seasoned with a few vegetables and herbs. Add the shredded beets, two tablespoons of vinegar, a teaspoon of sugar and half a dozen each of cloves, allspice and whole peppers. Let boil together a minute or so and add a bit of finely chopped parsley.

Place in the soup tureen one cup of very thick sour cream, add a little soup and mix well before pouring in the rest, or send the soup to the table and serve the sour cream separately in a sauce dish.

The amount of vinegar and sugar used depends on the taste, many preferring to omit one or the other. If a little smoked bacon or ham is cooked with the soup meat it gives a good flavor. Small slices of ham are then served in the soup.

MRS. D.B. MACGOWAN, Knoxville, Tenn.

TOMATO SOUP.

Heat one quart of tomatoes, when they boil, add one-fourth teaspoon of soda, then press through a colander. Return to the fire, add salt, pepper and celery seed to taste, also one tablespoon of butter, rubbed smooth with two tablespoons of flour.

Let all boil and add one pint of hot sweet milk and serve at once.

MRS. JOSEPH W. OWEN, Bristol, Tenn.

TOMATO SOUP.

One quart can tomatoes, one pint of hot water, one tablespoon of sugar, one teaspoon salt, four cloves, four pepper corns. Put all on the stove, let cook till tomatoes are soft enough to strain.

Melt one tablespoon of butter in a saucepan, add one tablespoon chopped onion, let cook till onion is yellow, then add one tablespoon of flour, slowly add tomato mixture, add one tablespoon chopped parsley, cook till slightly thickened or simmer about ten minutes. Strain through a sieve and serve at once with crouton.

CONTRIBUTED.

TOMATO AND RICE SOUP.

Boil one-half cup of rice until very soft. To one quart of good beef stock, which has been already seasoned with vegetables and herbs, add the soft rice and about half a can of tomatoes, which have been stewed with a sliced onion and a small piece of bacon or ham.

Boil together a few minutes and season with salt and pepper. Pour a little of the soup on a cupful of thick sour cream and mix thoroughly, then pour in the rest. Or serve the soup in the tureen and send the cream to the table in a sauce boat separately.

This soup can be made very thick with rice and tomato. The beef stock may also be omitted if an extra bit of bacon be added to the tomato and sufficient water be poured in to thin it. The soup looks nicer if the tomatoes are pressed through a colander.

MRS. D.B. MACGOWAN, Knoxville, Tenn.

VEAL SOUP.

Put a knuckle of veal into three quarts of cold water with a small quantity of salt and one small tablespoon of cooked rice. Boil slowly, hardly allow simmering, four hours, when the liquor should be reduced to half the quantity. Remove from the fire. Into the tureen put the yelk of one egg and stir well into it a teacup of cream, or in hot weather, new milk; add a piece of butter size of a hickory nut; on this strain the soup, boiling hot, stirring all the time. Just at the last, beat it well for a minute.

MRS. J.S. DONNELLY, Shoun's, Tenn.

VEGETABLE SOUP.

Equal quantity of carrots and turnips, one-half can tomatoes, two quarts of soup stock made of beef, and one pint ham essence. Add butter, pepper and salt to taste, a little celery improves it.

MRS. R.S. HAZEN, Knoxville, Tenn.

PUREE OF VEGETABLE.

Use one medium sized Irish potato, one stalk of celery cut into bits, one-fourth of a carrot, scraped and cut into dice, one-fourth of an onion. chopped, one-fourth of a turnip cut in dice. Fry onion and turnip in one tablespoon of butter, add the rest of the vegetables, cover with boiling water, cook till soft enough to strain, thicken slightly with flour, rub through a sieve, season with salt and pepper and serve with croutons.

CONTRIBUTED.

WHITE VELVET SOUP.

Put a good hen, not too fat, in a saucepan with three pints of cold water, cover closely and simmer (never boil), for two hours, while cooking, add one small onion and two cloves.

When the chicken is tender strain the soup and add to it one large head of celery and about four sprigs of parsley, set it back on the stove where it will only steam, not boil, keep covered. When the celery is tender. strain again and add to it one large cup of chicken breast, chopped very fine, and one large cup of blanched almonds, chopped, and one pint of cream, salt and cayenne pepper

SWEET SAUCES

SAUCE.

One egg, one cup sugar, one heaping tablespoon flour, one cup each of milk and water, one tablespoon butter, one-half teaspoon vanilla and one-half teaspoon lemon. Mix in order given, mixing flour smoothly, stir until commenced to cook well or smooth, add butter just before taking from the fire, add extracts when it is cold, may be cooked in double boiler.

MRS. E.J. BRISHELL, Marion, Ala.

A DELICIOUS SAUCE.

One pint sweet milk, one-half cup of sugar, a piece of stick cinnamon, a small piece of butter. Let all come to a good boil, then stir in a full teaspoon of corn starch, dissolved in a little cold water. Everything made of milk should be cooked over water.

MRS. J.T. McTEER, Knoxville, Tenn.

BURNT SUGAR CARAMEL.

Three cups granulated sugar, one and one-half cups sweet milk, three-fourths cup of butter thoroughly washed and worked in several waters to get all salt out. Put this on the stove and at the same time put one cup of white sugar in a skillet and stir until it melts. By this time the other should be at the boiling point. Stir the boiling milk slowly into the skillet of melted sugar, then put the mixture in sauce pan and boil until rather thick. Let partly cool and beat up til creamy. Flavor with vanilla.

MRS. ERNEST BRISCOE, Knoxville, Tenn.

SAUCE FOR CREAM PUFFS.

Heat the puffs and serve them on hot plates, pouring over them this sauce. One quart of brown sugar, one egg, broken whole, lump of butter, size of a hickory nut, three tablespoons of cream, flavor to suit taste. Beat very hard and then just let simmer; if too thick add more cream.

MRS. ELIZA BRANNER, Knoxville, Tenn.

FAIRY SAUCE.

Two cups granulated sugar, one cup butter, one yelk. Beat egg, sugar and butter together until very light and creamy, set in boiling water and stir constantly, beat the white very light and stir thoroughly into the sauce, flavor with whiskey; if too thick, thin with hot water.

LUCH ASHMORE, Sanibel, Fla.

HARD SAUCE.

In a tablespoon of butter rub two teacups of white sugar and a wine glass of wine, heap upon a plate and grate nutmeg over it.

MRS. T.W. FLEMING, Knoxville, Tenn.

HARD SAUCE.

One and one-half cups powdered sugar, small piece butter, chop together a minute, pour on a tablespoon of boiling water and beat hard, add a dash of salt and half teaspoon of vanilla extract.

CONTRIBUTED.

HARD SAUCE.

One-third cup of butter, one cup pulverized sugar, two tablespoons hot water, one teaspoon of vanilla. Beat hard and long.

MRS. LUCY BROWNLEE, Knoxville, Tenn.

LIQUID SAUCE.

One cup sugar, one-half cup butter, beat well together, add to it the white and yelk of one egg, beaten separately and three-fourths of a cup of boiling water, adding but little at a time and stirring constantly to prevent curdling. Put on the fire and let it boil until it thickens. Flavor with wine or brandy.

MRS. E.S. McCLUNG, Knoxville, Tenn.

LIQUID SAUCE.

To two eggs well-beaten, one-half cup of butter, one cup sugar well mixed, pour in a tumbler of boiling wine.

MRS. RHODA WILLIAMS, Knoxville, Tenn.

SAUCE FOR PUDDING.

Two eggs well-beaten, one-half cup butter, one cup sugar, pour in a cup of boiling wine.

MRS. T.W. FLEMING, Knoxville, Tenn.

SAUCE FOR PUDDING.

Whites of two eggs, one cup of sugar, beaten together, add one teaspoon of vinegar, beat well, then add three tablespoons of wine, just as it goes to the table add two-thirds of a cup of sweet cream.

MRS. J.G.M. RAMSEY, Knoxville, Tenn.

SAUCE FOR PUDDING.

One and one-half pints boiling water, molasses enough to color the water, one cup brown sugar, one-third of a cup of butter, cinnamon, nutmeg and lemon to suit the taste, thicken with flour or corn starch.

MRS. J.A. RAYL, Knoxville, Tenn.

PUDDING SAUCE.

Two tablespoons of butter, ten of sugar, work until light, flavor to taste.

MRS. B.J. STEPHENSON, Knoxville, Tenn.

PUDDING SAUCE.

Two ounces butter, four tablespoons fine white sugar, white of one egg, one gill boiling water, one glass of wine, grated rind of half a lemon. Cream the butter and sugar, add the white of the egg, well-beaten, and pour on the boiling water, add the wine and grated lemon.

MRS. T.W. FLEMING, Knoxville, Tenn.

PUDDING SAUCE.

Yelk of one egg, tablespoon of flour in a tablespoon of cold water, one cup boiling water, poured over egg, flour and water and stir piece of butter size of a walnut, cup of sugar, flavor with lemon juice or nutmeg. Beat this into the beaten white of the egg just before serving. This sauce is especially for Raisin Puffs.

MRS. H.P. WYMAN, Bristol, Tenn.

WINE SAUCE.

Have ready some rich, thick melted butter, and the moment you take it from the fire, stir into it two large wine glasses of white wine, two tablespoons of white sugar and a grated nutmeg.

MRS. R.S. HAZEN, Knoxville, Tenn.

WINE SAUCE.

Two teacups of sugar, one tablespoon of butter, one wine glass of wine, one tablespoon of flour, put in the sugar, one cup of cold water, heat to boiling point. Put wine in after taking off the stove.

MRS. ELIZABETH GILLESPIE CASWELL, Knoxville, Tenn.

A DELICIOUS DRESSING.

"Devonshire cream" is an English accompaniment of tarts. It is especially nice served with blackberry tarts, which are really large open pies of blackberries, sometimes made with simply a border of paste and no upper crust. These pies may be made of canned or preserved blackberries or raspberries or of the dried fruit, soaked out and stewed. Devonshire cream is made from perfectly fresh milk set in a pan in a cool place for twelve hours, then heated slowly to the boiling point, but not allowed to boil. The milk is then removed from the fire, and in the same vessel is kept for six hours longer in a cold place. The cream that rises is peculiarly sweet in flavor, and firm. It is specially nice with fresh or preserved fruits as well as with tarts. The Devonshire dairy folk claim that the art of preparing this cream has come down to them from the times of the Roman conquerers; and it is said to have been a favorite way of preparing cream among the Greeks in the most ancient times.

CONTRIBUTED.

BROWN SUGAR SYRUP.

Two cups brown sugar, half a cup of water. Put water on and when boiling hard add sugar and boil till thick enough. This is very nice.

MRS. S.B. BOYD, Knoxville, Tenn.

VEGETABLES

TABLE OF TIME FOR COOKING VEGETABLES.

All green vegetables, such as peas, cabbage, spinach, lima beans, onions, yellow and white squash, string beans, asparagus. and cauliflower should have a pinch of soda added to the water in which they are boiled in order to preserve the green color.

Green peas, ten to twenty minutes.

String Beans, forty-five minutes.

Asparagus, forty-five minutes.

Onions, cabbage, squash and cauliflower, thirty minutes.

Spinach, fifteen minutes.

Irish potatoes should be put in cold water to which a teaspoon of salt is added and boiled from twenty to thirty minutes. All other vegetables should be put in salted boiling water.

MRS. A.S. BIRDSONG, Knoxville, Tenn.

TO BAKE APPLES.

Peel and core the apples, place in dish over which grate a little nutmeg and pour over a thick syrup of sugar and water. Bake moderately fast, when about half done turn the apples over to keep one side from getting too brown.

BAKED APPLES AND NUTS.

For a half dozen large apples, a good three-fourths cup of nut meats (butternuts, black walnuts or hickory nuts) will be required. Chop the meats fine and add a half cup or sugar. Core the apples and fill the centres with the nuts and sugar. Bake in a rather deep pan with a cupful of boiling water added. When tender remove carefully from the pan, place in a pretty dish, pour the juice over the apples, and crown with whipped cream or a meringue made from the whites of two eggs. Put a red or green cherry on top of each apple.

BAKED BEANS.

One quart white beans, soak in water over night. In the morning, drain and cover well with fresh water, adding a chunk of pork about four inches square. Boil gently about two hours, until when you blow on a few beans in a spoon, the outer skin curls, they are then ready to bake. Place in a pan with the liquor in which they were boiled, put the pork in the centre, add one tablespoon black molasses, one teaspoon mustard, one teaspoon salt and bake about two hours in a moderate oven.

MRS. A.S. BIRDSONG, Knoxville, Tenn.

TO COOK SNAP BEANS.

String and snap fresh, green beans (those that have large beans and will shell out are best), parboil a few minutes, put a pinch of soda the size of a pea in and immediately drain and wash. Put in a piece of bacon, (half a pound is enough to cook a half gallon of beans after they are snapped), cover with boiling water and cook until tender, about two hours, with a good fire or a moderate fire, four hours.

MRS. W.N. PATTON. Bristol, Tenn.

CREAMED CABBAGE.

Cut cabbage fine, as to fry and cook in clear water until tender, with a scrap of red pepper, season with butter and rich milk or cream, thicken with a little flour, add a dash of salt.

MRS. J.S. DONNELLY, Shoun's, Tenn.

CABBAGE PUDDING.

(A Vegetable Dish from the *Virginia Housewife*.)

Take a firm head of cabbage, put it in a deep bucket, pour over it boiling water and let it remain half an hour, then turn one-third of the leaves back, cut out the heart, chop it up with a stuffing of bread crumbs, butter, pepper and salt, put this in the centre and fold the leaves over, tie it up in a cloth and boil it well, take out and put on it a lump of butter, it is then ready for dinner.

MRS. GEN'L A. ANDERSON, Knoxville, Tenn.

SCALLOPED CABBAGE.

Cut cabbage as for slaw. Put a layer in a dish, sprinkle with pepper and salt and bits of butter, then layer of bread crumbs, then a layer of cabbage and continue till the dish is full, having the crumbs last. Pour over the whole a pint of sweet milk and bake till done.

MISS MARY FRANCISCO, Knoxville, Tenn.

STUFFED CABBAGE.

Take a large fresh head of cabbage, cut out the centre, fill the vacancy with a stuffing made of chopped ham, bread crumbs, chopped centre, highly seasoned with sweet herbs mixed with the yelk of an egg. Tie the cabbage firmly in a thin cloth and boil in salt water two hours. Keep the kettle closely covered.

MRS. W.K. VANCE, Bristol, Tenn.

STUFFED CABBAGE.

Take a nice white head of cabbage, a white head is the best, boil it in clear water and salt, tie a string around it to keep the leaves from becoming ragged. When it is thoroughly done put out on a flat dish, turn four or five of the outside leaves back and cut the heart out, and chop it very fine. Have already chopped very fine, any cold meat you may have, a piece of cold beefsteak is the best, two hard boiled eggs, about half a teaspoon of celery seed and if you have it, one or two stalks of celery, butter, salt and pepper to taste. Mix all together well, then place it in the centre where you cut the heart from folding the leaves over it, it will have the appearance of a whole head of cabbage. Pour over it a teacup of drawn butter and milk and let simmer on the steamer till you are ready to serve.

MRS. J.W.S. FRIERSON, Knoxville, Tenn.

CAULIFLOWER.

Wash and clean a head of cauliflower, cut into pieces, boil until tender in salted water. Make cream sauce with milk and butter with a little flour to thicken.

Cauliflower may be served with a tomato sauce or with drawn butter. The cream sauce is made with one-half pint of milk and a tablespoon of butter, rubbed into a tablespoon of flour, boil until it thickens.

MRS. JOS. S. DONNELLY, Shaun's, Tenn.

CUCUMBER, STUFFED - See Tomato Stuffed.

BAKED CORN.

One quart corn, canned or fresh, two eggs, two tablespoons each of cream and butter, one large tablespoon sugar, pepper and salt to season highly.

MRS. M.K. BURNS, Bristol, Va.

TO BOIL CORN.
Shuck and silk and put on fire in cold salted water, only let it remain from four to six minutes after it has reached the boiling point; if young, only four minutes.

CONTRIBUTED.

ESCALLOPED CORN.
A delicious dish and one not commonly known is escalloped corn. This dish is prepared the same as escalloped oysters, except that canned corn or fresh sweet corn in its season is used instead of oysters. Butter a pudding dish and place therein alternate layers of cracker or bread crumbs and corn, having the crumbs for first and last layers. Use a generous allowance of butter with pepper and salt to taste. Pour milk over the whole and bake in a moderate oven.

MRS. W.K. VANCE, Bristol, Tenn.

CORN FRITTERS.
The corn must be young. Grate six or eight ears from the cob. Stir the beaten yelks of three eggs into three tablespoons of milk, then the corn, with salt and pepper and two or three tablespoons of flour, stir together thoroughly and at the last add the beaten whites. Have lard and butter boiling hot, put in the mixture, forming in small cakes, size and shape of an oyster.

MRS. W.K. VANCE, Bristol, Tenn.

CORN FRITTERS.
Grate one dozen ears of corn upon a coarse grater, and with a spoon scrape the cob in order to obtain the milk which adheres to it. Add salt, a tablespoon of flour, two tablespoons of milk and two eggs. Drop the mixture from a spoon into boiling fat and fry them a nice brown. Drain them and serve very hot.

CONTRIBUTED.

GREEN CORN FRITTERS.
To six ears of corn take four eggs, grate the corn from the cob, beat the whites and yelks separately, salt to taste. Fry at once in lard. Some cook them as doughnuts.

CONTRIBUTED.

CORN FRITTERS TO TASTE LIKE FRIED OYSTERS.
Take green corn and grate it in a dish, about twenty ears for a large family. To one pint of this put one egg, beaten, one teacup teaspoon pepper, mix them well together. A spoonful of the mixture will be about the size of an oyster, which must be fried to a light brown.

C.C.

CORN OYSTERS.
Six ears of fresh young corn, grated, two eggs, one tablespoon flour, one tablespoon corn starch, one teaspoon baking powder, one teaspoon sugar, butter size of a walnut, salt and pepper to season highly. Mix and drop in very hot dripping, a teaspoonful at a time. Sufficient for five people.

MRS. M.K. BURNS, Bristol, Va.

CORN PUDDING.
One teaspoon sugar, one teaspoon flour, one teaspoon salt, one teaspoon baking powder, one tablespoon melted butter, one cup sweet milk, two eggs, six ears grated corn.

MRS. RACHEL ROGERS, Knoxville, Tenn.

CORN PUDDING.
Grate six ears of corn, to this add three eggs, two tablespoons of butter, one pint sweet milk, salt and pepper to taste. Beat the corn pulp, eggs and butter well, add milk, salt and pepper and if you use field corn, a level teaspoonful of sugar. Pour into a baking dish and bake about one-half to three-quarters of an hour, or until it is all "set".

MRS. W.N. PATTON, Bristol, Tenn.

TO STEW CORN.
Cut the corn off the cob, place on stove with enough water to cover and boil till done. Make a dressing ,of cream, butter a little salt and pepper, pour the water off the corn and pour over it this dressing, let it come to a boil, then take off and serve in a heated.

CRANBERRIES.

Wash a quart of cranberries and stew them with a teacup of water, stirring them often. When berries are broken, press through a colander, add sugar and boil till the syrup is thick and rich. Cranberries require a great deal of sugar, but a less quantity if cooked this way.

MRS. W.K. VANCE, Bristol, Tenn.

BAKED EGG PLANT.

Peel, slice and boil the egg plant till tender, put in colander and mash. Place in bowl and beat with three eggs, butter size of a walnut; salt and pepper, one small onion, one-half cup milk, thicken with cracker crumbs.

MRS. JAMES A. HENSLEY, Knoxville, Tenn.

TO COOK EGG PLANT.

Peel, slice and boil the egg plants, it is better to soak the slices in salt water two hours before boiling. When done, mash and add two raw eggs, butter, salt, pepper and a little sugar, a cup of sweet milk and a few bread crumbs. Put in a baking dish, sprinkle bread crumbs on top and bake.

Or you can add a little flour when ready to balm, make into small cakes and fry in lard or butter. The addition of a little onion improves it in both cases.

MRS. E.S. McCLUNG, Knoxville, Tenn.

FRIED EGG PLANT.

Pare and cut egg plant into slices half an inch thick; Cut these into quarters; dust quickly with salt and pepper; dip them at once into beaten egg, roll in bread crumbs and fry in hot fat; dry on brown paper and serve at once. Egg plant looses its crispness after standing a few minutes. Under no circumstances soak egg plant in salt and water, as this draws out the juice, makes the fibre tough and robs it of its dietetic value.

Cucumbers and squash may be cooked in the same way.

MRS. WILL BEWLAY DUENNER, Bristol, Va.

MINCED EGG PLANT. (FINE.)

One egg plant about the size of a cocoanut; peel and cut slices and boil until tender, about thirty minutes, mash very fine, and while hot mix with one tablespoon of butter, one-fourth cup sweet milk, one teaspoon chopped onion, one cup bread crumbs, salt and pepper to taste, two eggs well beaten together. Bake in a pan, first covering the mixture with a covering of roasted crumbs, bake about twenty or thirty minutes.

MRS. LILLIAN RODGERS, Knoxville, Tenn.

STUFFED EGG PLANT.

One egg plant, three full tablespoons butter, one-half small onion, chopped fine, one small tomato, chopped fine, one and one-half cups cold meat, chopped fine, one egg, grated bread or cracker crumbs.

Cover egg plant with water and simmer twenty minutes, remove from water and cut in halves, scrape out inside to have a firm shell, press out moisture from pulp, melt one and one-half spoons of the butter, add onion, heat until softened, then add meat (veal or chicken with a little ham is best), stir in tomato, also pulp of egg plant mixed with equal quantity of bread crumbs, add beaten egg, salt and pepper to taste, cook about fifteen minutes, mixing well.

Fill the two shells, shaping up and round over top, cover with bread crumbs, mixed with remaining one and one-half spoons of butter. Bake until brown and serve very hot.

MRS. L.H. OTEY, Bristol, Va.

CREAMED HOMINY.

Soak one quart of ground hominy over night in warm water; in the morning drain and put to cook in a double boiler or in a vessel set in a pot of boiling water; cover well with boiling water and cook for five hours without stirring. If more water is needed, add it cautiously while boiling hot, so that the hominy will not lose its consistency. Do not salt until just before dishing, or the hominy will turn dark. Dress with rich cream instead of butter.

MRS. WILL BEWLAY DUENNER, Bristol, Va.

FRENCH KRAUT.

Cut half a head of cabbage in shreds, cover with vinegar and cook slowly for half an hour, then add salt, pepper and a piece of butter.

MRS. W.K. VANCE, Bristol, Tenn.

MACARONI AND CHEESE.

Three-fourths cup macaroni broken in pieces, two quarts boiling water, one tablespoon salt, one-half cup white sauce, three-fourths cup grated cheese, three-fourths cup of buttered crumbs. Cook macaroni in boiling salted water until tender, pour into a colander and run cold water through it.

WHITE SAUCE FOR MACARONI.

Two tablespoons butter, two tablespoons flour, one-half teaspoon salt, one and one-half cups hot milk. Melt butter, then add flour and salt, then hot milk. To this sauce add macaroni and cheese. Put in baking dish, covering the top with bread crumbs. Bake in moderate oven until crumbs are brown.

MRS. R.M. HOSKINS, Knoxville, Tenn.

DISH OF MACARONI.

A plate full of macaroni, break in pieces, boil till tender, after washing, salt to taste, do not let it scorch, when done pour on this a pint of sweet milk, tablespoon of grated cheese, butter, a teaspoon of mustard and pepper to taste. Stir all this and pour in a buttered dish. Set it in the stove to bake—it will take only a short time.

TO MAKE MOCK MACARONI.

Take a plate of crackers, break them up, pour over boiling milk, let them stand till nearly cold. Drain the milk off and use as macaroni.

MRS. GEN'L A. ANDERSON, Knoxville, Tenn.

ITALIAN MACARONI.

Boil one-third of a package or spaghetti in salt and water till tender, drain, cut in small pieces and put where it will keep hot.

Put in a pan one tablespoon of butter, add to it a heaping cup of grated cheese, one can of Campbell's tomato soup, add the spaghetti and season to taste with salt, cayenne and tobasco sauce. Stir and cook till thick and serve very hot.

MRS. CHARLES SIMMS, Knoxville, Tenn.

ITALIAN MACARONI.

Two packages macaroni, two pounds round steak, one pound butter, two two pound cans tomatoes, two bunches garlic, two large onions, one-half pound dried mushrooms. canned will do, cheese, one pinch each of sage, cayenne pepper, black and red pepper, salt to taste.

Cut all fat from the steak and brown it in the butter, put steak in a pot and boil till it cooks to pieces. To this liquor add the tomatoes, the butter in which the steak was cooked, the onions, garlic, meat and mushrooms, all of which chop very fine, then add the seasoning and let it cook until thick. An hour or so before serving, cook the macaroni in hot salt water till tender, drain through a colander and serve on hot dishes, a layer of macaroni and a layer of the gravy, a layer of grated cheese, Edam is best. Serve with lightbread, tobasco sauce, wine and strong coffee. Some think lemon improves it. You may repeat the layers as often as you wish on same dish. This makes a whole meal.

MRS. B.B. BURNS, Bristol, Va.-Tenn.

STEWED OKRA.

Wash the okra, about a quart, and cut off the ends. Place in a saucepan a tablespoon of butter, a finely minced onion and a green pepper, cut up; let all cook for six or eight minutes and then add three tomatoes, chopped fine, also the juice of the tomatoes. Season to taste with salt and pepper, a dash of cayenne and a teaspoon of chopped parsley. Now add the okra and let all simmer slowly for twenty or thirty minutes. Place in a hot dish and serve.

MRS. MARY JONES, Knoxville, Tenn.

OKRA AND TOMATOES.

Pour boiling water over tomatoes, skin and slice. Cut up the same quantity of young okra. Put in a pan without water, chop a little onion fine and add. Season with butter, pepper, salt and sugar to suit the taste. Excellent.

MRS. A.P. WHITE, Knoxville, Tenn.

176

STUFFED ONIONS.

Scoop the hearts out of large onions so that cups are formed. Mix the pieces of onion that have been cut out and mince with meat, sausage is best, but any other kind of meat will do with a little bacon. Add a few bread crumbs, salt, pepper and a tablespoon of cream, staff the onions with this and bake for an hour, basting often with melted butter.

Take each onion out carefully without breaking. Squeeze half a lemon into the juice in the baking pan and add a tablespoon of browned flour, when this comes to a boil add four tablespoons of cream and pour over the onions.

MRS. ROBERT KELLY, Bristol, Va.

PARSNIP FRITTERS.

Boil four or five parsnips, when tender take off the skin and mash fine, add to them a teaspoon of flour and a beaten egg, season with salt and pepper, and fry in hot fat until brown.

This is preferred to salsify or oyster plant by some. The oyster plant can be served the same way.

MRS. JOS. S. DONNELLY, Shoun's, Tenn.

FRIED PARSNIPS

Parsnips make a delicious dish if parboiled until quite tender, after which slice them, dip into maple syrup and fry a golden brown in hot butter.

MRS. DANIEL BRISCOE, SR., Knoxville, Tenn.

STUFFED PEPPERS.

Cut stem ends from six peppers, remove the inside, scald fifteen minutes and drain. Mix thoroughly one cup bread crumbs, two tablespoon melted butter, one-half teaspoon salt and one egg, add one cup cooked meat or fish, moisten slightly with water, fill peppers and place in buttered pan and bake half an hour. Serve on toast or with sauce.

MRS. PARHAM, Chattanooga, Tenn.

"THE PORTLY POTATO."

Boil and mash white potatoes and form into a mound on a platter that can withstand heat. Take out a cupful of potatoes from the top of the mound, leaving the cavity in the centre. Brush the mound and the inside of the cavity with the white of an egg and set it in the stove to brown. Melt half cup of butter, stir it into four tablespoons grated cheese, and when this melts pour it gradually upon the beaten yelks of two eggs. Pour the cheese sauce into the cavity without removing the potatoes from the oven. Sift crumbs over the entire mound and return to the oven for five minutes before sending to the table.

CONTRIBUTED.

POTATO BALLS.

When new Irish potatoes are quite small, boil or steam until tender, drop three into a piece of cheese cloth. Gather up the edges and twist until the potatoes are blended into one, which should look dry and mealy. Drop into a hot dish, season with melted butter.

POTATO CHIPS.

The secret of having nice crisp chips is to have all the starch soaked out of the potatoes, and then have plenty of good lard and "worlds of patience."

If you are to prepare very many, cut the potatoes the night before, select the large ones and wash and peel and put into a pan of cold water, then have your cutter ready, gauged the thickness you desire, chip a few and get the thickness you like best, but if they are very thin they are apt to scorch.

As fast as you chip, throw them into a bowl of cold water, washing them through several waters, till the water seems free from starch, then set them in very cold water out of doors; if the weather is so warm that the water will not remain cold put a lump of ice into it, then when you are ready to fry them they will be crisp and firm.

In the morning take them from the water, put them in a sifter to drain, have a large towel or piece of old table cloth spread on the table, take the chips from the sifter one by one and place on the cloth, then spread a cloth over them, pressing hard upon them as you would a blotter, so as to absorb all the water from the chips.

Have ready an iron pot, such as usually comes with a range, put it on the range with enough lard when melted to be about half full, when it is thoroughly hot, put in the chips, a few at a time, have a wire egg beater to dip them out as soon as they are as brown as you like; as you dip them out put them on a cloth, spread over a large dish; the cloth absorbs the grease. As you put them on the cloth, while they are hot sprinkle a little salt on them. The main point in good potato chips is in the preparation.

MRS. J.W.S. FRIERSON, Knoxville, Tenn.

POTATO CROQUETTES.
One pint hot mashed potatoes, one tablespoon butter, one-half saltspoon white pepper, a few grains of cayenne, one-half teaspoon each of salt and celery seed, a few drops onion juice and yelk of one egg. Mix thoroughly and beat well, add one tablespoon of chopped parsley, let stand till cold, shape, crumb, egg, crumb, brown in deep fat, drain and serve. Rice may be used instead of potatoes.

CONTRIBUTED.

POTATO SNOW.
Mash one dozen boiled potatoes while hot, add one cup hot cream and a lump of butter. Cream with a fork till foamy, then press through a colander, letting them fall into a hot dish.

MRS. W.E. BELCHER, Knoxville, Tenn.

POTATO SOUFFLE.
Season two cupsful of hot mashed potatoes with butter, salt, pepper and a little minced parsley. Beat in a half cupful of milk and stir until the mixture is smooth, fold in the whites of four eggs beaten stiff, turn into a buttered dish and bake about ten minutes, or until the souffle is puffed and brown. Serve it immediately. The work will be done more speedily over hot water than if the potato is in a state of cooling. The parsley may be omitted if not liked. Grated cheese sometimes is sprinkled over the top.

CONTRIBUTED.

BOILED IRISH POTATOES.
Scrape or peel the potatoes, boil till a fork can be run through them easily. Make a dressing of cream, butter and salt, which heat and pour over them, after draining off the water.

If the potatoes used are old, when done make a dressing of cream, salt and butter, mash the potatoes and pour this dressing hot over them, then beat till very light. They can be served this way or put on a dish and baked till a light brown.

CONTRIBUTED.

TO BOIL POTATOES.
Put potatoes in boiling water and let boil moderately until soft enough to pierce through with a fork. Drain off all water immediately and thoroughly or the potatoes will become soggy, losing their mealy quality. Sprinkle with salt. Shake the vessel up and down well, dislodging and separating each potato and in the process exposing each to the air for a few seconds.

Cover over with a napkin or clean, dry towel, and set on the range shelf to keep hot for five minutes before serving. New potatoes should stand in cold water for half an hour before putting them on to cook; old potatoes for one hour. These last, if much shrunken or wilted, may be put down to cook in cold water instead of boiling water.

CONTRIBUTED.

CREAMED POTATOES.
One pint of cold potatoes, cut into cubes or dice. Put them in the chafing dish, cover with milk and cook until the potatoes have absorbed the milk, then add one tablespoon of butter, one-half teaspoon of salt, one-half saltspoon of pepper and a little chopped parsley.

CONTRIBUTED.

ESCALLOPED POTATOES,
Slice six Irish potatoes, after peeling, put half in a baking dish and sprinkle with flour, salt and pepper and bits of butter, cover with the rest of the potatoes and again sprinkle well with flour, salt and pepper and add the butter, over all pour a teacup of sweet milk and put in oven to bake until done.

MRS. DAVID DUNN, Bristol, Tenn.

POTATOES AU GRATIN.
For one and one-half pints cooked potatoes cut in small pieces, make a sauce as follows: Melt two tablespoons of butter in sauce pan, add three tablespoons flour and pour in gradually one pint of milk, stirring constantly. When thickened and smooth, season with a teaspoon of salt and cayenne, add two-thirds of a cup of grated cheese and mix gently with the potatoes. Place in baking dish and cover with one-third cup of cheese and brown the top.

MRS. PARHAM, Chattanooga, Tenn.

POTATOES WITH GREEN PEPPERS.

To your usual hashed brown potatoes, try adding a little chopped bacon and some minced green peppers. You have no idea how appetizing it is.

CONTRIBUTED.

IRISH POTATOES MASHED AND BAKED.

Mash the potatoes well while warm, season with cream, butter and salt to taste, beat until smooth and light, put in the stove and let them brown.

MRS. B.J. STEPHENSON, Knoxville, Tenn.

SCALLOPED POTATOES.

Put a layer of cold, boiled, sliced potatoes in suitable dish and season with salt, pepper and a little onion, sprinkle over with a little flour, then another layer of potatoes, etc., continuing this until you have desired quantity. Heat enough milk to cover and pour over before putting in the oven, cover and bake half an hour and then remove cover and brown. Raw sliced potatoes may be used by cooking longer.

MRS. L.H. OTEY, Bristol, Va.

SWEET POTATOES CANDIED.

Boil the potatoes, then slice them and put a layer of potatoes with sugar, butter and a little nutmeg and repeat this until the dish is full, pour warm water over them, then put them in the stove for half an hour or until a syrup is formed.

MRS. B.J. STEPHENSON, Knoxville, Tenn.

CANDIED SWEET POTATOES.

Boil potatoes till nearly done, peel and slice, put in pan and make a dressing of three tablespoons of sugar, two of butter, a little flour, nutmeg or cinnamon if you prefer. Pour over the potatoes and add enough boiling water to cook them. Bake in a moderate oven.

MRS. H.N. SAXTON, JR., Knoxville, Tenn.

STUFFED SWEET POTATOES.

Choose medium-sized smooth potatoes; wash and bake in a moderate oven until they begin to soften, but are not thoroughly done.

Take out, cut a slice from one side, and with a spoon scoop out the inside; mash in a bowl, beating with a fork and seasoning plentifully with butter and a little salt and pepper; replace in the skins, lay on the slice, and set it in the oven until thoroughly heated. If they are very dry, moisten with a little thick, sweet cream before putting back in the skins.

In Virginia, small sweet potatoes are boiled in their skins, peeled while hot, halved, laid in a vegetable dish, seasoned with salt and a sauce of melted butter and cream poured over.

MRS. WILL BEWLAY DUENNER, Bristol, Va.

TO BOIL RICE.

Wash in several waters one large cup of rice. Put in quite a large pan with one quart of cold water, set on stove twenty minutes before serving, after it comes to a boil five minutes will cook it. As soon as the grains will mash, drain off all the water, give it a stir, cover the pan and set on back of stove to dry and burst.

MRS. E.S. McCLUNG, Knoxville, Tenn.

SALSIFY FRITTERS - See Parsnip Fritters.

SLAW.

One head white cabbage, three hard-boiled eggs, two tablespoons each of butter and sugar, one teaspoon each of salt, pepper, and made mustard, one teacup vinegar, two teaspoons er-earn.

This is good for lettuce or slaw.

MRS. ANN BELL, Knoxville, Tenn.

SLAW.

One-half head of cabbage, cut fine, sprinkle with salt and pepper. One-half cup of vinegar, two eggs, piece of butter size of a nut, a small tablespoonful of sugar. Take half the vinegar, put it on the stove with the other ingredients and stir till thick, mix in cold vinegar and when cool pour over the cabbage.

SQUASH OR CYMLING.

Cut yellow squash in halves and white squash in quarters and boil until tender in salted water with a pinch of soda added, drain and cover with a drawn butter made in this way: Melt one tablespoon of butter in a granite pan, add a tablespoon of flour, stir until smooth, then add one and one-half cups sweet milk and a good pinch of salt, stir until thick and pour over the squash. This sauce is suitable for cauliflower, cabbage, asparagus, spring onions, lima beans and if one likes, string beans and spinach, though the two latter are usually dressed with a tablespoon of butter.

MRS. A.S. BIRDSONG, Knoxville, Tenn.

SQUASH, STUFFED - See Tomatoes Stuffed.

SQUASH PUDDING.

Two young squashes, peeled and seeded, stew till mellow, then mash. Mix in two whole eggs or two yelks, a pinch of salt, a half cup butter, one-half cup sugar and one-half or two-thirds cup sweet milk, quantity depending on the dryness of the squash. Bake slowly in a buttered pan. Eat with vegetable course. If not liked so sweet use less sugar.

MRS. HATTIE KERN TAYLOR. Bristol, Tenn.

JELLIED TOMATO.

One quart tomato juice, one onion, boiled till soft and mixed with tomato juice, let stand over night. The next morning take about one-third of a box of gelatine, dissolve in a gill of water, let your tomato and onion come to a boil and pour over the gelatine, season with salt and pour into moulds. When set turn out on lettuce leaves, make a well in the centre and fill with mayonnaise dressing.

ST. NICHOLAS HOTEL, Cincinnati, Ohio.

BAKED TOMATOES.

Choose six large smooth tomatoes, cut a slice off the stem ends, scoop out the seeds, mix together one-half cup of ham or any other meat two heaping tablespoons of bread crumbs, one tablespoon of chopped parsley, one-half teaspoon of salt, dash of cayenne, one tablespoon melted butter.

Fill the tomatoes with this mixture, heaping it in the centre, sprinkle over the top with bread crumbs, place tomatoes in a granite baking pan, baste with melted butter, bake in hot oven thirty minutes.

MRS. ARCHER A. PHLEGAR, Bristol, Va.

BREADED TOMATOES.

Select rather green tomatoes and cut in thick slices. Dip each in sifted and seasoned bread crumbs, then in beaten egg, then again in crumbs and fry in hot fat till brown, drain well and serve plain or with a cream sauce.

MRS. PARHAM, Chattanooga, Tenn.

CREAM TOMATOES.

Cut fine ripe tomatoes in thick slices, season with pepper and salt and fry them slowly in hot lard and butter. When done put them on a flat dish, have a piece of butter; mixed with a spoonful of flour, put this into a pan with a cup of cream or milk and let come to a boil, pour over the tomatoes.

MRS. W.K. VANCE, Bristol, Tenn.

FRIED TOMATOES.

Cut a small piece from top and bottom of ten medium-sized tomatoes, ripe or green; then cut each across, dip each side in flour, and fry in two tablespoons of butter. Lift out when done on to a hot platter and sift a large spoonful of flour into the frying pan, stirring briskly until brown; add slowly a cup of milk or stock and half a teaspoon of salt and half that measure of pepper. Cook until smooth, pour over the tomatoes.

MRS. WILL BEWLAY DUENNER, Bristol, Va.

STUFFED TOMATOES.

Have large ripe tomatoes, peel them and take out the core and a little of the inside. Fill up the cavity with bread crumbs, a little cold meat of any kind, chopped fine, pepper, salt and a little mixed mustard, put a piece of butter on top. Bake in a deep dish, adding a little water and a piece of butter.

MRS. W.K. VANCE, Bristol, Tenn.

STUFFED TOMATOES.

Mix half a pint of stale bread crumbs, half a cup of finely chopped nuts, a grated onion, a level teaspoon of salt, a saltspoon of pepper, and a tablespoon of butter, melted.

Cut the stem end from six large tomatoes, and take out the seeds and the centres; stuff the tomatoes with the mixture and stand them in a baking pan; add half a cup of water and bake in a quick oven for thirty minutes, basting once or twice.

This same mixture may be stuffed into cucumbers or squash.

MRS. WILL BEWLAY DUENNER, Bristol, Va.

STUFFED TOMATOES.

Six large tomatoes, slice off top, remove the pulp and drain. To the yelks of four hard boiled eggs, mashed smooth with butter, add a tablespoon vinegar, teaspoon mustard, salt and pepper. Chop whites with tomato pulp, one cup cracker crumbs, one cup grated ham. When all is well mixed stuff the tomatoes, set on ice till served.

MISS NELLA C. MOSS, Knoxville, Tenn.

STUFFED TOMATOES.

To stuff six large tomatoes take one large apple, not quite a pint of peanuts and celery enough to flavor, all of which run through a meat chopper, moisten with any good dressing and fill in the centres of the scooped out tomatoes.

MISS ANNA J. DOUGLAS, Washington, D. C.

ALICE EVELYN HAZEN'S HANDWRITTEN RECIPES

CAVIAR SANDWICHES OR CANAPES
2 tablespoons of lemon juice
2 tablespoons of olive oil
Mix thoroughly and add to a quarter of a pound of caviar. Mush and beat till it is creamy. Spread on toast. Grate yellow of an egg on top and garnish with a ring of stuffed olive.

PECAN COOKIES
2 eggs
1 lb. sugar
1 lb. butter
1 scant teaspoon baking powder
2 tablespoons
2 qts. flour

Cream butter & sugar. Add well beaten eggs & water. With first quart of flour, add baking powder. Then add enough flour to [page torn]. Cut with [page torn, remaining recipe lost]

PRALINES
3 cups sugar
½ cup canned milk
Butter siz e of an egg

Boil sugar, canned milk, and butter. 1 cup sugar browned in a skillet. Pour into other mixture.
After you put the two together add ½ teaspoon soda, dissolved in water. While cooking, add 2 teaspoons vanilla and 1 ½ cups of pecans. After taken off stove, shape with tin forms or weathered marble.

PRALINES
4 egg white, real stiff
Fold 2 cups Brown Sugar
1 pound pecans

CHILE SAUCE
12 large ripe tomatoes
4 ripe or 3 green peppers
2 onions
2 tablespoons salt
2 tablespoons sugar
1 tablespoon cinnamon
1 cloves + all spice
3 cups vinegar

Peel tomatoes and onions. Chop tomatoes, onions, and peppers. Boil one and a half hours.

ACKNOWLEDGEMENTS

Researching and editing this cookbook in many ways followed the example set by the women of First and Central Presbyterian Churches as it relied upon the contributions of numerous individuals. First, I am grateful to the board of directors at the Hazen Historical Museum Foundation for the privilege to serve as Executive Director. Each board member has donated their time and energy to ensuring that the historic fabric of Mabry's Hill and Bethel Cemetery endure for generations to come. Mabry-Hazen House, its incomparable collection and dramatic family stories are a cultural treasure chest that I am humbled to research and interpret. Without the opportunity, I never would have rediscovered this rare piece of southern Appalachian culinary history.

I also want to thank Storyhaus Media for undertaking this project and helping the Hazen Historical Museum Foundation restore a nearly forgotten cookbook from a century ago. Thank you to Stephen Zimmerman, Christian Pennisi, and Tyler Dippel. Their enthusiasm and dedication to enriching our lives through storytelling has been a well-spring of inspiration.

I owe Storyhaus' Doug McDaniel a deep debt of gratitude for his patience, guidance, and support. Without our late-night conversations, I could not have fully envisioned this path for Mabry-Hazen House. His consistent encouragement and constructive critiques have furthered my growth as a public historian and storyteller.

Along the way, interns assisted me in the editing and researching of this project. In addition to researching the cookbook, William Oaks dedicated many evenings to the tedious, monotonous work of rekeying chapter after chapter into workable formats. Samuel Burgess aided me by investigating several of the contributors and helped bring them to life. Emily Weddle deserves more gratitude than she'll receive here for countless hours of sorting and cataloguing the extensive family collection. Her commitment has allowed me to pursue other projects, like this cookbook.

Others I would like to thank include our former executive director, Calvin Chappelle, for his trust and friendship, my graduate cohort for the laughs and fellowship, and the several readers of early drafts who made this a stronger book than it could have been otherwise. I also feel fortunate to have access to an extraordinary repository of East Tennessee history at the Calvin M. McClung Library.

Most importantly, I want to thank my mother and father, Mark and Angie Hollis. They are a cornerstone to my successes and their unwavering confidence helped me along when things were difficult.

Thank you all.
Patrick J. Hollis